FAITH,
HOPE &
CHARITY

> Leading a charity well is not a necessary evil to be endured, but a vital aspect of effective leadership and integrity for any organisation. Paul Martin's book will become a 'must read' for anyone seeking to engage in charitable endeavours well. From his excellent introduction to what a charity is all the way through to issues of good governance and due diligence, Paul sets out a road map of great clarity for those who want to ensure that what they do and the way they do is of the very highest standard. *Faith, Hope & Charity* is practical, accessible and deeply relevant. Its author has a wealth of experience and a deep passion for the life of charity to be vibrant, well-structured and built upon excellent foundations. I cannot commend it highly enough. Every trustee and leader of a charity should buy this book, read it, discuss it with their board and make it a consistent companion in discussions and decisions about how to do things well.

Rev Malcolm Duncan FRSA
SENIOR PASTOR OF GOLD HILL BAPTIST CHURCH AND CHAIR OF TRUSTEES;
CHAIRMAN OF SPRING HARVEST PLANNING GROUP; BOARD MEMBER MEMRALIFE;
GOVERNANCE AND LEADERSHIP CONSULTANT; AUTHOR, BROADCASTER AND LECTURER;
GOVERNMENT ADVISOR ON ISSUES OF FAITH, SOCIETY AND COMMUNITY COHESION;
SPECIAL ADVISOR ON ISSUES OF FAITH AND CIVIC LIFE

> Just as the Father, Son and Holy Spirit does not operate when we choose to ignore any one person that exists within the Trinity, so too do I believe that Charity without Faith or Hope can never survive. By writing the book *Faith Hope & Charity*, Paul Marin has created THE handbook that should be used by all who desire to start a charitable organisation. In fact, this book should be mandatory in all tertiary curriculums, that are prone to raise professionals, drawn to the field of charitable work. This book is long overdue …

Leon Schoeman
DIRECTOR OF CHANNELS TBN UK

> Paul Martin has done the churches a great service by drawing on his years of experience as a charity lawyer to give us a thorough and helpful guide to all the practicalities of sound church governance. This is an ideal book for church leaders to own and consult in order to avoid many of the heartbreaks and headaches that can accompany church leadership and will be an excellent guide for all trustees of church-based charities and governing bodies.

Dr Hugh Osgood
FREE CHURCHES MODERATOR AND
CO-PRESIDENT CHURCHES TOGETHER IN
ENGLAND

"For anyone who finds themselves in governance of a charitable organisation, *Faith, Hope & Charity* is an ideal book. For getting to know the ropes, what better than an insider's step-by-step guide? Paul Martin is not only an expert in charity law: his lucid, readable style demystifies the world of charity law and makes his extensive knowledge available to a wider public. This is a valuable and up-to-date reference work, especially apt for a time when the charity environment has become increasingly complex.

Andrea Minichiello Williams
CHIEF EXECUTIVE, CHRISTIAN CONCERN, CHRISTIAN LEGAL CENTRE, FAITH, TRUTH & HOPE

"Increasingly, there seems to be less and less charity about many of the new laws governing charities, though some of the legislation is overdue and welcome. But how does the average individual, church or charitable organisation navigate their way through the icy waters of charity law, without spending a small fortune in trying to build the unsinkable charity, only to hit unforeseen icebergs? Well, help is at hand in this clear, concise, accessible and right up-to-date book by Paul Martin, a lawyer who so well understands charity law, and wants it to work in tandem with the grace of God. Your investment in this book will, I believe, be repaid many, may times over. I will be personally recommending it near and far!

Dr Steve Brady
PRINCIPAL, MOORLANDS COLLEGE, CHRISTCHURCH

"Good governance is not just a tool to ensure compliance with the requirements of being a charity. It is the way charities achieve their purpose. This book will help charities to be robust, vibrant, independent, innovative and sustainable and maintain the trust and confidence of the wider community. It will be a valuable reference for trustees and managers well beyond the UK as charities all over the world seek to be more effective in their selfless service to the public.

Murray Baird
ASSISTANT COMMISSIONER AUSTRALIAN CHARITIES AND NOT-FOR-PROFITS COMMISSION

"Over the last 20 years I have been surprised by how often the church has needed good legal advice. Paul Martin has consistently and helpfully guided us through a range of different situations. I would like to endorse this very practical and accessible handbook — a great resource in handling the legal complexities of running a Christian charity.

Steve Tibbert
SENIOR MINISTER KINGS CHURCH CATFORD AND BOARD MEMBER NEWFRONTIERS

"Paul Martin has created an important resource for practitioners, academics and anyone who is interested in the charitable sector. This well-written encyclopedic study of the charitable sector provides coverage of a number of important issues and a level of specificity not covered in most introductory texts. Anyone involved in the development of the charitable sector, especially foreign jurisdictions developing their own charity legal framework, will treasure this book and find it particularly instructive.

LI Yinglu
ASSOCIATE DIRECTOR, RESEARCH CENTER FOR CHARITY LAW, BEIJING NORMAL UNIVERSITY CHINA PHILANTHROPY RESEARCH INSTITUTE

" Paul's previous book *The Christian Charities Handbook* was an invaluable component in the trustee's toolbox. This latest work addresses the major implications of more recent legislation and is an absolute 'must have' for trustees who need to keep abreast of the changing world of charity structures and governance requirements. In what can sometimes feel like riding on a constant roundabout of change, Paul's logical and methodical approach provides a welcome sense of calm and perspective. "

Robert Hyde
ASSEMBLIES OF GOD PROPERTY TRUST

" Charity Trustees don't always know where to turn to find out how to act and take correct decisions. This new, second edition of a vital book will help them do that superbly! It covers virtually every known circumstance, is completely up-to-date at time of publication, and merits again the very loud applause the author gained for his initial work. You can't be without it! "

Peter Brierley
CHURCH CONSULTANT: BRIERLEY CONSULTANCY

" Christian charities, ministries and churches are renowned far more for their Godly output than for their effective and efficient processes or for their excellence in handling modern necessary bureaucracy. Paul Martin has made an astounding contribution by suggesting to all us leaders how to do things so much better, bringing even more glory to God. This second edition is bang up to date and right on the mark. "

Richard Meryon
CHAIR OF MILITARY CHRISTIAN ORGANISATIONS AND PAST DIRECTOR OF THE GARDEN TOMB JERUSALEM

" This book could not have come at a better time. It is a comprehensive tool for those involved in the running of charitable organisations. Based upon many years of practical experience in this area, Paul has simplified every aspect of running a charity. It really is an answer to the cry for help from many pastors who want to do what is right but don't know how. I would highly recommend this book; I particularly recommend it to the evangelical churches who have wondered how to run their churches properly and efficiently. Certainly an excellent book! "

Agu Irukwu
SENIOR PASTOR OF JESUS HOUSE, LONDON; CHAIR OF REDEEMED CHRISTIAN CHURCH OF GOD UK

FAITH, HOPE & CHARITY

**The A to Z of governing
a charitable organisation**

PAUL MARTIN

malcolm down
PUBLISHING

Faith, Hope & Charity

Published by Malcolm Down Publishing,
Sovereign Court, 230 Upper Fifth Street,
Central Milton Keynes, Bucks, MK9 2HR

ISBN 978 19107 8660 4

Section 21, Safeguarding Issues subsection, pages 299–304
contributed by David Pearson of CCPAS

First published 2008 under the title *The Christian Charities Handbook*
Completely revised and reprinted 2016

BRITISH LIBRARY CATALOGUING IN PUBLICATION DATA
A catalogue record for this book is available from the British Library

Design and layout by Tony Cantale Graphics
Printed in Poland

CONTENTS

FOREWORD

Without a doubt, charities in the United Kingdom are making an incredible difference in the lives of millions of people. As I have travelled the country over the past 30 years in my role as Chairman of Care for the Family, I have observed the single-minded, enthusiastic commitment of countless people whose vision to "make a difference" has resulted in them either starting a charity or getting involved in an existing one. They and their charities have, unquestionably, changed the landscape of the society in which we live.

However it is not all good news: the charitable sector is, perhaps more than ever, in the spotlight for negative reasons. We hear reports of charities that are involved in excellent work but facing compliance failures, disagreements, funding problems, personality issues and investigations by the Charity Commission or HMRC.

Many charities are small, and are normally started or run by those who have a personal – and passionate – interest in the cause they champion. It is easy for such charities to feel overwhelmed by the demands of proper organisation and compliance. Often problems are caused by a failure to establish the charity correctly in the first place, and then by failing to understand the law and required practice going forward. Such matters can seem boring: changing the world is exciting; keeping minutes of board meetings, less so! But even large charities run into difficulties – and perhaps it is easy to become complacent. However, we ignore these issues at our peril, for when things go wrong they not only affect the charity that is close to our heart but the general reputation of the sector.

I welcome this book and recommend it wholeheartedly. Paul Martin is experienced, both as a lawyer specialising in charity law and as a charity trustee of over 40 years. He has seen the good, the bad and the ugly, and I believe he has done the entire voluntary sector a great service by producing *Faith, Hope & Charity*. It is a handbook in a practical format that clearly sets out the A to Z of how to actually run a charity.

This book will help charities to succeed – for unless our foundations are strong we build on sand. If it fulfils Paul's aim in writing it then it will enable us not only to operate our charities effectively, but *wisely*.

Rob Parsons OBE
Chairman, Care for the Family

INTRODUCTION

R ECENTLY I WAS JUST FINISHING a talk on charity law to a group of lawyers and businessmen in Beijing when one attendee stood up and volunteered this comment: "An active charity sector is a sign of a well ordered society." As he said this I began to reflect on the impact of charitable activity in the world. Increasingly charities face some of the toughest problems that our world throws up and they do so with an enthusiasm and diligence that is in marked contrast to the risk averse, short termism so often in evidence today.

Who else would:

- Take relief supplies and medical care into the war-torn countries of the world?
- Raise monies to provide food and shelter for the victims of natural disasters, famine, or the displaced and homeless?
- Commit themselves to the essential work of providing clean water, education, social development or caring for the sick and dying?
- Invest in the long-term development of people and communities in order to re-humanise them and give them hope?

Churchill once said, "Give us the tools and we will do the job." Many charities would claim that the "tool" they need is money, but this book challenges that thought with the notion that financial resources are but one of many "tools" that a charity needs today. In the sections that follow (drawing on over 40 years of involvement in charities as both a volunteer and a lawyer specialising in the sector), I am of the opinion that the "tools" of good governance, careful administration and compliance with the law are probably more critical to the effectiveness of a charity than a healthy bank balance.

The charity sector has experienced significant growth in recent years. There are now almost 170,000 registered charities in England and Wales together receiving a total income in excess of £70 billion per year. Clearly the charitable sector is a significant part of society today. The law relating to charities has therefore needed to develop in order to keep pace with this growth. The standards for compliance are, if anything, stricter in the charity sector than in almost any other part of society. Our well-meaning intentions count for little if we are doing our charitable work in contravention of the law.

In this book I have endeavoured to simplify and apply the law as much as possible in order to provide practical, pragmatic guidance. It is not a book to be read from cover to cover in one sitting, rather it is laid out in an accessible way so that the reader can locate the area that is of concern or interest and find the help they need. In one particular area I have gone beyond the strict remit of this book in order to offer some personal thoughts on an issue that is of growing concern in faith-based charities, namely "why leadership/ organisations fail". You might not agree with every point made, but I have seen the excellent work of too many charities undermined by these issues – to say nothing of the reputational damage to the sector as a whole and the values that particular charities stand for. If the monies and abilities that have been consumed by these disputes had remained in the sector, then how much more could have been achieved?

Given the complexities of the law today, I have been very grateful for the input of others – experts in their particular areas – who have willingly contributed their expertise to this book. Without them this book would not have been the resource that it intends to be. If you are looking for specialist help in their areas of expertise, then in my opinion they are the best around! Permit me to mention their names:

Jennifer O Brien contributed the section on Data Protection. This is a subject of increasing relevance to charities, whatever their size. Jennifer demonstrates the clear, logical thoughts that are the hallmark of her work. I get to see that work on a daily basis as she works in my office at Wellers.

Rosalind Nunoo spends her working week advising on Immigration matters, again with my firm. Her knowledge and experience in this important area is well reflected in her section.

Peter Drown is an accountant who advises businesses and charities throughout the UK. Having been in practice for almost 40 years, latterly as senior partner of Beavis Morgan LLP in London, there are few accounting situations that he has not experienced. Peter's advice is always practical and helpful.

Mark Bainbridge is the go-to man on employment issues. In his section Mark also develops his theme to include discrimination: surely a hot topic today. Mark also works for Wellers.

Andrew Meade has spent a lifetime in Financial Services and has developed his practice helping individuals and charities in this complex and highly regulated area. Andrew, together with his colleagues Dan Atkinson, Damien Lardoux and Hayley Jarvis are treasured resources of EQ Investors in London.

David Pearson founded CCPAS many years ago and under his leadership they are probably the foremost experts in the whole area of safeguarding today. Their work in advising government, local authorities and charities throughout the country is testament to David's leadership and commitment to this vital subject. Charities that ask CCPAS to help them in the area of Safeguarding and follow their advice are unlikely to go wrong.

Finally I would like to record my grateful thanks to two other people who have made a massive contribution to this book. Tony Cantale has worked imaginatively on the design and layout of the book in order to make the contents accessible to the reader. I hope that you agree that Tony has done a great job? Secondly, a big thank you to my wife Claire for all her hard work in producing the manuscript and index. Claire's ability to record my thoughts, correct my split infinitives and come up with the completed manuscript is a testament to her ability to multitask. Claire also went along with my idea of going somewhere warmer than Kent in January in order to write this book. Despite being battered by three tornadoes during our sojourn in Florida, we stuck to the task and here is the result.

Despite my best efforts mistakes will remain and for these I humbly apologise.

The law is as at September 2016.

Paul Martin

Charity Begins at …

Compliance

Property

Dispute

Accountability

Safeguarding

Reliance

Merger

essential services. The development of this thought was further enhanced in 2010 by the Conservatives' "Big Society" theme and a new Charities Act followed in 2011 – to "consolidate the Charities Act 1993 and other enactments which relate to charities."

Following the Lord Hodgson's Report in 2012 into the development and regulation of charitable activity in the UK, the Charities (Protection and Social Investments) Bill becomes law in 2016. The Act is intended to strengthen the powers of the Charity Commission, regulate public fundraising and give charities the power to make social investments.

So, charity law has a long heritage spanning over 400 years of legislation and case law. But, although the Statute of Elizabeth in 1601 formed the foundation of what we know as charity law today, there were established charities before the 16th century. Amongst the oldest charities that are still operating today are King's School, Canterbury which was founded in AD 597, St Peter's School, York (AD 627) and St Bartholomew's Hospital, London (AD 1122).

What Is a Charity?

The legal definition of "charity" is "an institution which is established for charitable purposes only, and falls to be subject to the control of the High

Charitable Purposes

A "charitable purpose" (henceforth referred to as "Charitable Object") is one which (a) falls within the list set out in the Charities Act 2011 and (b) is for the public benefit.

The Charities Act 2011 lists 13 charitable Objects:

- The prevention or relief of poverty.
- The advancement of education.
- The advancement of religion ("religion" includes a religion which involves belief in more than one god and a religion which does not involve belief in a god).
- The advancement of health or the saving of lives (including the prevention or relief of sickness, disease or human suffering).
- The advancement of citizenship or community development (including promotion of civic responsibility, volunteering or the effectiveness or efficiency of charities).
- The advancement of the arts, culture, heritage or science.
- The advancement of amateur sport (meaning sport which promotes

aimed at charities that charge fees for their services. The guidance does not state that charities cannot charge fees at all, but where charges are so high that they effectively exclude people on low income, then this is likely to affect the charity's ability to satisfy the public benefit test. The guidance distinguishes between fees charged and other forms of financial contribution. For example, membership of a Christian charity or church may involve a contribution in the form of a tithe. Provided the benefit someone receives from membership is not dependent upon the contribution, this will not affect public benefit. However, the guidance does warn that, "public benefit might be affected in circumstances where there is significant pressure placed upon beneficiaries to make a financial contribution, or where the financial contribution needed to benefit is substantial compared to the financial means of the contributor, even though benefit is not legally dependent upon such a contribution being made." The guidance includes specific examples of ways in which direct benefit might be provided to people on low incomes.

Any private benefit must be incidental. The guidance does not state that a charity can provide no private benefit, but that any private benefit must be incidental to carrying out the charity's purposes. Examples given include paying reasonable salaries to the charity's staff, or a business making a limited profit as a result of charitable regeneration projects. A problem may arise in this regard with charities that have a membership structure. The Charity Commission will want to satisfy itself that the organisation does not exist primarily for the advantage of its members, but that the structure has been adopted as the most effective way of the organisation delivering public benefit, as well as administrative convenience.

It is not possible for a charity to be set up for some purposes that are charitable and some that are not; they must all be charitable.

From a practical point of view this means that trustees and those that manage the charity must ensure that they:

- are satisfied that the charity carries out its work in a way that benefits the public and that they understand the ways in which its Objects are beneficial;
- manage the risk of any detriment or harm to the charity's beneficiaries or the general public that might result from the charity carrying out its Objects;
- make clear decisions about who will benefit from the charity's Objects.

In other words, if only a certain section of the public can benefit, then the charity must have proper reasons for this restriction. This provision can also impact a charity's membership provisions (see section 9), physical access to facilities provided by the charity (see section 11), as well as any charges for the charity's service;

· make decisions to ensure any personal benefits are no more than incidental. (This provision could restrict a charity's ability to thank or encourage its volunteers.)

In addition to the above, the trustees must state in their Annual Report (part of the audited accounts) exactly how they have carried out the charity's Objects for the public benefit. The Charity Commission provides some examples of public benefit reporting but it is unwise to copy these slavishly. Rather, the public benefit reporting requirement gives the charity an excellent opportunity to explain the development, significance and achievements of the charity in the year in question. Bearing in mind that the public benefit report forms part of the charity's accounts which are themselves publically accessible online, potential grant-funders, collaborators and purchasers of the charity's service are more than likely to review these reports as part of their due diligence exercise. Future staff and volunteers of the organisation may do likewise.

The Charity Commission looks at these public benefit reports and doubtless uses them as a mechanism for reviewing the charity's compliance and ongoing status as a charitable organisation.

There is a clear relationship between the advantages of charitable status (tax benefits and public credibility) and the need for charities to be set up for purposes that are for the public benefit. The Charity Commission states that, "Charities are precious, and play a vital and unique role at the heart of our society, but like all bodies in which the public places its trust, they should be accountable to everyone for what they do. That is the essence of the public benefit test."

Prior to 2006, there was a presumption that charities established for the relief of poverty, the advancement of religion and the advancement of education automatically satisfied the public benefit test. This presumption was removed by the Charities Act 2006.

Under the old regime, where a charity's Objects fell into the "other purposes for the benefit of the community" category, the organisation had to prove to the Charity Commission that it satisfied the public benefit test, i.e. that its Objects would benefit the community, or a significant section of it, in a way that is recognised as charitable. Since 2006 this test is applied to all organisations applying for registration as a charity, as well as to existing charities on an annual basis throughout their life.

The only exception to the above is in respect of a charity whose Objects are exclusively for the prevention or relief of poverty. While such a charity does not have to prove public benefit, it still has to be able to prove that its work is beneficial: in other words, that what it does benefits those whom it sets out to serve.

In assessing whether or not an organisation satisfies the public benefit test, the Charity Commission pays particular attention to the relationship between the trustees and the beneficiaries. If a charity's Objects benefit named or specific individuals, it will unlikely be a charity. Similarly, it will not generally be a charity if the beneficiaries are related or connected to the people setting up the organisation; for example, if they are personal relatives, or connected through employment or common membership of a body such as a professional institute.

No organisation can be charitable if it is created specifically for the purpose of carrying out political or propagandist activities. In addition, it cannot be a charity if its purposes are against the public interest.

The Charity Commission is likely to take a "risk-based" approach in its public benefit assessments, focusing its resources on assessing the public benefit of charities which may have difficulty meeting the public benefit requirement. Specific examples given are charities affected by the changes in the law, fee-charging and religious charities and charities where "social conditions have an impact on the ability of those charities to demonstrate that their purposes continue to provide benefit to the public." It is likely that attention will continue to be focussed on independent schools and private hospitals, as well as religious charities, and they may be required to report more fully on how they meet the public benefit requirement.

A consultation carried out by the Charity Commission concluded that the public expects charities to, among other things, foster a sense of community. It states that people believe charities should promote "social cohesion" in the activities they engage in, being as socially inclusive as possible and engaging the wider community, "especially charities that cater for particular religious or cultural groups." Some commentators have interpreted this to mean that

Types of Charitable Organisations

2

There is a number of legal structures in which "charity" can exist. The choice of legal identity makes a considerable difference to the way in which the charity is governed and it is important to choose the most appropriate legal identity for the proposed activities.

When establishing a charity, any one of the following legal structures is possible:

- **An "unincorporated charity"** – this can be a Charitable Trust or a Charitable Unincorporated Association, both of whose main characteristic is that the organisation does not exist as a separate legal entity from its trustees. It can only operate through the individuals ("trustees") who have overall management and control. Its assets are held by those individuals on trust for the purposes of the charity.
- **A "charitable company"** – a form of company with members (but no shareholders) and registered both at Companies House and with the Charity Commission. It is established exclusively for charitable purposes (Objects) and its constitution (Articles) prevents the distribution of its assets among its members.
- **A "Charitable Incorporated Organisation"** – an organisation that has the advantage of limited liability for its members but is not registered with Companies House. It is regulated only by the Charity Commission.
- **A "Co-operative and Community Benefit Society"** – registered under the Co-operative and Community Benefit Societies Act 2014.
- **A "Royal Charter"**.

Each of these legal structures is discussed in more detail below. In addition, some information is provided at the end of this section about "Community Interest Companies". These are not charitable companies but they can be established to fulfil non-charitable purposes that benefit the community.

Irrespective of the structure chosen for the charity, it will have a "governing document". Technically it may be referred to as a Trust deed, Articles of Association or Constitution. The governing document should be prepared by the lawyer acting in the registration process and will contain the charitable Objects for which the organisation is set up, together with the specific powers to be given to the trustees in order to achieve those Objects. Time and money spent on having the governing document prepared specifically for the particular circumstances of the organisation will be well spent, as the "standard models" are unlikely to be an exact fit and this could lead to problems later.

Unincorporated Charities

Unincorporated charities, be they a Charitable Trust or a Charitable Unincorporated Association, share one important characteristic – they are not separate legal entities from their trustees. This means that in certain circumstances a trustee's personal assets could be at risk. (see also section 11 with regard to unincorporated charities owning property.) Looking at each in turn:

- **CHARITABLE TRUST**
  A trust is an obligation binding on persons ("trustees") to deal with "property" given by a donor ("asset") in a particular way for the benefit of others ("beneficiaries") of the trust.

  The trustees are the legal owners of the trust property. In the case of a charitable trust, the trustees are legally bound to look after the property of the trust in a particular way and for a particular purpose, which must be exclusively charitable and for the public benefit. Trustees administer the

A charitable trust would be a particularly suitable legal form for a charity where some or all of the following apply:

- the trustees are prepared to take the risk of being personally liable for its debts or liabilities;
- the organisation is founded by a single individual;
- the organisation will be controlled by a fairly small group of people, it envisages having few or no staff and its administration is going to be simple;
- the organisation will not be working or sending people overseas;
- the organisation will only be making grants or loans;
- the organisation will not be engaging in trading activities;
- new charity trustees are going to be appointed by the continuing charity trustees;
- the organisation is not going to rely on a membership for any part of its administration;
- land and buildings are to be held on trust permanently for the purposes of the charity;
- there is to be a restriction on spending capital.

charitable trust and decide how the property in the trust is to be used to achieve the charity's purpose.

If the activities of a charitable trust are within both the terms of its governing document and charity law generally, then any liabilities the trustees incur can be met out of the charity's resources. Any acts outside these provisions, whether wilful or negligent, will expose the trustees to claims that they are in breach of trust, and they can be sued personally to meet any liabilities of the charity which are a result of their actions.

In addition, if the trustees of a charitable trust enter into a contract on behalf of the charity, and as a result incur liabilities or debts in excess of the charity's assets, they may be sued personally by the creditors for the difference.

The property of a trust can include money, investments, land, buildings or other assets. The cash and investments held in the trust are also called the "capital" or "fund" of the trust. The capital may produce income, such as interest or dividends. In addition, the land and buildings may produce rental income.

Any property of a charity (cash, investments, buildings, or land), which the trustees may not spend because of a restriction usually set out in the governing document, is called its "permanent endowment". This means that the property must be held permanently and can only be used in furthering the charity's purposes or to produce an income for the charity. (See Appendix 1, paragraph 19). An example of permanent endowment is money given to a charity with the donor stating that it should be invested and only the income spent on the charity's Objects.

A charitable trust is normally established by the creation of a "trust deed", but a trust deed may also be known by other names such as a "declaration" or "deed of trust", or a "deed of settlement". A trust can also be established by a "conveyance" or under someone's Will.

A trust cannot own land or sign documents in its own name. Any land belonging to the charity will be registered in the names of the individual trustees who hold it in trust for the charity. Documents must usually be signed by all the trustees.

• CHARITABLE UNINCORPORATED ASSOCIATION

A charitable unincorporated association is normally used where a group of people decide to co-operate to achieve the organisation's goals, and wish to play a part in the organisation's administration.

A charitable unincorporated association is established by a "constitution"

are very few restrictions on the purposes for which a CIC can be used. The basic legal structure for CICs is a limited liability company, and it can either be established as a new company or converted from an existing one.

As CICs use their assets, income and profits for the benefit of the community, they are required to have some special additional features to achieve this:

- CICs must be subject to an "asset lock" which ensures that assets are retained within the company to support its activities or otherwise used to benefit the community. For example, this means restrictions on the payment of dividends to members, and a prohibition on distributing assets to members if the CIC is dissolved or wound up.
- A CIC must adopt a suitable constitution that complies with the legislation governing CICs.
- A CIC must make a "community interest statement" declaring that its activities will be carried out for the benefit of the community and describing how this will be achieved.
- A CIC must satisfy the CIC Regulator that a reasonable person might consider that the CIC's activities are, or will be, carried on for the benefit of the community. This is known as the "community interest test". The CIC will have to continue to meet this test throughout its life. A CIC will not satisfy the test if it carries on certain political activities, or if a reasonable person might consider that its activities are carried on only for the benefit of the members of a particular body or the employees of a particular employer.

Apart from the special features listed above, CICs will operate in the same way as regular companies – having a separate legal identity and the ability to enter into contracts and own assets in their own names, as well as having flexibility in borrowing and fundraising.

The directors of a CIC can be paid and will have the same rights and duties as any other directors.

The members of a CIC will have the same governance and decision-making role as in any other company, but they will be under a stronger obligation to consider the wider community that the company serves, and involve stakeholders in its activities to a greater extent than might otherwise be the case.

The asset lock and other features will give confidence to those funding

2

CICs (particularly those not looking for any financial return), that the assets will be used for the benefit of the community and not unduly benefit the CIC's members or employees.

For further information on social enterprises generally please see www.socialenterprise.org.uk

SECTION 3

Regulation

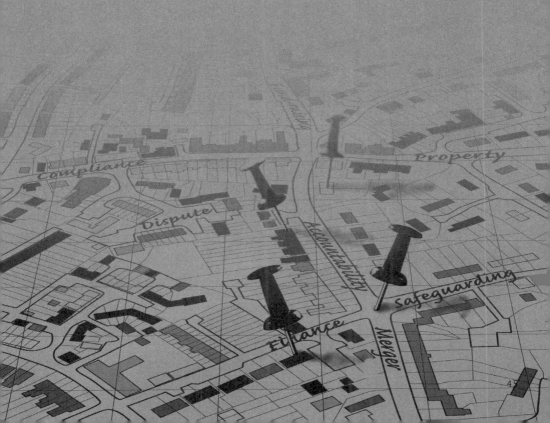

The Role of the Charity Commission

The Charity Commission is part of the Civil Service and is a "Non-ministerial Government department" meaning it is independent of ministerial influence. The Charity Commission is also independent of the charity sector which it regulates. It reports on its performance annually to parliament.

Structurally the Charity Commission is a charitable company consisting of a board, who set overall strategy and direction, and the directors group, which is concerned with the daily running of the operation, and is chaired by the Chief Executive. Board meetings are open and members of the general public can attend if they wish.

Under the Charities Act 2011 the Charity Commission has been given five specific objectives as well as six general functions. The specific objectives are to:

· increase public trust and confidence in charities (the "public confidence objective");
· promote awareness and understanding of the operation of the public benefit requirement (the "public benefit objective");
· promote compliance by charity trustees with their legal obligations in exercising control and management of the administration of their charities (the "compliance objective");
· promote the effective use of charitable resources (the "charitable resources objective");
· enhance the accountability of charities to donors, beneficiaries and the general public (the "accountability objective").

The general functions are to:

· determine whether institutions are or are not charities;
· encourage and facilitate the better administration of charities;
· identify and investigate apparent misconduct or mismanagement in the administration of charities and take remedial or protective action in connection with such misconduct or mismanagement;
· determine whether public collections certificates should be issued, and remain in force, in respect of public charitable collections;
· obtain, evaluate and disseminate information in connection with the performance of any of the Charity Commission's functions or in meeting any of its objectives;

- give information or advice, or make proposals, to any Minister of the Crown on matters relating to any of the Charity Commission's functions or to meeting any of its objectives.

The Act also sets out guidance in the way it should perform those functions.

Charitable status does confer benefits – most notably tax advantages and the public reassurance of accountability to the Charity Commission. But enterprises operating as charities must also accept the obligations which come with that benefit, including:

- the requirement to satisfy the "public benefit test" (see section 1);
- the need to justify any payment to charity trustees (including directors of charitable companies);
- rules on trading and investment that can significantly limit charity activities;
- tougher regulation, to protect the rights of its beneficiaries, donors and other stakeholders.

Charities receive considerable sums by way of public donations and therefore a robust compliance mechanism makes them accountable to the same public. The Charity Commission sees its role very much as sustaining the public's trust and confidence in the sector as a whole.

Specific Functions of the Charity Commission ("the Commission")

- **AS REGULATOR**
  The Commission describes its role as regulator as (including) "securing compliance with charity law and dealing with abuse and poor practice, enabling charities to work better within an effective legal, accounting and governance framework, keeping pace with developments in society, the economy and the law, and promoting sound governance and accountability."

  It promotes legal compliance through its online publications and casework. A higher expectation of compliance is placed on larger charities that have paid staff and access to professional advice. The Commission increasingly employs a "name and shame" concept to encourage charities to provide the reporting information required by the appropriate deadlines.

- **AS INVESTIGATOR**

  The Commission sees intervention and enforcement as important and works with other regulators (e.g. HMRC), as necessary. It evaluates complaints against charities and, if it believes things have gone seriously wrong, will open a formal investigation. Examples include where there has been serious misconduct or mismanagement, or where charitable assets are at risk of loss, damage or misuse. The Commission's stated aim is to ensure that "the charity is back on track to carry out its work for the future", although that may not always be apparent to the charity being investigated! The Commission also publishes reports of all its inquiries "to help other charities learn lessons". This can in turn sometimes fuel high media attention, particularly if the subject of the investigation has already attracted significant media coverage.

- **AS PUBLISHER**

  The Commission publishes a series of helpful Guidance notes for charities, which are updated periodically, as well as Alerts, Decisions, Statements on live cases, Inquiry reports and Regulatory case reports. All of these make for interesting reading.

The Charity Tribunal

The Charity Tribunal provides charities with a low cost/low risk means of challenging decisions of the Commission.

There is the ability to appeal to the Tribunal if the Charity Commission:

- refuses to register a charity;
- removes a charity from the Register;
- refuses consent to change a charity's governing document;
- has made another decision that the applicant wishes to challenge, for example, to open an Inquiry.

The Tribunal is independent of the Government and appeals can be decided on the basis of written submissions or oral evidence. The time limit for appealing is within 42 days of the date of the Commission's original decision. The National Council for Voluntary Organisations has some helpful guidance notes on how to submit an appeal.

When it hears a case, the Tribunal will consider all the evidence that was originally before the Commission and also other evidence. If it considers it appropriate, the Tribunal can send the case back to the Commission for them to make a fresh decision on the basis of the Tribunal's findings.

If an applicant considers that the Tribunal's decision is wrong in law it can apply for permission to appeal to the Upper Tribunal (Tax and Chancery Chamber).

The Charity Tribunal will not deal with customer service complaints in relation to the Commission. These will continue to be dealt with by the Commission's internal complaints system. Details can be found on the Commission's website.

Charities (Protection and Social Investments) Act 2016

The bill extends the Commission's power in a number of areas including:

· extending its ability to disqualify charity trustees;
· power to issue an official warning to a charity or a charity trustee;
· power to extend a trustee's or a charity employee's suspension from office to a maximum of two years;
· power to remove a trustee who has resigned – stopping trustees avoiding disqualification by resigning before they can be removed;
· power to wind up a charity following an Inquiry.

In addition it contains important provisions concerning fundraising and the ability of a charity to make social investments.

HMRC

We have already seen that one of the main advantages of charity registration is the tax reliefs that are available. With Gift Aid currently costing the Exchequer £2 billion per annum, HMRC are keen to ensure that the whole of a charity's income is expended for charitable purposes only.

HMRC, therefore, look at charities' accounts, and in particular their expenditure, to ensure that monies are expended for charitable purposes. In section (1) of this book, the 13 main charitable purposes (Objects) are set out. Broadly, HMRC will be concerned to ensure that each item of expenditure by a charity is in furtherance of at least one of those Objects (it does not necessarily have to be the Object[s] for which the particular charity exists!).

If HMRC find that a charity has expended its resources on items that are for non-charitable purposes, then they will treat such expenditure as non-charitable expenditure and will seek to recover tax from the charity at the appropriate rate on the sum expended. They will contact the charity seeking clarification on particular items of expenditure before drawing a conclusion.

Expenditure incurred in the administration of the charity is classed as being for charitable purposes. Likewise investments that a charity makes or loans which are in furtherance of the charity's Objects would not be classed as non-charitable expenditure.

Basically non-charitable expenditure would include:

· expenditure not incurred for charitable purposes only (this would include expenditure that is partly for charitable purposes and partly for non-charitable purposes);
· payment to an overseas body where the charity has not taken reasonable steps to ensure that it will be applied for charitable purposes (see section 21);
· trading losses arising from non-primary purpose trading (see section 24).

If a charity accumulates income or builds up reserves, HMRC may challenge this on the basis that the income has not been applied for charitable purposes. If, therefore, a charity is accumulating income over a period, with a view to undertaking a major expenditure in the future (e.g. a large property transaction), then it would be important for the charity to explain in its Trustees Annual Report (part of the accounts) the reasons why the income is being accumulated.

For charities that exist to advance religion, HMRC consider that such definition includes:

· the provision of places of worship;
· raising awareness and understanding of religious beliefs and practices;
· carrying out religious devotional acts;
· carrying out missionary and outreach work.

HMRC are of the opinion, however, that advancement of the Christian faith does not include acts that are simply in keeping with expected Christian behaviour, such as generosity of spirit. So just being generous, in their mind, is not charitable.

Some of the areas that HMRC take particular interest in include:

- **Employment** – in addition to reviewing employment records, they are particularly interested in any payments that are made to volunteers – (SEE section 15).
- **Expenditure** – areas such as unnecessary travel expenses, loans to staff, trading for non-primary purpose, as well as welfare payments made to needy members of a church have all attracted their attention and, in some cases, been disallowed as charitable expenditure.
- **Money sent overseas** – for a fuller treatment on this subject please see section 21.

- **Accounting records** – missing vouchers, incomplete documentation or lack of adequate explanation have all led to items of expenditure being disallowed.
- **Entertaining** – the provision of meals as an integral part of a religious activity (for example, an Alpha Course meal) would be allowable as a charitable expense. A party for church members using the charity's funds would not.
- **Sale of merchandise** – sale of recordings of the church services would be regarded as within the purposes of the charity. Selling merchandise such as T-shirts or baseball caps would not.

In the event that a charity's income is spent on non-charitable expenditure, then the tax exemptions are removed and the charity must pay tax on an amount of income equivalent to the value of the non-charitable payments.

HMRC have also demonstrated a reluctance to grant tax relief on expenditure that is partly for charitable purposes and partly for non-charitable purposes.

Other areas of non-charitable expenditure can include:

- a loan to a third party (e.g. a member of staff);
- payment to an overseas body where the charity has not taken reasonable steps to ensure the payment will be applied for charitable purposes (see section (2);
- trading income from non-primary purpose trading (see section 24).
- payments not specifically authorised by the terms of the charity's governing document;
- payments made that are specifically prohibited by the charity's governing document.

If as a result of a review of a charity's accounts HMRC decide to investigate further, they will instigate a compliance check. This can be done either over the telephone or in writing, and HMRC will inform the charity exactly what they are checking. During the period of a compliance check, the charity should not stop sending returns or making payments to HMRC when they are due, although they may find that HMRC suspend Gift Aid claims until the outcome of the compliance check.

If HMRC find that the compliance check has not satisfactorily answered their questions, then they may decide to open a formal inquiry. Again, they will write to the charity and state their intention to do so and set out the areas they are interested in.

At this point, it is recommended that the charity should appoint a lawyer or accountant to liaise with HMRC, particularly as the outcome of such an inquiry could be very expensive as far as the charity is concerned.

If as a result of the formal inquiry HMRC decide that there are items of non-charitable expenditure made by the charity, then their powers include:

- the ability to charge a penalty of up to 100% of the sums in issue;
- a claim for back tax together with interest on that sum;
- suspension of Gift Aid;
- extrapolation – this means that if, for example, HMRC find that 5% of a charity's expenditure in the year in question was for non-charitable expenditure, then they can claim that the same percentage would apply to other years as well. Bearing in mind HMRC can go back seven years in their investigations, it means that the payment that the charity may have to make for the year in question could be multiplied by seven.

Steps that a charity could take to minimise non-charitable expenditure being made would include:

- enacting specific policies, binding on all members of the charity (trustees included), concerning expenditure;
- having adequate internal control systems;
- a thorough check before making payments to overseas bodies;
- refusing to make any payments without proper and complete vouchers/ receipts;
- undertaking a risk management analysis (see section 26).

The Image of the Charity

The Charity's Name

Naming a charity can be a challenge! Some names are descriptive of the activity of the charity: "Youth With A Mission", some define the charity's area of operation: "London City Mission", and some invoke a scriptural theme: "Good Shepherd Church".

When selecting a name for a charity the following should be taken into consideration:

· the name must be distinct from other registered charities so as not to cause confusion for the public;

· the name should not include words or phrases that could cause offence in English or another language;

· the name should avoid using misleading names, i.e. suggesting the charity does something or works in a particular location when that is not true;

· a name that includes certain words may be more difficult to register (e.g. Royal, International or King's) and some words may not be allowed by law, (for example, indicating support for an illegal activity).

Before applying to register an organisation as a charity, it is wise to check the proposed name against those existing on the Register of Charities on the Charity Commission website.

The words "charity", "charities" or "charitable" can form part of the name. However if the charity is to be a charitable company then Companies House will need written proof that the Charity Commission does not object to the use of these words in the name.

The registration of a name does not give the charity any rights to that name under general law. Furthermore the Charity Commission will not guarantee the continued use of that name following registration. A name is always open to a subsequent challenge by others who may claim to have used the name (even as a "working name") over a long period in respect of an unincorporated charity. For example the charity "British Province of the Unitas Fratrum" protects the name "Moravian Church" and would preclude the use of the Moravian name by a subsequent charity.

The Charity Commission has the power to require the charity to change its name if:

· the registered name is the same as, or too similar to, the name of an existing charity;

- the charity's name is likely to mislead the public as to the true nature of the purposes or activities of the charity;
- the charity's name includes a word or expression that in the Charity Commission's opinion is likely to mislead the public as to the status of the charity (for example words which denote national or international status or royal patronage);
- the charity's name is likely to give the impression that it is connected in some way with H.M. Government, a local authority or some other body to which, in fact, it is not connected;
- the charity's name is offensive.

If the Charity Commission orders the charity to change its name after registration, then, notwithstanding that the name may have been available at registration, they will not indemnify the charity against the costs of the change or the reprinting of any stationery or marketing material.

If the organisation is to be a charitable company then similar restrictions will exist with regard to its name. A prior review of the Companies House website is advisable.

Use of Sensitive Names

- **"Royal"** – to include this word in the title of a charity would be extremely difficult. Prior consent to use the name would need to be obtained from The Ministry of Justice before the Charity Commission would register.
- **"International"** – evidence of the proposed charity's activities (or intended activities) in at least two overseas countries will be required.
- **"Charity"/"Charitable"** – the use of these words in the title requires the approval of the Secretary of State for Trade and Industry and, in the case of a registration as a charitable company Companies House will require the Charity Commission's prior written consent as well.

Name Change

Many charities change their name without remembering to notify the Charity Commission. As a result, difficulties can arise.

For any charity to change its name, the law requires a resolution to be passed. For a charitable company this will require a "special resolution" of the company. For an unincorporated charity or CIO, it will require an "ordinary resolution" to be passed by the trustees.

- **FOR AN UNINCORPORATED CHARITY**
  An unincorporated charity's name as contained in its governing document (e.g. "Sovereign World Trust") is part of the charity's trust and any unauthorised alteration is therefore technically a breach of trust! Such a breach can be remedied as follows:

  · If the unincorporated charity has power in its governing document to change its name, then an ordinary resolution should be passed by the trustees and, subject to the new name being acceptable to the Charity Commission, the Register of Charities can be altered.
  · If the unincorporated charity does not have power in its governing document to change its name, then it will require a Scheme of the Charity Commission as it is effectively changing the trust of the charity. However the Charity Commission is unlikely to be enthusiastic about such an application given that Charity Commission Schemes (to say nothing of their time) are usually reserved for more serious issues.
  · The pragmatic approach might be to allow the charity to use the new name as a "working name" and to keep the old name as the registered one. The new name can be entered onto the Register of Charities as part of the required details of the charity, and the charity is then free to use the new name on its letterheads, reports and published documentation, although it is wise to also quote the registered name, perhaps in small print, on each document.

- **FOR A CIO**
  The points above relating to unincorporated charities could equally apply to a CIO; however a CIO must contact the Charity Commission for them to finally approve any change of name.

- **FOR A CHARITABLE COMPANY**
  A special resolution to change the name of a charitable company must first be filed with the Registrar of Companies, and the change will not be completed until the Certificate of Incorporation on Change of Name has been issued by the Register of Companies. The Registrar of Companies retains the power to object to a new name and therefore any name change should be checked in advance with the Companies House Register.

A copy of the special resolution is then filed with the Charity Commission who, subject to agreeing the name, will change the Register to reflect the change. It is advisable to check the Charity Commission website to see that the new name is available beforehand.

Many charities decide to use a shortened version of their name or a "working name" to be the name by which the charity will be known in every day activity. (e.g. RCCG are the initials by which the charity Redeemed Christian Church of God is known.) The abbreviated name will usually be entered on the Register by the Charity Commission. The charity cannot use a name that it had been prevented from registering as an abbreviated or trading name, due to its similarity to an existing registered charity.

Publicity

It is wise for every charity or charitable company to include its full name and charity number on its letterheads, emails, publicity material, cheques and website. Furthermore, under the Charities Act 2011 a registered charity (providing its gross income for the last financial year that exceeded £10,000) should include the fact that it is a registered charity on:

· all notices, advertisements and other documents issued by and on behalf of the charity to solicit money or other assets for the benefit of the charity;
· all cheques, promissory notes, endorsements and other orders for money or goods, signed on behalf of the charity;
· all invoices rendered by it and all its receipts and letters of credit.

Any person (trustee and/or senior staff of the charity) falling foul of 1 and 3 above or any persons signing a document falling within 2 above, is guilty of an offence and liable to a fine if prosecuted.

Publicity for a charity should be produced with the object of only advertising the charity and the work that it does. It is considered unwise for a charity to take a "position" on certain political, international and otherwise controversial issues, simply because that is unlikely to be the main Object for which the charity exists and complaints by members of the public are likely to lead to the Charity Commission requiring the controversial material to be removed.

Care should also be taken when third-party material is offered on a charity's website, or otherwise endorsed by the charity's publications, as again the charity could suffer from being too closely aligned to a particular person/opinion. The Charity Commission has upheld complaints concerning the endorsement made by some charities (and opened formal Inquiries into the charity's activities), ultimately requiring the charity to disassociate from certain publications that it had formerly promoted.

The above guidance is to be distinguished from instances where, for example, the charity's Object is to advance the Christian faith by reference to a particular set of beliefs. It would be entirely consistent for the charity in those circumstances (subject to compliance with the law) to take a particular position on conduct or beliefs that are inconsistent with the stated beliefs of the charity.

In the case of an unincorporated charity, its trustees are well advised to ensure some degree of influence over the charity's position on certain subjects, as ultimately they are responsible.

Logos and Trademarks

In instances where the charity's officers wish to protect its name, beyond the very limited protection given by its existence on the Register of Charities, they may wish to consider registering either the charity's name and/or its logo as a trademark. Registration in this way would be a deterrent to those who might otherwise try to plagiarise the name for fundraising or marketing purposes.

Registration of a trademark is possible on a DIY basis (www.ipo.gov.uk); otherwise it is wise to consult a specialist Intellectual Property firm who can advise on the best forms of registration, particularly if the name to be protected is to be used worldwide. (See also section 14.)

Governance and Management

5

What is the Difference?

Governance has been defined as "the process by which a governing body ensures that an organisation is effectively and properly run .... Governance is not necessarily about doing; it is about ensuring things are done" (Sandy Adirondack, *The Good Governance Action Plan*, National Council for Voluntary Organisations, 2002).

The charity's effectiveness in both the achievement of its Objects and the way in which it functions will depend largely upon the ability of its board of trustees (or directors) to govern efficiently. Many of the issues encountered by charities, in both their administration and function (some of which require Charity Commission intervention) can trace their origins back to deficiencies within the governance and management structure of the charity.

Primarily, governance is the responsibility of the board of trustees and it includes: setting policy and long-term strategy; safeguarding the charity's vision and values; ensuring its financial viability; understanding the external environment and evaluating the performance of the charity towards achieving its stated Objects.

Management of a charity refers largely to the day-to-day administration and includes:

· implementation of the plans or policy whereby the charity pursues its Objects;
· guiding trustees on compliance;
· the delegated authority for the implementation of financial policy, performance evaluation and risk management;
· reporting fully to the trustees on the activities of the charity.

The trustees have certain specific roles which are discussed in section 6. However the simple principle is that trustees govern and managers manage.

It is, therefore, important that the trustees work to develop a good relationship between themselves and those who are managing the process of carrying out the Objects of the charity (staff or volunteers). There are certain relationships that are key:

· between the chair of trustees and the Chief Executive or minister;
· between the trustees themselves – particularly if they bring key skills to the organisation, which they could use to monitor certain activities of the charity (for example, finance, legal or human resources).

For the trustees to be effective in their governance role they will need to take time together to reflect on the "bigger picture". There does not exist an ideal model of governance for charities, simply because charities come in various sizes and have different approaches. However for a fuller discussion on various model forms of governance, the National Council for Voluntary Organisations (NCVO) have published helpful material on the subject. (see also Appendix 2 where some models of church governance structures have been set out.)

Many smaller charitable organisations do not have full or part-time staff and therefore it is not practical for the board to concentrate exclusively on governance, as they need to be involved in both governance and management. However, even in smaller charities the fundamental role of the trustee does not change – it is just that they have other responsibilities as well! It is suggested that trustees in small charitable organisations should identify those activities for which they have a governance role, those for which they have a management role and those for which they have a volunteer role, and strive to preserve the distinction.

There is specific responsibility for governance placed upon each trustee or director of a charity and they should commit to work as part of the trustee team to ensure:

- the charity pursues its Objects, for the public benefit;
- its financial integrity, including ensuring its financial viability;
- compliance with laws, in the UK, and overseas (if applicable);
- that management are held accountable;
- the long-term strategy;
- stewardship of the resources of the charity;
- the appointment (and dismissal) of the Chief Executive;
- careful decisions on major issues that have a significant impact on the charity;
- they identify situations that might pose undue risk to the charity's resources or reputation;
- they act in the charity's best interest at all times;
- they act with reasonable care and skill.

Some practical outworkings of these principles will include:

- developing and agreeing a long-term strategy;

- setting up operational plans and budgets and then monitoring progress and spending;
- recruiting new board members to meet the changing needs;
- understanding and complying with all legal and regulatory requirements;
- regularly identifying the major risks to which the charity is exposed and putting in place systems to manage those risks;
- managing conflicts of interest and maintaining independence of decision making;
- listening and responding to the views of the charity's supporters and those it exists to serve, (including visiting the charity's work overseas, if applicable).

Conflict Between Trustees and Management

If the board and the management have carefully defined their respective roles and have worked on building a good working relationship, then the possibility of conflict is minimised. However, both the trustees and the management should recognise that relationships and responsibilities are an evolving process, and from time to time areas of potential conflict will arise. Good governance is demonstrated when those issues can be identified and addressed before they become a significant distraction.

In a great many charities, however, the pressure of day-to-day activity, together with the limited amount of time that the board of trustees can invest in their role, can mean that there are areas of responsibility that have never been correctly agreed and defined, and problems can arise. This is particularly illustrated when a growing charity hires its first administrative employee. The trustees may continue to work on various management and practical issues, and the new employee is therefore unclear as to their own area of responsibility. The challenge for the board of trustees will be to delegate the day-to-day management (within clearly defined limits of authority) to the new employee, and re-focus their energies on the governance issues.

The American author John Carver[*] is noted for his development of the model for boards of directors. Carver's model distinguishes between the organisation's goals and the means that the organisation employs to achieve those goals. In his model, it is the board's job to decide the goals and the Chief Executive's job to determine the means to achieve the goals.

[*] Boards that make a difference; a new design for leadership in non-profit and public organisations
by John Carver, second edition San Francisco: Jossey-Bass (1997)

Carver also contributes some excellent thoughts on the board/CEO relationship, the board's responsibility for itself and the need to institutionalise excellence in the culture of the organisation. Although written primarily for the American charity sector its principles are not limited to that country and boards wishing to explore this important subject in more detail would benefit from reading his book.

The Founder

"Charities with dominant individuals often experience serious governance problems"

Charity Commission News, December 2015

In the charitable sector, it is often the case that the energy and vision behind the establishment of a charity derives from one person – "the founder". Many of today's charities trace their origins back, not to a committee or to a business plan, but to an individual, who had both the vision about how change could be brought about and the drive and commitment to ensure that an organisation was birthed to achieve that vision.

In both the birth and the establishment of the charity, the founder's vision, zeal, single-mindedness and ability to attract resources, often in the face of significant opposition, is probably the single reason why the charity exists. However, notwithstanding all those great qualities that enabled the charity to be established and to grow, in the longer term the founder has to be accountable and a team player with the trustees, management and staff of the growing charity, if the new charity is to be sustained and be accountable to its beneficiaries, rather than being the personal project of the founder. Often the founder will be a trustee of the charity but that is not always the case. Whether a trustee or not, the founder is often able to exert much influence and control.

Many charities and churches at some stage have to face the fact that the entrepreneurial, single-minded visionary leadership that gave birth to the organisation is not the only skill that is required to take the organisation forward. Sooner or later qualities of team-building, delegation, participatory management and accountability are those that must be developed in the charity, if the work is to be sustained and the baton passed to a new generation of leadership.

In cases where these issues are not addressed by the board at an early stage, the result can be that the founder continues to lead an organisation which is their own personal domain; either the management (perhaps under another leader), rises up and challenges the founder, or the founder remains in his or her role until they can continue no longer, staff leave and the organisation diminishes or closes.

It is difficult for trustees, who may have been appointed by the founder, to challenge the structure and style that the founder has established. However, just as there are parallels in both the business and political worlds where leaders have overstayed their time, the same applies in the charitable sector.

An examination of some of the instances where the Charity Commission has intervened in the affairs of a charity shows that a number of them had boards of trustees and staff positions that were populated by the founder, his or her family and friends. In such cases the Charity Commission has often found that the founder has been virtually unchallenged in his governance role and not held accountable by fellow board members. As a result, an unhealthy and possibly dangerous situation exists. In the writer's experience of over 35 years of legal representation of charitable organisations, the following conclusions have been drawn:

- It is inadvisable for both a husband and wife (or two other persons from the same household) to be trustees of the same charity.
- A minister or founder of a church should not automatically be made a trustee of the church charity, unless there is a very good reason for doing so.
- Appointments to the board should be made by the board or the charity's members and not by the founder.
- An active board rotation policy (to include the founder, if they are a trustee) is essential. See section 8;
- If the minister/founder is salaried by the church, albeit they are not a trustee, then the spouse should not be a trustee of the charity.
- Members of the founder's family (siblings and offspring) should not be on the board of the charity unless they are clearly outnumbered by independent trustees.
- If the founder is not prepared to operate under the above guidelines, then it is best they are not a member of that board.

See also section 7 on accountability.

The Minister

The relationship between a church minister and the trustees of that church is a very special one and worthy of further consideration, as it exists as a cameo to illustrate the different perspectives that both the minister and the trustees bring to the charity.

The trustees are accountable to the authorities (Charity Commission, Companies House and HMRC) for the charity. The provisions of the charity's governing document show that they have control of the charity, its property and assets, and are responsible for governing the charity in such a way as to ensure the assets are used towards achieving the Objects for which the charity was set up. The minister, as an employee of the church, will be employed upon terms that are agreed and monitored by the trustees. He or she will consider that they are accountable to God for fulfilment of the call on their life and the responsibility for the people under their care in the church.

Difficulties can arise when the trustees, in order to meet their responsibilities, appear to control the minister ("after all he is our employee"). The minister, however, reacts to this by bypassing the trustees and trying to make their position irrelevant.

The challenge is as follows:

· For the trustees – how can they ensure they are discharging their responsibilities as trustees without creating unnecessary friction with the minister?
· For the minister – how can he or she operate responsibly within the constraints placed on them by the trustees without compromising their call and ministry or operating in a way that makes the trustees feel irrelevant?

When the minister has felt threatened in his position, some typical reactions I have seen have included:

· The keeping of the church's cash instead of allowing it to be paid into the bank or allowing an independent person to monitor it.
· Intimidation of the trustees to submit to the minister's will.
· Refusing to attend a trustees meeting to explain his or her vision, plan and budget.
· Keeping the church's account as a personal account, sometimes as sole signatory, or ensuring that a trustee signs blank cheques for the minister.

· Operating a parallel administration to sideline the trustees.
· Openly preaching about the problems of the trustees from the pulpit.
· Gossiping to other church leaders.

Some of the responses of trustees that again I have witnessed have included:

· Seizing the accounts, records and cheque book and frustrating the minister's effectiveness.
· Deciding to instigate the removal of the minister.
· Speaking ill of the minister to third parties.

It is valid for the trustees to look to the minister (if he or she is also a trustee) for guidance to the board on spiritual matters relating to the church charity. Apart from this, however, it is clear that ministers who are also trustees should only have the same level of involvement and participation in decision-making as all other trustees. In other words, the minister's opinion should not outweigh the view/opinion of the other trustees. Decisions should be taken by the board of trustees acting together. Each member has only one vote; the minister does not get two!

On a practical point the minister needs to ensure that he or she is able to devote the necessary time to properly discharge their duty to the board as a trustee. Perhaps they need to examine their reason for wanting to be on the board of trustees – in many cases the benefit of his participation might be delivered in other ways, without their having to take on the onerous role and responsibility of trusteeship.

The minister cannot expect or require the trustees to do anything which is in breach of either the governing document or the law of the land. Trustees on the other hand must bear in mind the spiritual direction of the church. See also section 7 on accountability.

Spiritual Responsibility and Legal Responsibility

The power-play illustrated above between the trustees (legally responsible) and the minister (spiritually responsible) for a church begs a fundamental question: who is ultimately responsible in the charity?

Clearly as far as the UK law is concerned, the trustees of the charity are answerable for the charitable trust that they govern and for all the activities that go on within it. As stated above, the minister or spiritual leadership is responsible to a higher call and there are occasions when the spiritual direction in which they are taking the church can result in strains and stresses. Here are some examples:

- The spiritual leaders may decide that the church no longer needs an annual general meeting as they seek to downplay the ability of the membership to vote on major issues. That may well conflict with the charity's governing document (and the members' expectations) and potentially puts the trustees in breach of the law.
- The spiritual leadership decide to embark on a major expenditure (for example, the purchase of a new building), the complexity and expense of which causes some disquiet among the trustees. Given that the trustees would need to be a party to the acquisition and any associated financial arrangements (the latter possibly involving them in personal liability), they feel that it is beyond the historical performance of the charity to date to support the project that the leadership envisage.
- The trustees feel that they need to make an executive decision – perhaps on a staff matter – which the spiritual leadership do not agree with.
- The spiritual leadership are running the church and taking important decision without consulting with, or otherwise informing, the trustees; the trustees feel that, as ultimately they are responsible, they cannot allow the spiritual leadership to commit them to obligations they are unaware of, or unwilling to enter into.

The above are just some examples of issues that can separate those who are legally responsible and those who are spiritually responsible. If conflict and a possible split are to be avoided, then both parties need to establish principles in the early days of the relationship that will prevent the establishment of "camps". These could include:

- Meetings between the minister/spiritual leadership and the trustees in order to allow greater understanding of each other's roles.
- Commitment to the shared vision and mutual accountability.
- The inclusion of a clause similar to that set out in section 9 (page 126) being included in the charity's trust deed.
- Clear definition and agreement of roles of the trustees ("Governors") and of those who are responsible for the spiritual life of the church ("Management").

· An accountability/mentoring relationship to an outside third party for those responsible for the spiritual side (e.g. an outside minister), who can bring wisdom and objectivity into the scenario.

Appointment of the Leader

Most charities will have one person who acts as its "Leader". Whether called a Chief Executive, General Secretary or minister, they are accountable to the board of trustees as a whole. As mentioned earlier the board chairman needs to establish a good personal working relationship with the leader.

It has been suggested above that a church minister should not automatically be a trustee. However, they or the charity's leader (if not a trustee), can and should be invited periodically to trustees meetings, both to report on the progress of the organisation, and so that they can understand the trustees' perspective on some of the decisions that they are seeking to make (and vice versa!)

The roles and responsibilities of the chair of the board and the leader need to be defined and agreed at the outset. Given that there is the possibility of a degree of suspicion between the board as a whole and the leader, the relationship between the chairman of the board and the leader is critical to overcome such suspicion. Their relationship should include regular meetings and agreed methods of communication between those meetings.

While the chair of the board should not be too involved or interfere with the day-to-day running of the organisation, he/she needs to be aware of what is going on, in order that he/she can in turn report back to the board.

The chair will be responsible for the annual appraisal of the leader.

It would be wise for the board to ensure that the relationship between the charity and the leader is covered under an applicable service contract. This contract should be professionally produced to ensure that it deals with all of the issues with which the charity should properly be concerned, (see section 15). For example, if the leader is allowed to take outside speaking invitations and is given an honorarium for so doing, does that belong to the charity or the leader? In like manner, if the leader writes books (albeit in the charity's time) is he to be allowed to keep the royalties or do they belong to the charity? Failure to deal with these issues in the proper way has been grounds upon which the Charity Commission has investigated charitable organisations.

The setting of the remuneration of the leader is not without its challenges.

The charity will wish to pay at a level that is sufficient to recruit suitable candidates, yet remuneration levels in charities are historically lower than those in the commercial world. Clearly the final decision is one for the board of trustees as a whole, and salary levels may differ from charity to charity. There are websites that publish median salaries for many positions in the charity sector and these can provide guidelines to charity trustees who are seeking to discover the "going rate". Further benchmarking may be obtainable from other similar-sized charities. The comparables can be a useful evidential backup for instances when the charity is specifically asked, "who set the level of remuneration of the leader?"

Larger charities are beginning to replicate the commercial world by the establishment of remuneration committees comprising representatives of the board and senior management. If such committees are used, it is recommended that the charity trustees produce an appropriate protocol that governs the setting up and the limits of the committee.

Leadership/Organisational Failures

These are personal reflections gleaned from over 40 years involvement within charitable activity, with over 35 of those spent acting as a lawyer for charitable organisations.

Leadership/organisational failures have a significant effect on the credibility of faith-based organisations and have diminished society's respect for their message and the biblical values they claim to adhere to. The damage caused to those within the organisation, (particularly church members) and other beneficiaries of the charity are enormous. Many innocent casualties bare emotional scars that can last a lifetime. The trustees of a charity, as its governors (and often as the employer of a leader who may have failed), have an important role to play.

Perhaps the board and the leader could work to embed some important values into both the board and the DNA of the organisation, to be adhered to by the board and the leader. These could include:

· commitment to God and His principles;
· commitment to family and its core values;
· accountability to the church members;
· commitment beyond the law;

Seven Reasons

I have observed seven possible reasons why faith-based charities and their leaders experience problems:

- The lack of accountability of the leader.
- An ineffective board – unwilling to ask the difficult questions or make the hard decisions.
- Too much deference to the minister as spiritual leader. Spiritual abuse has been defined as "coercion and control of one individual by another in a spiritual context". The pressure to conform; misuse of scripture or the pulpit to control behaviour, or the suggestion that the leader has a "divine" position, have all contributed to leadership failures.
- Insecurity of the founder – this can include blocked goals, when the leader feels that everything he suggests or wants to do is being undermined. Insecurity may take many forms, including the leader's fear of being replaced. (Many church leaders' worst nightmare is the possibility of being voted out by a church meeting, and they all know colleagues or situations where this has happened!).
- Moral failure – Billy Graham once remarked that "75% of the men of God with the greatest gifting and potential were destroyed by sex."
- Incompetence – sometimes the leader or organisation just makes bad decisions.
- Lack of balance as to achieving the vision – i.e. "we must do this at all costs." Perhaps this results from a fear of God's judgement for failure?

- respect for the worth and dignity of individuals;
- transparency, integrity and honesty;
- responsible stewardship of resources;
- commitment to excellence and maintaining the public trust.

"As a matter of fundamental principle, the non-profit and philanthropic community should adhere to the highest ethical standards because it is the right thing to do. As a matter of pragmatic self-interest, the community should do so because public trust in our performance is the bedrock of our legitimacy. Donors and volunteers support charitable organisations because they trust them carry out their missions, to be good stewards of their resources, and to uphold rigorous standards of conduct. Non-profit

Seven Suggestions

Seven suggestions to minimise the risk of failure:

- A robust board of trustees – willing to ask the awkward questions, pursue the right answers and make the hard decisions.
- Accountability – both regular and effective.
- Realistic goals/aims – (maybe God is more interested in what we are like than in what we achieve)?
- Understanding and acceptance of the roles and responsibilities of the Pastor/leader.
- Understanding the full effect of failure on other people. A leader I know keeps a list at the back of his Bible of the numerous people who would be affected and the damage caused if he were to fail morally. Others use browser blockers such as "K9 web protection" or "Covenant Eyes" to hold them accountable for their use of the internet.
- Ensuring the right people with the right skills are in the right roles – God is more interested in character than charisma.
- Early warning – whistle-blowing is the technical term used in other contexts; however, perhaps early warning from other staff who work closely with the leader would enable issues to be addressed before it is too late.

5

and philanthropic organisations must earn this trust every day and in every possible way. But organisations are, at base, people, and it is up to the people of the independent sector – board members, executive leaders, staff and volunteers – to demonstrate their on-going commitment to the core values of integrity, honesty, fairness, openness, respect and responsibility."

(Covenant Partners Inc. USA)

The principles set out above will not prevent every failure. Indeed the Bible reminds us that failure is something that God has made allowance for in His relationship with mankind. However, it does seem that in recent years instances of failure – both in churches and by leaders – has risen significantly and maybe this suggests that we have either become too casual or have failed to spot the warning signs at an early stage.

Faith-based charities have long enjoyed the support of the community at large in going about their work. However, reputational damage (which in today's world goes viral almost as the norm) means that damage is caused to the sector as a whole and not just an individual charity. Ultimately this devalues the message and the Biblical values that the organisation seek to advance/ live by. If the response of the community is that "we cannot hear your message because what you are is speaking more loudly"; then that begins to undermine everything for which the organisation stands.

Policies

Good governance in the charity sector is greatly assisted when the charity develops its own clearly-documented policies dealing with how it will manage and deal with various aspects of its work.

There is no complete set of policies that a charity must adopt; rather it will be for the board to decide which policies are necessary for that particular charity. The objective is to have policies that fit the particular organisation and are practical and workable, rather than have a long list with a view to impressing others as to how efficient the organisation is! Some of the more common policies include:

- Health and Safety – including fire safety and staff working conditions – see section 15.
- Equal Opportunities – including statements on harassment, discrimination, and advancement – see section 16.
- Data Protection – see section 13.
- Risk Assessment – see section 26.
- Volunteering – including expenses – see section 15.
- Employment – including staff expenses, loans, appraisals, grievance, sick leave etc. – see section 15.
- Safeguarding – including whistle blowing – see section 18.
- Fundraising – see section 23.
- Finance – see section 22.
- Governance – including committees, use of outside consultants, job descriptions and conflicts of interest – see section 5.

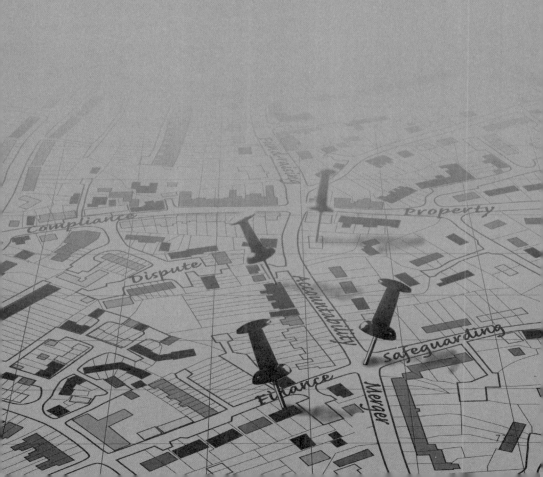

SECTION 6

6

The Board

A well-run charity is one that is directed by a clearly identifiable board of trustees who take responsibility and are accountable for governing the organisation, so that it is compliant as well as economically and effectively run. The role and responsibilities of trustees are set out in the previous chapter. Depending on the nature of the charitable organisation, the "trustees" may also be known as directors, board members, council members, governors or executive committee members. (Hereafter they are referred to collectively as "trustees".)

Most trustees volunteer for the role and receive no payment (other than reimbursement of any necessary out-of-pocket expenses incurred in carrying out their trusteeship). As trustees have the ultimate responsibility for running the charitable organisation, it is vital that charities give high priority to the recruitment, selection and training of the trustees.

Role and Recruitment of a Trustee

The individual trustee's responsibility has been summarised in the preceding chapter:

- **THE QUALIFICATIONS FOR TRUSTEESHIP**

The candidate must:

- be at least 16 years old;
- not be disqualified from serving as a director under the Companies Act or have unspent convictions for dishonesty, be an undischarged bankrupt, or previously removed as a trustee of a charity by the Charity Commission or court;
- have the appropriate DBS certificate for working with children and vulnerable adults.

- **APPOINTMENT**

- By Resolution or Deed (depending on the governing document). (See section 8.)
- By recording the appointment with the Charity Commission (and Companies House, if applicable). (See section 8.)
- By signature of a Declaration of Willingness to Serve and Trustee Code of Conduct (see section 8).

If the organisation is a charitable company, then although the board members are called directors, they function as trustees for the purposes of the Charities Act; either name can be used. In the case of a charitable company, however, care should be taken by anyone who is not on the board yet who seeks to issue directions to the board as to how they should act. Such a person may well be acting as a Shadow Director and therefore responsible for sharing the liabilities of trusteeship (for example, they would share the liability for wrongful trading with the other trustees).

Many charities find the process of recruitment of new trustees a difficult task. As a result there is the temptation to recruit a board, perhaps from among friends or close contacts, and leave that board in place until someone retires. Given that today there is a significant weight of responsibility imposed upon charity trustees (and boards need to ensure that they can act in an effective way), often this will necessitate recruiting additional trustees who will bring skills of different disciplines to the board table. Indeed recent research has shown that efficient charities place an increasing emphasis on improving board recruitment practices by recruiting board members, not just because they are enthusiastic, but because they have the right skills and experience and the time necessary to do the job.

It is helpful to undertake a basic skills survey among board members in order to determine:

· what is needed to make the board as effective as it can be;
· whether it has the right mix of skills, experience, ethnic background, resources and age spread to enable it to deliver its service to its intended beneficiaries.

Very few charities who conduct a skills survey settle for the status quo. There then follows the task of sourcing and recruiting new trustees.

Traditionally charities have recruited new trustees through personal connections and/or word of mouth. The Charity Commission has published some helpful material on trustee recruitment in which they recommend other recruiting methods, such as advertising.

The following principles are suggested to assist in the recruitment process:

· Decide which member(s) of the board will take ultimate responsibility for leading the charity in the recruitment process.
· Prepare a job description for the trustee position that the charity is

seeking to fill. Be realistic in the job description as to the time commitment, skills and responsibilities required. New trustees cannot be expected to react positively if they find that the time and responsibility commitment is significantly above that which was represented to them.

· Prepare a pack that includes the job description, a copy of the charity's governing document, a copy of its most recent Annual Report and Accounts, together with an executive summary of the organisation and all recent publicity.

· Identify the target audience. Decide whether the position will be communicated by word of mouth and/or advertised.

· Prepare a comprehensive induction programme that can be offered to the new recruit to enable them to transition smoothly into the position. Possibly this would include the secondment of an existing trustee to act as a "mentor" to the new candidate.

When a potential candidate has been identified and they are responding to the initial overtures being made, seek (with the candidate's consent), to take up at least one reference on the candidate (unless they are personally known to one or more of the existing trustees).

A formal offer to the candidate should be subject to receipt of the aforementioned reference, proof that the candidate is eligible to act as a trustee (see section 8) and subject also to a clear DBS check (see section 8).

Qualities in a Charity Trustee

WILLINGNESS TO TAKE RESPONSIBILITY. This comes from an understanding of the governing document, an acceptance of the Objects for which the charity is set up and a willingness to discharge the role of trustee effectively.

AN ABILITY TO WORK WITH OTHERS. A board of trustees is made up of individuals but together they comprise a team. The overriding requirement on a charity trustee is to act in the best interest of the charity, in that he or she forgets personal considerations if they conflict with the good of the charity.

WILLINGNESS TO GIVE APPROPRIATE TIME. To serve on a board of trustees is not something that can be done adequately by giving "an hour or so each month". In addition to the scheduled board meetings, a trustee will need to give time to read briefing papers, give specific input from his or her specialisation to staff members of the charity and visit the charity's beneficiaries (this can include travelling overseas if the charity conducts its work there), in order to fully understand and evaluate the charity's performance.

CONFIDENCE TO ASK THE AWKWARD QUESTIONS FROM TIME TO TIME. Given that a charity trustee's primary responsibility is that of governance, they must be free to challenge and hold staff and volunteers accountable. If the trustee has any doubts or suspicions about the charity's function or personnel, they must share these concerns with the chair of trustees and if necessary put them in writing.

WORK TO UNDERSTAND AND DEVELOP THE TRUSTEES' ROLE WITHIN THE ORGANISATION. Following the completion of an induction course, the role of trustee will evolve with the organisation and each trustee is responsible for moving ahead with the organisation to ensure that it is pursuing its stated Objects.

DEMONSTRATE THE INTEGRITY THAT THE CHARITY IS EXPECTED TO MODEL. If the charity's success is in a large part dependent upon the effectiveness of the trustees, then it must follow that sloppy behaviour among the trustees is likely to lead to a poorly functioning charity.

The contribution that each trustee brings to the charity depends largely on the mix of trustees on the board. However, in general terms it will include the contribution of:

- **Advisor** – bringing the trustee's personal experience and qualification to advise the other members of the board and the staff of the organisation. Generally providing leadership for the organisation.
- **Ambassador** – making contacts and linking the charity's staff to outside persons and bodies that can assist in the charity's development. Generally supporting the Chief Executive and senior staff.
- **Advocate** – acting as a voice for the charity. The trustee will often be a visionary able to enthuse others towards achieving the Objects for which the charity was set up.

Induction and Training

An induction programme is an essential prerequisite of any aspiring trustee. There are two reasons for this:

- potential trustees can only be effective when they understand the organisation, its aims, its culture and what contribution the trustee is expected to bring;
- the charity needs to understand clearly the skills and contributions that the trustees individually and collectively can be relied upon to contribute.

A common reason for charity managers to express frustration with the board of trustees (and vice versa) arises out of an unrealistic expectation of the other. Very often this can be traced back to the absence of a clear induction policy.

There are two essential qualities that a new trustee must have at the outset of their period of service:

- a good understanding of the Objects of the charity and a positive desire to identify with those;
- the appropriate amount of time to contribute to the charity and fulfil their responsibilities as a trustee.

Given the charity trustee is responsible for the charity's assets and has a clear duty to act at all times in the charity's best interests, a prospective trustee would be unwise to take up responsibility unless they had read and considered:

- a copy of the charity's governing document;
- copies of the last three years' audited accounts;
- copies of minutes of trustees meetings for the same period.

A new trustee should be encouraged to meet with a cross-section of the staff and volunteers of the charity and to read some project reports, in order to get a good understanding of the way in which the charity functions.

It is also suggested that new trustees should receive:

- a copy of the original positional description, amended as may be necessary;
- a copy of a description of any organisational structure;
- details of all other trustees together with their contact information;

- copies of any strategic plans;
- copies of any major fundraising proposals/grant applications;
- copy of any trustee code of conduct.

In addition to the written information, a structured induction programme could include:

- informal time with other trustees and senior staff of the charity;
- visits to one or more of the charity's projects;
- an opportunity for the new trustees to feed back what they have seen and heard and what conclusions they have concerning the charity and its work.

A board that does not value the new trustee for the fresh ideas and views that they may bring to the board is missing out on a great resource. Just because the charity has run in a certain way for many years does not mean that those ways are the best. It follows that new trustees must feel valued, and that the contributions they make (particularly new insights) will be well received and evaluated rather than dismissed with a "we've always done it this way" response. A disillusioned new trustee will not serve the charity well and will gradually withdraw from meetings and contributions they would otherwise bring. This in turn brings resentment among the other trustees and distracts the board of trustees from their essential work.

It is likely that new trustees will be particularly disillusioned by:

- lack of an advance agenda;
- trustees meetings that do not focus on key issues and are badly run;
- the lack of proper reports and detailed information that is passed to the board by the charity's workers;
- poorly thought out plans for fundraising and financing the charity's ongoing operations;
- estranged relationships between the trustees themselves or the trustees and the key staff;
- a closed mind to new ideas and suggestions.

The chairman of the charity has a key role, both in making new trustees feel welcome and in drawing them out at trustees meetings and ensuring their effective participation in the governance of the charity as a whole. It is suggested that the chairman can usefully schedule time to meet with a new trustee during their first year, to ensure their expectation of the charity and the charity's expectation of them is still intact.

For a fuller consideration of this subject the author recommends the publications of The National Council for Voluntary Organisations.

Meetings and Records

The frequency of trustees meetings will depend largely on the size and/or needs of the particular charity. It is suggested that the minimum number of trustees meetings each year should be two, and in reality quarterly meetings may be appropriate for most charities.

It is important that the chair and secretary prepare well and in advance of board meetings. Such preparation would include:

- circulating the proposed agenda at least seven days beforehand, together with any significant papers and reports to be discussed;
- preparation of an annual work plan for the board detailing the major items that would be covered at each meeting during the year. Such items would include certain reoccurring subjects such as:
    finance;
    review of activity;
    review of risk;
    compliance.

It is vital that trustees meetings are fully and accurately minuted. For this purpose it is suggested that an independent person is invited to be a minute secretary, so they can concentrate exclusively on capturing the important points without having to join in the discussion.

Comprehensive minutes are vital for the following reasons:

- to record any conflicts of interest, disclosed at the outset of the meeting;
- to confirm the discussions held and the decisions made;
- to record the agreed action and the responsibilities for carrying out those actions;
- to inform those trustees who did not attend the meeting, yet are bound by decisions made by the board;
- to remind those who did attend the meeting as to what they agreed to do;
- to provide a full record which would be reviewed by the Charity

Commission should it decide to challenge a decision made or otherwise enquire into the charity.

Following the meeting, the minutes should be prepared quickly (while events are still fresh in the mind) and checked with the chair of the meeting and thereafter circulated to all who attended and those who were entitled to attend but could not.

While it is important that the draft minutes are checked with the chair of the meeting, they should not be altered in any way that reflects a discussion or decision that did not in fact take place. The minute secretary should refuse to have any further part in the publishing of minutes that did not reflect the discussion and decisions that had been reached at a properly convened meeting.

Once the minutes have been circulated, it will not be until the next meeting of the trustees that they can be formally accepted (by means of a vote), and signed off by the chair of the meeting, at which time they will be taken as being a true and accurate record and placed in the charity's minute book.

The courts have held that a valid meeting normally consists of the quorum of trustees who can both see and hear each other. Telephone conference calls cannot normally be used to transact business if the governing document or the law itself requires a face-to-face meeting. For larger charities, particularly where the trustees are spread around the country or overseas, the governing document may permit electronic video conferencing whereby all trustees can see and hear each other.

Obviously not all the business of the charity has to be conducted at meetings. There may be times when trustees will conduct business by telephone, fax or the internet or by the circulation of papers (for example the written resolution procedure that can be utilised by a charitable company) – see section 9.

Conflicts of Interest

Given that a trustee has a clearly legal duty to act exclusively in the charity's best interest when making decisions as a trustee, it follows that, if there is a decision to be made in which the trustee has a personal interest (including one in respect of a connected person), then there is a conflict of interest and that will need to be managed.

Practical steps to both identify and manage a conflict of interest include:

- At the outset of every board meeting the chair should give opportunity for any trustee to disclose any conflict of interest in respect of any item on the agenda.
- If the conflict of interest is a major one then the board must find an alternative way to deal with the agenda item (without the contribution of the conflicted board member), and which does not involve the conflict of interest.
- If the conflict is a minor one then it can usually be managed by the conflicted member excusing themselves from the discussion and any vote (i.e. leaving the room completely).
- If the conflict is major and there is no alternative way forward that would remove it, or most or all of the trustees share that conflict, then the Charity Commission must be consulted and advise on the way forward.

It is strongly advised that the charity should have a conflicts of interest policy and also maintain a trustees' register of interests, under which a trustee's commitments and interests can be recorded, which would give some advance notice of a potential conflict. Clearly such a register needs to be updated regularly.

The minutes of the meeting should include a full explanation of the conflict of interest and the way in which it was dealt with and should show:

- what the conflict of interest was;
- which trustee or trustees were affected;
- an outline of the discussion;
- if anyone withdrew from the discussion;
- how the remaining trustees made the decision in the charity's best interest.

The Charity Commission has issued detailed guidance on managing conflicts of interest.

The Chair

(For ease of usage "chairman" is hereinafter employed)

The chairman is usually also a trustee. The terms of his appointment as chairman are usually governed by the governing document. The chairman is responsible for leading the trustees meetings through the business items that are on the agenda. Sometimes the governing document also gives the chairman a casting vote in the event of a deadlock.

At the outset of a trustees meeting the chairman should announce whether or not the meeting has a quorum (i.e. the minimum number of people that the governing document says must be present in person in order to make a valid decision at the meeting). If there are not enough trustees to form a quorum, then the meeting has no standing and the chairman should adjourn it.

As mentioned above, trustees meetings will be greatly assisted if an agenda is circulated to all participants beforehand, together with copies of any briefing papers or other reports or documents that the trustees will be considering. In that way trustees can prepare thoroughly before attending the meeting. Some chairmen decide that the element of surprise is an essential ingredient to a major decision and fear that by announcing a proposal in advance of the meeting it will allow time for opposition to the proposal to be mounted. Trustees in turn seldom like being surprised and may react to the surprise by deferring a decision!

It is for the chairman of the meeting to decide how much time will be allocated to each item on the agenda, and it is helpful if the chairman also indicates to the meeting whether a decision is being required on a particular matter at the meeting or whether the item is there for information only at that stage.

In advance of the meeting the chairman and the secretary can usefully spend time preparing for the meeting in the following way:

- Considering how the room could be set out and whether an overhead projector/flip chart/laptop and projector would be an assistance.
- Creating a seating plan around the table.
- Deciding whether refreshments will be offered before or after the meeting (it is suggested in any event that drinking water be placed on the table during the meetings).
- Setting the anticipated finishing time for the meeting (it is good practice to announce the timetable at the beginning of the meeting);

The chairman conducting the meeting needs to have a clear grasp of the procedural requirements of the charity's governing document and also must ensure that all discussions are channelled through the chair, so the chairman can exercise a degree of control over the meeting. If persons other than trustees are to be invited to come in and contribute to a section of the trustees meeting (for example a chief executive who is not on the board) then that person should be brought in at the appropriate time and should leave as soon as that part of the agenda has been completed.

The chairman should also ensure that before a vote is taken the proposal is clearly summarised, so that all board members understand what they are being asked to vote on.

If the meeting is adjourned before it is completed, then it can be reconvened at a later date and time without the need to circulate fresh notice.

The minutes of the meeting should record in reasonable detail the substance of discussions that led to major decisions being made. If the trustees have sought outside professional advice on a particular matter, then that advice should be referred to in the minutes and a copy of the advice appended to the finalised minutes themselves. An example of this would be where the trustees resolve to make a major purchase (a property say) and advice was sought from a surveyor, and perhaps the charity's accountants, as to the charity's ability to fund such an acquisition. Remember the decision affects not just the trustees who actually take it, but also their successors as trustees, who may carry the ramifications in the event that the decision taken proves to be a wrong one. If the minutes record a clear reasoning for the decision and show that the trustees took all possible advice before coming to a reasonable decision in all the circumstances, then the trustees are unlikely to be criticised by the Charity Commission.

If a trustee is unable to agree that the draft minutes are an accurate record of the meeting, they should draw their issue to the attention of the chairman before those minutes are signed. If the trustee is ultimately unable to agree the minutes, then their dissension on a particular issue should be noted and recorded as an addendum to the minutes before they are signed.

Minutes of a trustees meeting should be provided to all of the charity's trustees. It is wise to provide a copy of the minutes of the AGM to the charity's Auditors. It is not necessary to make the minutes of trustees meetings available for public inspection. However, please see section 13 with regard to Data Protection.

The minute book of the charity should be retained by the charity's secretary and should be kept in a safe place. It is recommended that the minutes of trustees meetings should be kept for the entire life of the charity.

A charitable company is permitted to retain its statutory books on computer.

Remember that although the trustees can invite non-trustees to a meeting (for example, a professional advisor or a staff member) those people cannot vote. Furthermore, charity trustees cannot nominate someone to vote on their behalf.

Code of Conduct

Increasingly charities are beginning to use a trustee code of conduct to improve the governance of the charity. The National Council for Voluntary Organisations publishes a model trustee code of conduct which is in effect a contract between the trustee and the organisation, whereby the trustee promises to observe the organisation's values, avoid conflicts of interest, protect the organisation's reputation and participate professionally in board decisions. The benefits of such a code of conduct include:

· defining the role of the trustee;
· improving the day-to-day governance;
· minimising the risk of misconduct against the organisation;
· highlighting certain dangers such as conflicts of interest;
· enabling the chairman to get alongside a trustee who is not complying with the code and thereby minimising "non-performance" by a trustee.

Payment to a Trustee

While for the most part charity trustees are unpaid for their services to the charity, there are occasions when a payment can be made to a trustee, and the circumstances surround this are carefully controlled by the Charity Commission.

There are five main instances when a charity may consider making a payment to a trustee:

· reimbursement of a trustee's expenses;
· payment to a trustee for a specific service given to the charity;
· payment to a trustee for serving as a trustee;
· employing a trustee or connected person;
· reimbursement of loss of earnings incurred while serving as a trustee.

Before the charity considers a payment under any of the above circumstances, there are some important considerations for the Board of Trustees to consider:

- Does the charity have the power in its governing document to make the payment? If it does not, then the governing document will need to be altered before any payment can be made (save for reimbursement of a trustee's expenses). For an unincorporated charity, this will necessitate an application to the Charity Commission for its consent. For a charitable company, the Articles can usually be altered by a Resolution.
- How will the conflict of interest be managed? Fundamentally a trustee must not put him or herself in a position where his or her personal interest conflicts with his or her duty to act in the best interests of the charity. It follows that any discussions about the possibility of making a payment to a trustee (other than reimbursement of necessary expenditure) must be carried out in the absence of the trustee concerned. The Board of Trustees must be satisfied that the proposed payment is in the best interests of the charity.
- How will the trustee's performance be measured to ensure the charity gets good value? This would be especially important if the employment of a trustee is long-term.
- How will the proposed arrangement be documented? A trustee providing a specific service may need a service agreement; a trustee being employed would need an employment contract; and other arrangements may need to be specifically documented in an agreement so that the understanding is clear on both sides.

Dealing with each of the five likely payments in turn:

- **REIMBURSEMENT OF A TRUSTEE'S EXPENSES**
Charity trustees are entitled to claim legitimate expenses in connection with their service as a trustee and the charity does not need specific authority in the governing document to make these payments.

From a practical point of view, a charity should not make any reimbursement unless the expenditure has been properly authorised and the claim supported by appropriate receipts.

Clearly it is impossible to define every area of expenditure that can be reimbursed, but the major ones would include travel costs, meals, postage and telephone calls incurred while on charity business, as well as items such as the reasonable cost of childcare or costs of dependants to enable a trustee to attend a meeting, or overnight accommodation and subsistence incurred while attending either a trustees meeting or undertaking work for the charity.

In practice, well-run charities will have a trustee's expense policy, which sets out a protocol for claiming expenses. The charity should always take care to ensure that it does not settle expense claims which are excessive or which do not relate exclusively to legitimate trustee activity on behalf of the charity.

- **PAYMENT TO A TRUSTEE FOR SPECIFIC SERVICES GIVEN TO THE CHARITY**
Fundamentally this applies to services that are given to the charity over and above the normal role of a charity trustee and covers not only a trustee providing these but also a connected person.

Examples of circumstances where a charity may wish to make a payment under this Section would include payment to a trustee for:

- delivering a talk;
- using a trustee's firm for building or decoration work;
- providing specialist services for the charity such as:
    estate agency;
    computer consultancy;
    translator;
    legal services.

A charity can make such a payment provided:

- there is a written Agreement between the charity and the trustee (or connected person) setting out the services to be provided and the exact or maximum amount to be paid;
- the trustee concerned has not taken part in any decisions made by the Board of Trustees concerning the making of the Agreement or the services to be provided;
- the payment for the services is reasonable in relation to the service to be provided, and that the trustees are satisfied that the payment is in the best interests of the charity;
- the total number of trustees who are receiving payment are in a minority on the Board;
- there is no prohibition in the governing document of the charity concerning payment to the trustee;
- the charity trustees have read and agreed to the Charity Commission Guidance on the subject, which is contained on its website.

Provided the charity can comply with the above conditions, then the Charity Commission's prior consent to the payment is no longer necessary.

While it is important that any proposed arrangement as above is also recorded in the charity's Minutes, that does not replace the need for a formal written Agreement between the charity and the trustee concerned, which will need to set out the proposals in detail and which should be prepared by the charity's lawyers. The Agreement will provide that the trustee concerned will not participate in any future trustee discussions concerning the Agreement, quality of service provided, or its commercial terms. The Agreement will need to be retained for at least six years, as it forms part of the charity's accounting records.

The level of payment for any service under this provision must be reasonable and have regard as to whether or not the charity can afford the level of payment, as well as the value to the charity of the service being provided. Best practice would suggest that the figure should be benchmarked against comparable services, and the comparisons retained as justification for the sum paid.

Fundamentally the charity trustees must remember that their duty of care towards the charity will mean that they must be able to demonstrate that they acted honestly and in good faith when making this decision and managing the ongoing conflict of interest. Professional advice is recommended.

If the trustees cannot comply with the conditions above, then they should not make any payment until Charity Commission consent has been sought.

- **PAYING A TRUSTEE FOR SERVING AS A TRUSTEE**
Under this provision, it may be possible for a Board of Trustees to pay a trustee for carrying out his or her service *as a trustee.*

Again, the charity will need to have authority in its governing document, and if this doesn't exist they should seek the consent of the Charity Commission. Failure to have this authority may make the trustees liable to repay all or part of the payment that is being made.

Payment under this provision may be a one-off payment (for example, to enable a trustee to attend a specific event) or on a continuous basis (for example, to enable duties to be carried out on an ongoing basis).

The payment under this provision will usually be in circumstances where the remaining trustees are convinced that there is a "clear and significant advantage" to the charity, and that such a payment will not have an adverse effect on the reputation of the charity among its supporters. An example of such a payment would be where the charity may be involved in an unusually complex area of operation in which a trustee must exercise a higher degree of responsibility and expertise. Payments that have been authorised under this section have included a Chair of Trustees of a multi-million pound operation, in circumstances where the Chair is required to devote a significantly increased commitment of time to the affairs of the charity.

In making an application to the Charity Commission for consent, the Board will need to show why the charity would be less effective without the payment being made, and if the payment concerned is in connection with the recruitment of a new trustee then it will need to show the steps it has taken to recruit trustees without payment, and why they have failed to secure the calibre of trustee that the Board feels is required.

- **EMPLOYING A TRUSTEE OR A CONNECTED PERSON**
From time to time a charity may wish to employ on staff someone who has previously served on the Board of Trustees in an unpaid capacity. In many instances, the employment of someone in this category may need to be approved by the Charity Commission.

Fundamentally the Board will need to justify the decision to employ the trustee, although this is often possible, given the trustee's detailed knowledge of the charity and its activities, which perhaps gives them an advantage over an outsider for the job in question. The trustees must however demonstrate that they have been open and transparent in their decision-making and there should be no question of any improper influence in the process. There will be a high standard for the trustees to demonstrate, both in the process that has led to the potential appointment and also the ongoing conflicts of interest which will need to be managed.

If the decision to employ the trustee has been taken while the person remains a trustee then the Charity Commission's approval of the employment must be obtained, failing which the employee/trustee concerned may have to repay any earnings to the charity. This is so even if the trustee later resigns from the Board before taking up the employment.

In applying for Charity Commission consent (which can be done online), the Board will need to demonstrate that the appointment is necessary for the effectiveness of the charity, and that the position has not been specifically created to fit the particular qualities of the trustee concerned. It will usually be necessary for the trustees to show that the job offer has been subject to an open and transparent selection process and that the charity will be obtaining good value for the money being expended and the service to be provided.

If the Charity Commission takes the view that there has not been an open and transparent recruitment process, then it may require one to be conducted for the post to be openly advertised.

On occasions a charity may wish to invite an existing employee to join the Board of Trustees. In these circumstances, given that the employment will have commenced some time before the person joins the Board, their salary is not deemed to be a benefit that flows from their being a trustee. However it is suggested that Charity Commission consent be obtained so that there are no questions raised on any increase in salary that may be awarded to the employee thereafter.

Again the Board of trustees must manage the conflict-of-interest carefully, and ensure that the employee who joins the Board does not have any influence on the terms and conditions of employment or salary reviews, or indeed the continuance of the particular post that he or she occupies.

The Charity Commission has in the past shown a reluctance to authorise an employee who happens to be the Chief Executive of a charity to join the Board, mainly because it has been concerned for the need for stronger governance arrangements so that the Board's decisions would be taken for the greater good of the charity without the influence of the paid Chief Executive, who is now sitting on a Board.

In circumstances where a connected person of a trustee becomes a paid employee of the charity, the Charity Commission's prior consent must be obtained.

- **REIMBURSEMENT OF LOSS OF EARNINGS INCURRED WHILE SERVING AS A TRUSTEE**

In some circumstances, the Board of Trustees may wish to compensate a trustee for loss of earnings which the trustee suffered while attending Board meetings or discharging other responsibilities for the charity. Provided the charity has authority in its governing document and there is a positive advantage to the charity in making such a payment, then it is enabled to do so.

Compensating a trustee for loss of earnings is not the same as reimbursing a trustee's expenses (see above). It may be that the governing document does not give specific authority to reimburse a trustee for loss of earnings and, in that case, the Charity Commission's authority must be obtained.

In seeking authority, the charity will need to demonstrate why the payment is being made and how it will benefit the charity, as well as give details of the sums involved. The charity will need to consider carefully the level of payment, as it may be that to reimburse a trustee for the amount of loss of earnings they have suffered would be out of proportion to either the charity's resources or for the particular contribution that the trustee has made on the day in question.

In summary:

- If the governing document of the charity prohibits a payment being made, then the Charity Commission's consent to alter the governing document must be obtained (in the case of an unincorporated charity), although, for a charitable company, the Articles will usually give authority for the amendment to the governing document without Charity Commission consent.
- The trustee who is the potential recipient of monies must not participate in discussions concerning the proposed payment (or their proposed employment by the charity).
- Payments to a trustee must be disclosed clearly in the charity's accounts.
- If the aggregate of the trustee's payments in any one year is less than £1,000.00, then the Charity Commission regards these as "small trustee payments" and their prior authority is not usually sought. "Small trustee payments" also include small one-off payments (honoraria) to a trustee, which may be made as a gesture for appreciation and goodwill for services that the trustee has rendered to the charity (for example, if they retire after a long period of service). Again, the trustees must demonstrate that such a payment (albeit less than £1,000.00) is in the best interest of the charity.
- Any payments in excess of £1,000.00 are treated in the same way as a payment to a trustee and the above provisions apply. Any one-off payments to a trustee should be notified to the charity's accountants to ascertain whether or not they are taxable in the hands of the recipient.

Delegation to Committees and Advisory Groups

The governing document of most charities will permit the trustee board to set up committees. These are small groups to which the board assigns a particular task or area on which to focus. The tasks delegated can include finance, administration, staff welfare, relocation or other major project. Their role is purely an advisory one, and ultimately they will report back to the board, who will make a decision as to whether or not to implement their findings.

The make-up of these committees can contain non-board members, although it is advisable for a committee to have at least one board member represented thereon.

If a charity is to set up a committee, then the trustees must ensure that each committee has a clear term of reference and that the committee is comprised of people who have the required skills base and experience to enable the committee's deliberations to benefit the charity.

Some boards also set up advisory groups. This is an opportunity for the charity to benefit from specialist knowledge and experience from people who do not otherwise have the time to commit to full board membership. These groups are usually comprised of non-board members and, while they have no official role or decision-making ability, they provide advice to the board based on their knowledge and experience. Often a charity will set up an advisory group that is comprised of specialist professionals who operate in the field in which the charity is working.

Some charities have a Patron, a Council of Reference or a Board of Governors. Generally speaking, these are well-known people who agree to lend their name to be associated with the charity. They add a degree of kudos and authority to the charity. As with an advisory group, they have no official role or decision-making powers. As a rule, charities that have Patrons, Boards of Governors or Councils of Reference should ensure that they keep those people updated with the activities of the charity, perhaps on a half-yearly basis. It can be embarrassing if a member of the public approaches one such person, only to be told that they have not heard from the charity for some time!

Lastly, it must be remembered that final decisions concerning a charity must be taken by the trustees acting together.

Blue Sky Thinking

Given that trustees serve in a voluntary capacity and use up some of their valuable free time to do so, it is highly unlikely that they will have additional time that can be donated to the charity for what may be considered unproductive endeavours. Despite this, however, many charity boards are now finding the benefit of being able to create a block of time (perhaps on an annual basis) when they can be together and think strategically without a specific agenda.

Usually one of the trustees will be a prime mover for such an activity, which takes board members out of the boardroom environment with its detailed agenda and time constraints.

Blue Sky Thinking enables the board to:

· review its performance as a board – perhaps against an agreed checklist (see section 29);
· review the performance of the charity against its stated Objects. In advance of this, it will be helpful to obtain some specific "beneficiary feedback" from those who are the direct recipients of the charity's activities;
· invite a guest speaker who can speak on either the specific area in which the charity is operating or perhaps on governance and management issues;
· interact with key staff who may also be invited to participate in all or part of day;
· have a small group discussion and review of case studies;
· share a meal or other fun activity;
· perhaps invite the chief executive of another charity working in a similar field to come and speak to the group and facilitate a sharing of ideas.

Fundamentally, a healthy board that is committed to the growth and development of the charity needs to take time to reflect, think and understand the environment that the charity is working in and to project future trends. Perhaps the old maxim can be applied specifically to charity trustees by saying "trustee boards that fail to plan, plan to fail."

Effectiveness of the Board

The effectiveness of the trustee board is something that the trustees themselves should take time to review regularly (see section 29). With many charitable organisations, the demands of fundraising, motivating and managing staff, and striving to achieve the charitable Objects, are more than sufficient for the board to cope with. To those trustees, "effectiveness" is perhaps measured in terms of whether or not the organisation is still existing at the end of the year!

Trustees can only act within the powers that are set out in the charity's governing document. It is essential therefore that each trustee is familiar with a copy of the charity's governing document and the board should ensure that a copy is available at every board meeting as the definitive guide to trustees' decision-making.

The trustees owe a duty of care to the charity, which includes acting reasonably and prudently and in the best interests of the charity. Trustees should understand the legal, financial and management issues that affect the charity and, from time to time, they may need to seek specialist advice on issues where they do not have a personal expertise. Where professional advice is taken, then a copy of that advice should be preserved with the charity's minutes to support the decision that was subsequently made. Charity trustees are responsible for compliance with the applicable Charity Law and, in the case of a charitable company, with Company Law.

A well-functioning board* has been defined as one in which:

· the board has a clear understanding of its role and responsibilities;
· the board has the right mix of skills and experience, and board members have the time to do the job well;
· the board and management share a common vision of how it should go about achieving its goals;
· the board and management periodically review how they are working together.

Financial Responsibilities of the Board

The trustees' financial responsibilities include:

· ensuring that the charity properly administers its income and expenditure;
· approving the annual budget and monitoring the charity's performance against budget;

* What Makes Boards Effective? An examination of the relationships between board inputs, structures, processes and effectiveness in non-profit organisations. *Corporate Governance: an International Review*, Cornforth, Chris (2001)

- establishing the charity's fundraising policy and monitoring its fundraising activities;
- ensuring that any investments are made in accordance with the charity's governing document, are made with the benefit of professional advice, and do not put the charity's assets at undue risk;
- ensuring that the charity's capital and income are used exclusively in furtherance of the charity's stated Objects;
- overseeing any trading activities and ensuring that all tax implications are properly managed;
- having correct systems in place within the charity to minimise the risk of fraud, money laundering or other irregularities;
- ensuring that correct systems are in place concerning the expenditure of the charity's monies;
- approval of the Annual Accounts;
- ensuring that the charity's resources are not applied to benefit a member of the board unless specific consent has been given.

When the Charity Commission inquires into the affairs of a charity, often the financial management of the charity occupies most of its attention.

Whatever the size of the charity, it is suggested that the following should be observed:

- provisions that ensure that every cheque or other outgoing money transfer document is authorised by two different people. Ideally it should be two trustees, but this may be impractical, (particularly in the case of small charities that do not have a functioning day-to-day office thereby necessitating the cheque or other document being transported several miles to find another signature). However, one of those authorising should be a trustee. Whatever system is in place, trustees are ultimately responsible. Therefore, any system for signing cheques and other transfers that departs from the "two people principle" needs to sit comfortably with all of the trustees. Charities are increasingly using electronic transfer mechanisms for payments out and therefore the trustees will need to ensure that a system is in place, ensuring that no monies can be transferred without their consent;
- it is recommended that blank cheques should not be signed in advance and given to another trustee to countersign;
- no one person (trustee or otherwise) should have sole authority to bind

the charity, or order goods or services, without the sanction of the board of trustees (save for items of up to an appropriate pre-determined limit);

· a policy be adopted to ensure that any cash or cheques received by the charity is counted and recorded by two individual people (neither of whom should be the treasurer). This is particularly important in the case of churches where offerings are received in cash. It is not acceptable for one person to take the cash home after a service, count it and then pay it into the bank. The offering should be counted before it leaves the building by at least two independent people, who should agree the total and sign a record to that effect. Those records should be kept and passed at the end of the year to the Auditor who compares them with the paying-in book.

· the charity's post should also be opened in the presence of two people;

· the charity's assets must be protected at all times (for example by adequate insurance policies).

These comments are not intended to suggest any impropriety but rather that trustees must be prepared to go the extra mile to show that there is little or no opportunity of any irregularity or loss taking place;

Liabilities of Trustees

If trustees act carefully, lawfully and in accordance with the charity's governing document, then any liabilities they incur as trustees can be properly met out of the charity's resources. If the trustees do not so act, then they may be in breach of trust and can be personally responsible for the liabilities that have been incurred by the charity. As the trustees act together as a board, they will usually be responsible as a board to meet any liability to a third party.

The above principles hold true regardless of the legal structure of the charity. For example, in the case of a charitable company, although the company is a separate legal entity to its directors, the directors will still be liable under charity law if they fail in their duty and a breach of trust occurs.

An example of a breach of trust could include:

· spending the charity's monies on activities that are not permitted by the charity's governing document;

· making a bad investment decision – entering into a contract or liability that is out of all proportion to the charity's resources at a time when there is no realistic prospect of the charity having the necessary funds to honour it;

- undertaking a course of action that was contrary to professional advice that the trustees had received.

In addition the directors (trustees) of charitable companies can also be liable for wrongful or fraudulent trading.

The Charities Act 2011 permits the Charity Commission, in circumstances where a charity trustee (or its Auditor or independent examiner) is or may be personally liable for a breach of trust or a breach of duty, but that he has acted honestly and reasonably, to make an Order relieving that person wholly or partly from any liability. However, this relief does not apply in relation to any personal contractual liability of a charity trustee. Conceivably, therefore, the charity trustee who signs a mortgage deed in favour of a lender to charge the charity's asset to that lender as security for a loan may, if the charity defaults, be excused from liability by the Charity Commission. However, because he will have signed a personal promise to pay the mortgage under the mortgage deed, he could still be held liable in that personal capacity to the lender.

Charity trustees may be permitted under the governing document to effect trustee indemnity insurance (see section 26). However the Charity Commission is keen to ensure that if a trustee acts with total disregard for their responsibility as a trustee, then they should not be covered by trustee indemnity insurance. An area of high risk to charity trustees is where the charity has a subsidiary trading company, and great care needs to be exercised in the supervision of the activities of that company.

Succession Policy

This is one area in which most charities struggle. The point has already been made that it is difficult enough to recruit trustees for small to medium-size charities and the thought of having to find replacement trustees gives most boards a degree of concern.

However, there are charities existing today that have on their board people who may have served in that capacity for 25 or 30 years, in circumstances where it is questionable whether they can take an objective view about the charity's competencies and activities. Such a person may, by weight of their longevity on the board, be a limiting factor for the board moving forward and act as a disincentive to new trustees who would otherwise bring fresh ideas and experience to the charity.

Possible solutions to the issue would include:

- enforcing a fixed retirement age: the charity's governing document may require a charity trustee to step down when they reach a certain age. Given that people today often retire from their jobs at between 60 and 65 years of age, many of them are open to serving on a board of trustees once they have retired. They undoubtedly bring the great benefits of experience and time, and it would be short-sighted to exclude them from serving by having a retirement age that was the same as the normal retirement age in business. Equally to have trustees still on the board when they reach 80 years of age could be stretching things a little too far. Perhaps a compromise at, say, 72 years of age (the retirement age for judiciary) would be acceptable;
- agreeing service as a trustee for a fixed period. This would apply if the charity were to adopt the rotational method set out below;
- a systematic rotation policy: this is a methodology favoured by the Charity Commission, whereby one third of the members of the board automatically come up for retirement at each AGM. They can offer themselves for re-election to serve for, say, two more periods of three years after which they must leave the board. (see also section 8).

Whichever methodology is ultimately adopted, the charity needs to weigh carefully the benefits of having new people and ideas refreshing the board on a regular basis, with the burden of the lack of continuity in the personnel of the board caused by constant change.

Perhaps pragmatically changing demographics, whereby people are less likely to stay in one place for life, means that there will naturally be a rotation in board members, although whether this is enough to ensure that the board of trustees remains invigorated and focused is something that the board in each charity will need to decide for themselves.

There may be a temptation to think of offering the founder of the charity a seat on the board for life. For reasons already discussed in section 5 this is not a good idea. However they could always be offered the position of Patron which is a largely ceremonial position, with little opportunity to influence decisions.

A trustee board considering its succession planning could well benefit from asking themselves three foundational questions; the honest response to these would help in preparing a job description to be given to a possible new candidate:

- what kind of organisation are you?
- where have you come from and where are you going?
- what is the role of a trustee in your organisation?

What If ...?

6

The board of trustees need to review their "What If ...?" strategy on a regular basis – perhaps annually. For example:

- What if ... the Chief Executive leaves? – does the charity have people who are being mentored to take on such a responsibility? What would be the effect on the charity and its programmes? Should there be Key Person Insurance on their life?
- What if ... the charity failed to raise sufficient funds to discharge its obligations for the current year? Can the activities be scaled back and restricted to the level of income that could be raised?
- What if ... a major donor or a major grant provider withdrew their support? Could the charity disengage from contractual responsibilities without penalty? Would the trustees need to borrow monies to disengage?
- What if ... a claim was made against the charity by an ex-employee? or by the family of a worker who was killed or kidnapped overseas? Or as a result of a Safeguarding breach?
- What if ... there were a fire at the charity's headquarters and all the records were lost? Is the system backed up? Could the charity continue to function from another base?

The above are only samples of the contingencies that could arise. More detailed analysis of risk management is contained in section 26.

The important principle for charity trustees is that where considerable reliance is placed on people, systems, and the goodwill and cooperation of third parties trustees would be unwise to pretend that everything is guaranteed to turn out just as they planned!

Nowadays, a well-run charity should have a crisis management policy in place detailing the authority structure, media spokesperson and other roles that may become necessary as a result of a crisis in the charity. (See section 26 and Appendix 1.)

Corporate Trustee

Remarkably, it is possible for a corporate trustee (i.e. a company or a body that does not itself need to be a charity) to be appointed as sole trustee or one of the trustees of a charity. In the case of one being a sole trustee this would seem to be curious given the basic provision in charitable organisations, whereby trustees can be personally liable for breach of trust (whether they are trustees of an unincorporated charity or directors of a charitable company).

Some local charities do have their local authority as sole trustee, but they cannot be a trustee for an Ecclesiastical charity or one set up to relieve poverty. The responsibilities and liabilities of trusteeship are with that corporate body but the body itself needs to act through individual persons (directors) in order to express its will, although those persons are not themselves trustees of the charity.

The directors of the corporate trustee company will not be held liable by the charity itself, although they could be held liable to the company for any liability the company has incurred in respect of the charity. The directors of a corporate trustee should therefore be familiar with the charity's governing document and also the general requirements affecting charity trustees.

It is important to ensure that the governing document of the charity allows for the appointment of a company as a trustee, whether jointly with other individual trustees, or as a sole trustee. If the governing document does not permit this, it may be possible to modify the deed under the provisions of the Charities Act or upon application to the Charity Commission. It is also important to ensure that the corporate body that is to be appointed to act as a charity trustee has the power under its own Articles to do so.

Fundamentally, the test before effecting the appointment of any corporate trustee is to consider whether or not the appointment will be in the best interests of the charity. Possible grounds for such an appointment would include:

· if the charity is having difficulty in appointing individual trustees and considers that such difficulties will continue into the future;
· if the appointment of a corporate trustee will bring to the charity the benefit that corporation has had either with similar charities, or in the specific field in which the charity is operating;
· if the charity has a separate charitable body that holds the title to the charity's premises and seeks a corporate trustee to be the sole trustee of that charitable body.

For further discussion on the advantages and disadvantages of a corporate trustee company the reader is directed to the Charity Commission guidance paper on the subject.

Custodian Trustee

This is defined as a corporate body that has been appointed to have the custody of property on behalf of a charity. As such, the custodian trustee holds the title to land, shares etc., receives the income and remits it to the trustees. The actual functioning of the charity is then carried out by the managing trustees.

An example of this arrangement is where a body holds the ownership of a church building yet leaves the day-to-day running of the church itself in the hands of the local managing trustees.

- **OFFICIAL CUSTODIAN FOR CHARITIES**
In circumstances where there is likely to be a regular rotation of trustees of a charity it may be decided that the title to any freehold or leasehold property should be vested in the Official Custodian for charities who will hold it on trust for the charity. The Official Custodian will have no power to take part in managing the land vested in him. This procedure avoids the need to update regularly the ownership details at the Land Registry.

- **TRUST CORPORATION**
Trust Corporation is a particular type of corporate trustee being one either appointed by the court or under the Public Trustee Act 1906 to act as a custodian trustee. A trust corporation is often used where there is a need for a sole trustee of a charity which holds land. A Charity Commission Scheme, or Order that appoints a corporate body as trustee will have the effect of conferring that trust corporation status on that body, in respect of the charity for which it is appointed to be trustee.

For further reading and helpful insight in the effectiveness of the board and the charity generally, please see *The Code Of Good Impact Practice* published by the National Council for Voluntary Organisations and available on its website.

Accountability 7

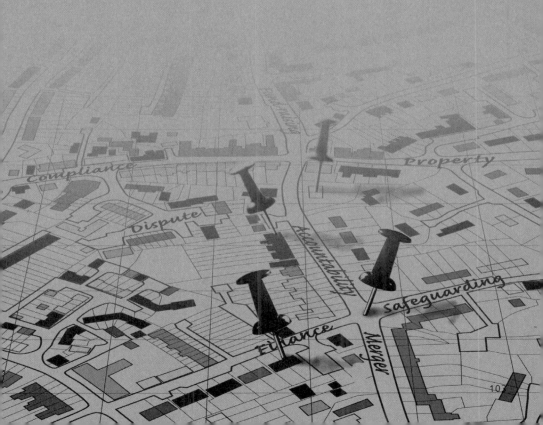

Charitable organisations exist, not for the benefit of the founders or the trustees, but for the benefit of others. Charities have the potential to exercise considerable power or influence, yet at the same time can risk failure of one form or another if they are unclear as to whom they are answerable.

Accountability can be defined as being responsible to a person or persons and giving honest account as to actions, motives, decisions, activities and performance. Perhaps above all accountability is an attitude. Accountability can be either personal or corporate (i.e. to the charity).

It is helpful to explore two specific areas of accountability within a charitable organisation.

Accountability of the Leader

Myles Munroe makes the valid point that "the key to good leadership is the power to influence through inspiration not manipulation. The danger of leadership is its potential for wielding power without answering to anyone else. Dictatorship can materially occur in the absence of a leader's submission to an authority."*

In faith-based charities there is arguably a greater need for accountability, given that leadership in such organisations often includes the element of "calling" or "vocation". In some organisations, the notion that the leader should be accountable to others does not sit comfortably with their position as leader of the organisation. However as we have seen in section 5, an unnecessary stand-off between the trustees and the leader can follow the perception that one or other party is acting in an independent way.

The essential protection of the leader (to say nothing of the charity and its beneficiaries) is in the voluntary submission of the leader to a trusted authority. A leader seeking to be accountable should consider establishing a group of mature, experienced and willing people, who are prepared to spend time with the leader, to understand the vision, the charity itself and the constraints under which the leader works and as a result, to offer counsel, challenge, rebuke, correction, encouragement and example. It is suggested that for the relationship to work the following principles will be relevant:

- A written list of the areas (both personal and for the charity) that the accountability will cover should be produced.

* Dr. Myles Munroe, *Spirit of Leadership*, Whitaker House (2005)

- The group should consist of no more than four people, and not all should be close friends of the leader!
- The group should function in the same geographical community as the leader, in order that they can observe and understand the wider picture.
- The group, or perhaps individuals from it, should meet with the leader regularly to build a relationship and interact, including spending time in a leisure activity.
- The leader must be willing to trust the group implicitly, be open and honest and heed their input.
- Use of computer linkages such as "K9 Web Protection" or Covenant Eyes" to monitor the leader's use of the internet should be part of the accountability relationship.

A wise leader who is prepared to be accountable in this way will find that it forms a secure base from which he or she can operate, and it will enable the leader to innovate and take the appropriate risks, which are the hallmarks of effective leaders within charities.

If a leader is not prepared to be accountable in this way then perhaps the question to ask is: why? – what are they hiding? – of what are they afraid?

Accountability of the Board of Trustees/Directors

Trustees are accountable for:

- the exercise of their powers to govern the charity;
- utilising the resources that they have within the charity to pursue its stated Objects.

They are legally accountable both under charity law and to the Charity Commission, for submission of an Annual Return and accounts.

In the case of charitable companies they are legally accountable under Company Law (as well as charity law) and to Companies House for submission of the Annual Return and accounts.

In addition to their "legal" responsibilities, charity trustees can also be accountable to a variety of people and groups including:

- The charity's donors – whether individuals, organisations, local authorities, corporations or government.
- Large donors – many now require an independent evaluation of the

effectiveness of a charity's programme as a condition to their ongoing support.

- The charity's members (see section 9).
- The general public who are the potential beneficiaries of the charity's activities. It follows that if the charity is not fulfilling its stated Objects, then its services or facilities will not be taken up to the extent that they could be.

The board will also need to consider how it will hold both staff and volunteers accountable.

A salutary reminder that the principle of accountability has not been universally embraced by Christian organisations can be had by visiting the Charity Commission website and viewing the section entitled "Charity Commission Inquiry/Case Reports". Reported cases concerning Christian organisations show that, in the majority of the cases, the issues that have arisen can be traced back to a lack of accountability among the leaders and/or the trustees of the particular charity.

If faith-based organisations, given their affinity to biblical principles, cannot give a lead in such matters, then it brings into question their integrity in the eyes of the secular authorities, and the principles for which they claim to stand. See also section 9.

SECTION 8

Administration

Address/Registered Office

Each charity needs to have a registered address that is notified to the Charity Commission and at which information addressed to the charity can be sent. In addition, a charitable company is required to have a registered office that is notified to Companies House. The registered address receives official correspondence from the Charity Commission and, in the case of a charitable company, from Companies House. Furthermore, the address is designed to receive service of any legal actions.

Care should be taken if the registered address is that of a residence belonging, say, to one of the trustees. If that trustee moves or resigns from the trusteeship, important communications from the Charity Commission and/or Companies House may go unanswered, thereby ringing alarm bells with the Charity Commission, and in the case of a charitable company, possibly resulting in that company being struck off the Companies House register for non-compliance. The efforts to reinstate the organisation can be costly, in terms of both time and expense. Increasingly the Charity Commission uses the charity's email address and this too needs to be monitored and updated when necessary.

The registered address forms part of the charity's details that are disclosed to the public. A visit to the Charity Commission's website gives access to much information about a registered charity, and this information may even include a telephone number for the charity's registered address or their correspondent.

Some charities appoint their lawyers or accountants to provide their registered address so that official documentation will be passed immediately to the persons who need to act on them. The registered address should be a specific street address and not a post office box.

Appointment of Directors/Trustees

The initial trustees are appointed when the charitable organisation is first registered. Usually they have been recruited by the founder as being people who identify with the aims of the organisation and can bring necessary skill, vision, leadership and governance to it.

The governing document of most charitable organisations provides that subsequent trustees are appointed by either the members or the existing trustees, although nominations may be submitted to the trustees from other sources. In circumstances where the governing document for the organisation does not provide a mechanism for the appointment of subsequent trustees, then an application may need to be made to the Charity Commission for assistance.

In the case of unincorporated charities who own property, special care should be taken to ensure that those trustees in whose name the property or lease was first registered, have correctly passed on the title to their successors. For example, the title to a charity's property may be registered in the names of "A, B and C as trustees for the AnyCharity". If any of those trustees subsequently resign their trusteeship, then the charity will be in difficulty when it comes to dispose of the property, particularly if those trustees can no longer be found. This issue can be resolved in one of two ways that should be undertaken at the time the trustee concerned leaves:

- by a formal Deed of Retirement and Appointment of New Trustee. This is signed by both the retiring trustee and the newly appointed trustees and is produced to the Land Registry to ensure that the registered title is updated; or
- by the retiring trustee signing a formal transfer document in favour of the new trustees, which would then be registered at the Land Registry.

In both courses of action a Land Registry fee is payable but not Stamp Duty Land Tax.

Special care needs to be taken if an unincorporated charity holds a lease on a property, as it is likely that this lease will have been granted to "A, B and C as the trustees of the AnyCharity". If a trustee retires, then it may be necessary to obtain the landlord's consent for the lease to be assigned to A, B and D (as the new trustee of the charity). This is because the retiring trustees will have made covenants in the lease that cannot be released without the landlord's consent. Unincorporated charities proposing to take a leasehold property may therefore consider it wise to incorporate as a charitable company or convert to a CIO before completing the lease. There are reasons why a CIO may not be the best vehicle to use for a charity acquiring property or a lease – for a fuller treatment on this subject, see section 11.

In the case of a charitable company or a CIO, the title to a freehold or leasehold property is registered in the name of the charitable company or CIO and therefore when its directors/trustees rotate there is no need to change the registered title.

Trustees of an unincorporated charity, who wish to overcome the problems associated with transferring land each time the trustees change, can consider applying to the Charity Commission for a certificate incorporating the trustees as a body corporate. (Known as a Part 12 Incorporation under the Charities Act 2011) If the Charity Commission considers that it is in the interests of the charity, they can grant such a certificate whereupon the charity becomes a corporate body and may transact business in that corporate name. However the trustees of the charity, notwithstanding their incorporation, shall still be accountable personally for their own actions and for the due administration of the charity and its assets.

The size and make-up of a board of trustees is critical to the charity's effectiveness. Many charities have too few trustees (three is the absolute minimum, but in the event of one of those retiring, the charity is immediately plunged into crisis until a new trustee can be found and appointed). Alternatively, many other charities have a board of trustees that is too large and the board therefore lacks flexibility and it becomes difficult to involve all of the trustees.

There is no definitive answer as to the ideal size for a board of trustees, although it is suggested for most small- to medium-sized charities (i.e. gross income of up to £3 million), a board comprising between five and nine trustees would be sufficient. Having an "odd" number of trustees minimises the chances of a voting deadlock!

Trustees may be appointed in many different ways. Depending on the governing document, these may include:

- being elected at an Annual General Meeting, or General Meeting, by a vote from the membership of the charity;
- being co-opted on to the board by the board of trustees themselves;
- being nominated by an outside organisation that has a significant interest in the work of the charity, for example a local authority who funds the charity;
- by virtue of the office ("ex officio") that a person holds, for example the leader of a charity.

It is important that the appointment of trustees is recorded correctly. In the case of a charitable company, this involves the filing of a company form (AP01) with Companies House, and in the case of an unincorporated charity or CIO the notification is given to the Charity Commission, and can be completed online on the Charity Commission website.

Trustees who are either nominated from outside or serve on the board in an *"ex officio"* capacity should be particularly careful in circumstances where a conflict of interest may arise between their position as a trustee and their responsibilities or loyalties to the organisation that has nominated them. Their priority as a trustee must always be to do what is in the best interest of the charity. If the conflict of interest is irreconcilable, then at the very least they will need to withdraw from the discussions concerning the issue in hand or in some cases resign their trusteeship completely. See also section 6.

A person is disqualified from acting as a charity trustee if they:

- have unspent convictions for offences involving deception or dishonesty (a conviction is "spent" between six months and ten years after conviction, depending on the offence; however, custodial sentences in excess of two and a half years can never be "spent");
- are a discharged bankrupt;
- have in the past been removed from trusteeship of a charity by the Charity Commission or the Court;
- are disqualified from being a company director under the Company Directors Disqualification Act 1986;
- fail to make payments under a county court administration order;
- have come to an arrangement with their creditors and have not been discharged (e.g. an individual voluntary arrangement).

In addition to the above, a person is disqualified from acting as a director of a charitable company if they:

- have been persistently in default of company requirements for filing accounts and documents;
- have been found guilty of fraud or fraudulent trading.

The charity's governing document may contain a restriction on who may be a trustee, and, for example, require a person to be of a particular religious denomination.

A cautionary tale involves the status of the first trustees of a charitable company. It is likely that the first trustees ("Directors") of a charitable company include the person(s) who at registration signed the Memorandum and Articles of Association of the organisation as "subscribers". These subscribers are the first members of the company. When they eventually resign as directors, it is possible that they will forget to resign their status as *members*

8

of the company. Given that the members of the charitable company may be those who confirm the appointment of directors of the company, there have been cases where subsequent directors have been held to have been incorrectly appointed, and therefore decisions that those "directors" have made have not been valid. The authority for appointment had in those circumstances remained with the original subscriber(s), who by then may have very little to do with the organisation.

Disclosure and Barring Service Checks (DBS)

Charities which are either (a) working with children and/or (b) concerned with the care of vulnerable adults, in circumstances where the trustees have access to such vulnerable adults in carrying out their normal duties, need to pay special attention to the requirements for DBS checks on the trustees, to ensure that a trustee is not barred from working with children or vulnerable adults.

The charity's trustees are responsible for ensuring that trustees, staff, independent contractors and volunteers are legally able to work in positions involving children and vulnerable adults:

- if they come into contact with children and /or vulnerable adults they are eligible for an Enhanced DBS check;
- if they will be in "close contact" with children and/or vulnerable adults then an Enhanced DBS check that includes a check against the Children's/ Adults Barred List is appropriate.

Trustees of all charities would be wise to obtain a DBS check on staff/volunteers where this is possible, as it is an indicator of a person's suitability to work within the charity.

The requirements of the Disclosure and Barring Service continue to change to reflect new legislation and practice. Trustees will therefore keep up to date with changes and implement them as appropriate. The DBS website contains more details (www.gov.uk/disclosure-and-barring-service).

Fundamentally, each charity and its trustees must decide whether they are legally allowed to carry out DBS checks or whether they are legally required to do so. The burden is therefore on the charity and its trustees to ensure compliance. It is an offence to offer a regulated position (including position as a trustee of a children's charity) to an individual who is barred from working with children, even if the person offering the position did not know that the candidate was so disqualified.

These requirements clearly have implications for churches as, in the majority of cases, churches are also charities.

A DBS certificate has no expiry date. There is a DBS update service available online that lets charities keep their DBS certificates up-to-date.

Where people do not qualify for a DBS check, Basic Disclosures (Scotland) can be used to obtain basic disclosures on an applicant in the UK. (www.disclosurescotland.co.uk)

Retirement/Removal of Trustees

The governing document of the organisation may prescribe a length of time for which a person should serve as a trustee. Difficulties arise in cases where the governing document is silent on the point, particularly if the trustees of the charity have served in that capacity for many years! This fact in itself can serve as a serious deterrent to new trustees joining the board.

The Charity Commission now favours wording in an organisation's governing document limiting the period for which a trustee can serve, although permitting that trustee to stand for re-election for a further period. It is suggested that perhaps an initial period of three years, with the ability to be re-elected for a further three years, is a good starting point. At the end of the period the trustee would be required to stand down from the board for a period (not less than two years), before being able to offer themselves for re-election. Furthermore, a correctly structured rotational policy for the board means that new faces are continually being recruited and ensures that the board benefits from new ideas and new skills.

The disadvantage of a rotational policy can be that it can make it difficult for the trustee board to gel (given that it perhaps meets two or three times a year), as its members are constantly rotating. Furthermore, new persons joining the board feel that their period of service is more akin to being on a conveyor belt than sitting on a board of governance.

If the governing document does not contain adequate provisions for retirement, (whether after a set period of service or upon reaching a certain age), then those provisions can be added by a resolution of the board. The governing document will need to be carefully reviewed; as such an alteration may require Charity Commission consent (see Appendix 1 paragraph 20).

In the case of a charitable company a copy of the duly revised Articles of Association needs to be filed with Companies House after the resolution has been passed.

A charity will need different skills of leadership as it grows in size or scope.

Other factors such as ill-health or an inability to attend trustees meetings regularly may cut short a trustee's period of service on the board. Given the responsibilities now placed on charity trustees, it is suggested that any trustee who is absent from three consecutive trustees meetings may need to seriously consider resigning (for their own sake as well as the charity's).

The Charity Commission has the power to remove a trustee who has been found guilty of an offence under the Safeguarding legislation.

If the governing document of the charity permits, then a trustee can be removed from office by resolution of the other board members. If the governing document does not contain the power to remove a trustee, then specialist advice will need to be sought. In the case of a charitable company, then the members of that company can vote at an AGM/GM for the replacement of all or part of the board. The Charity Commission can remove trustees, often instituting an Inquiry into the charity, and concluding that there has been misconduct or mismanagement, and finding that it is necessary or desirable for the protection of the property of the charity.

In circumstances where there is not a clear majority of trustees to vote for the removal of a trustee (or perhaps that trustee is the only one left on the board), then an application to the Charity Commission may be necessary.

The Role of Secretary

The responsibilities of the secretary include sending out meeting agenda and board papers, taking the minutes at board meetings and an AGM/GM, and undertaking other duties that may be delegated to the secretary by the board or its chair. In addition, the secretary will often complete and file the annual return with the Charity Commission.

Unless the Articles of Association of a charitable company specify otherwise, a private company does not need to have a company secretary. However someone will need to take responsibility to keep up to date the register of members, the register of directors, the register of charges, notify Companies House of changes, complete the company's annual return and ensure that the company's documents are kept securely.

Specific details of the secretary's responsibilities include:

- ensuring that proper notice is given of the charity's various meetings (with reference to the charity's governing document and the required period of notice for any particular resolutions that are being proposed);
- ensuring that when the election of officers is to take place, nominations are received by the appropriate date in advance of the meeting.
- agreeing with the chairman the proposed agenda;
- ensuring that any relevant papers are made available to the charity trustees in good time for a board meeting;
- at the meeting itself, ensuring that any arrangements for a vote, or poll which may be needed, are in place, that there is the appropriate quorum present throughout the meeting, that apologies for absence are noted and that all decisions made at the meeting are minuted;
- the production of the minutes after the meeting, agreement of the same with the chair and their circulation to all those entitled to receive the same.

See also section 9.

The Role of Treasurer

The treasurer's responsibility is to oversee the financial affairs of the charity, report to the board on the charity's financial viability and ensure that the correct financial records are maintained. This will include interpreting the accounts and the accounting policies to other members of the board in a way that is easy for them to understand.

The treasurer is responsible for liaising with the charity's Auditors/independent examiners, producing the financial records for Audit, and ensuring they have all information and clarification that they require to do their job properly.

The treasurer should have sufficient technical expertise to understand and guide the financial affairs of the charity. In a small charitable organisation, the treasurer is likely to prepare the financial reports and budgets. The responsibility of treasurer is very often given to a member of the charity's board in order to provide a level of expertise at the board table. Church treasurers are very often deacons and serve in a similar capacity.

In larger charities, where the charity has investments, the treasurer will be the person primarily responsible for liaising with the charity's financial advisors and monitoring the investments on behalf of the board to ensure best possible return. Larger charities may well have a full-time employee serving as a finance director or chief financial officer. In such cases, the treasurer will provide practical interface between the finance director and the board.

It is suggested that the job description of a charity's treasurer could include ensuring the following responsibilities are undertaken, although depending on the size of the charity, not all of this will be applicable:

- maintaining the appropriate book-keeping system and a petty-cash system;
- responsibility for making the bank reconciliation;
- maintenance of a system for recording and paying bills;
- responsibility to ensure all income due to the charity is received (this includes legacy income);
- keeping a record of all vouchers for production to the Auditor/independent examiner;
- keeping the charity's cheque book and possibly acting as one of the (two or more) cheque or transfer signatories;
- monitoring the charity's money held on deposit and ensuring a good rate of interest;
- preparing the annual budget for the charity, together with budgets for any specific projects;
- preparing management accounts for the trustees, showing both the "budget" and "actual" figures;
- liaison with the charity's accountants/independent examiner in order to obtain the audit/examination of the accounts;
- ensuring the audited/examined accounts are signed off, presented at the AGM/GM and filed with the Charity Commission (and Companies House if applicable);
- ensuring appropriate reports are made to the charity's main grant-funders;
- liaison with charity's fundraisers and monitoring the charity's fundraising projects;
- monitoring the charity's payroll scheme and ensuring that all returns are made to the HMRC, and tax and National Insurance is paid;
- ensuring the trustees are fully aware of all issues relating to the employment of staff (salaried, freelance or volunteers);
- ensuring appropriate insurances are maintained;
- coordinating and monitoring the charity's financial and reserves policies.

Annual Return

Trustees of all registered charities are required to send an annual return to the Charity Commission. Usually a reminder is sent by the Charity Commission to the charity's email address or registered office and the charity is required to complete its Annual Return within a prescribed period. The Charity Commission maintains a record of charities that are persistently late in filing their annual returns and have adopted a "naming and shaming" policy on their website; and often use that default as a reason for contacting the defaulting charity.

Charitable companies are also subject to Company Law which means they must submit and return a Companies House annual return, again within a prescribed period. This is in addition to the one they will also file with the Charity Commission. Companies House annual returns tend to be in a fairly consistent format, often pre-populated, whereas the Charity Commission tends to vary both the format and the questions asked.

In the case of a charitable company's annual return, this is a public document, a copy of which can be obtained readily from Companies House. At present the Charity Commission does not make a charity's annual return available to the public. The Charity Commission's annual return is due ten months after the end of the financial year, and a charitable company's annual return to Companies House is to be filed within nine months of the end of the financial year. Failure to file Companies House annual return can result in the directors being personally fined. The Charity Commission's sanction is to consider removing a charity from the register if that return is six months late, as well as taking further action.

Compliance

Trustees of charities (be they unincorporated charities, CIOs or charitable companies) have a duty to comply with the law. A brief summary of the main areas is set out below:

- All charity trustees must be eligible to serve as trustees (e.g. not disqualified).
- Charity trustees are responsible for ensuring proper compliance with reporting and accounting requirements.
- Charity trustees must ensure the charity complies with the law relating to trading and fundraising.

- Trustees of a charitable company are also company directors and therefore subject to the Companies Act requirements relating to directors. In addition to the reporting requirements to Companies House, there is an overriding responsibility on them to act in the best interests of the company (irrespective of their personal position). They must ensure the charitable company does not continue to trade if the trustee knows or should have known that the charitable company is insolvent (i.e. not be able to pay its debts when they fall due).
- If the charity employs staff, then issues relating to employment law, health and safety and taxation will be relevant.
- Trustees of charities owning property need to be aware of environmental issues.

- Charities working with children and vulnerable persons need to comply with the relevant Safeguarding provisions.
- Data protection issues may relate to the charity's database and other confidential information.
- Charities that trade are subject to the appropriate trading standards and legislation relating to the supply of goods and services.
- Trustees of charities need to ensure that the charity has a Reserves policy and report on it in their annual report and accounts each year;
- All trustees of charities have a responsibility to ensure that the charity's expenditure is for items that are fully charitable. (See section 3 for a fuller treatment of HMRC's position on non-charitable expenditure).

See also the sections on Risk Management (26), Charities Working Overseas (21), Intellectual Property (14) and What Can Go Wrong? (25).

Trustees are not expected to have an in-depth knowledge of all the legislation that can affect the charity. However it is important to be aware that legislation exists and ignorance of the law is no defence. Trustees must take independent legal and accounting advice on the issues that relate to their particular charity and to retain such written advice with the charity's records and keep it reviewed on a regular basis. One of the trustees should be responsible for making sure that the charity is both aware of, and complies with, the relevant legislation. The websites of the National Council for Voluntary Organisations, Third Sector, as well as the Charity Commission are all good resources.

It is not a defence for charity trustees to say that they delegated responsibility for compliance to executive staff or other persons. (For further details on this subject see section 6).

It is good governance practice for trustees to have written policies covering issues such as health and safety, risk management, kidnap and ransom, reserves and child protection. (See also section 5). The Charity Commission constantly reminds charities of the major issues and encourage them to have systems in place to respond appropriately. Should the Charity Commission undertake a review visit or open an inquiry it is likely to ask for a sight of the written policies.

Records

A charity should keep a record of its accounts and the supporting papers for a minimum period of six years from the end of the financial year in question. It is not sufficient to point to the fact that the accounts have been filed with the Charity Commission and/or Companies House; the supporting papers themselves must be preserved.

It is good governance practice to keep copies of annual returns, contracts and important correspondence for a similar period.

Although there is no minimum period for which a charity should keep records of minutes of its trustees or board meetings, it is suggested that these should be kept indefinitely. I recently had good cause to be thankful that the records for a particular charity included the minutes of a trustee's meeting in 1895. The existence of these enabled the charity to establish title to a piece of land, the sale proceeds of which greatly enriched the charity!

Many charities keep their major records on computer in an effort to reduce the dependence on paper. The computers should be backed up on a regular basis and the back-up programmes kept off site, in case of fire at the charity's main office.

The charity's records should be available for inspection by the current trustees, who should be afforded access to records going back to the period before they were appointed to the board.

Charities are obliged to send copies of their accounts to anyone who asks for them (although they are allowed to make a small charge for copying and postage).

As part of "risk management", many charities are now backing up their entire accounting records in order that a virtual office could be recreated at another location in the case of destruction of the charity's main office. It is now considered excellent practice for a charity to periodically power up the virtual office in order to ensure that the back-up is fully functional. Backing up the records ensures a seamless transition. In cases of emergency, it would be extremely frustrating if the back-up did not allow the charity to continue to function.

Freedom of Information Requests

Many charities are now receiving requests from members of the public or other organisations for the disclosure of specific information that the charity hitherto had regarded as confidential. For a fuller treatment on this subject please see section 13.

Persons with Significant Control (PSC)

Companies (including Charitable Companies but not CIO's or Unincorporated Charities) are now required to keep a register of individuals or legal entities that have control over them and to deliver this information annually to Companies House.

The definition of a PSC includes a person who "directly or indirectly holds the right to appoint or remove the majority of Directors" or "otherwise has the right to exercise, or actually exercises, significant influence or control." Such a definition may therefore include:

- A donor to a Charitable Company that seeks to influence it by way of his or her donation or grant.
- Situations where a third party has the right to nominate or control appointments to the Board of a Charitable Company.

Directors of a Charitable Company should regularly review to see if there are persons who have the right to exercise, or actually exercise, "significant influence or control over the Company."

For more information concerning the regulation please see the Companies House website – www.companieshouse.gov.uk

SECTION 9

Membership

9

Who Are the Members?

In an unincorporated charity, any rules concerning membership of the charity will be set out in the governing document of the charity. The governing document also identifies the founding trustees (who are also members) and explains the procedure for the appointment of new trustees and the retirement of the existing ones.

The governing document of a CIO will likewise define and set out the rules for membership.

The governing document of a charitable company is called the Articles of Association (or "Articles"). This document will also define who are the members, stipulate the number of members that the charitable company is to have, and provide that the members are responsible for electing or re-electing the trustees (usually known as directors) at each Annual General Meeting (AGM)/General Meeting (GM), if the Articles require directors to retire by rotation at the AGM/GM.

Since the Companies Act 2006 came into force, private companies (which include charitable companies) no longer need to hold an AGM unless their Articles require it to be held. However, for reasons set out below it is advised that a charitable company continues to hold what is now referred to as a General Meeting (GM).

Those setting up new charities can decide how many voting members the charity will have, i.e. will membership be limited only to the trustees ("closed membership") or to a wider group of people ("open membership")? Those members in turn determine the composition of the trustee board. It is possible for very large charities with considerable income and influence to be regulated by a small number of members who hold complete power. No outside donor or beneficiary of the charity can become a member unless recruited by the existing members.

A charity with open membership can have a significant democratic influence over the activities of the trustees. In other words, membership can hold the directors/trustees accountable and this is a function that some major donors and grant-makers to a charity are keen to see.

Some charities maintain a large membership and admit to membership almost anyone who has had any meaningful relationship with the charity, be they a donor, a beneficiary of the charity's activity or those who have expressed a keen interest in and a desire to be part of, the charity's work. It is suggested that a large membership can prove to be unwieldy and potentially damaging to the charity. Given that all members are entitled to attend and vote at the charity's AGM/GM, it makes for not only lengthy meetings, but the possibility that partisan voting could end up replacing one or more of the trustees at an AGM/GM of the members, resulting in a lack of continuity from year to year.

Charities with a closed membership restrict the membership to the actual directors or trustees for the time being, in which case those people hold the dual role of directors/trustees and members.

The issue of trustee accountability is addressed elsewhere in this book, (in section 7) but it is good discipline for the board of directors/trustees to question, on a regular basis, whether in fact they are held accountable for their actions in a meaningful way by the members of the charity, or elsewhere.

Some charities have great difficulty in determining who exactly are the members of the charity. The Charities Act 2011 gives the Charity Commission the power to determine who are the members of a charity, either on the application of the charity itself or following a statutory Inquiry by the Charity Commission. In practice they seldom appear keen to do so and charities may have to go the High Court to obtain a ruling on this point.

Some UK charities have established subsidiary charities in other parts of the world and regard those subsidiaries as members of the parent charity. Periodically, the parent charity will convene a conference in which all the subsidiary charities are invited to participate, and very often issues of significance for the whole organisation are debated and voted on. In such cases, the governing document of the parent charity should define exactly what voting influence each subsidiary would have. For example is it to be one subsidiary one vote, or would the voting rights be in proportion to the number of staff controlled by each subsidiary, or perhaps the amount of income that each subsidiary attracts from year to year etc.?

Alternatively, it may be provided in the governing document that the subsidiaries have no decision-making power but are considered to have a powerful influence on decision-making by voicing a regional or field-led view on important policy issues.

Confusion may exist: (1) in the role of membership in a charity and (2) the identity of the members themselves. Charities seeking to build a high public profile (both for fundraising and to promote their charitable Objects) should consider developing an active and engaged membership. Potential benefits include:

· Members help keep the trustee boards fresh and accountable.
· They can help to generate income for the charity because of their perception of being involved.
· An active and engaged membership enables member-led lobbying and campaigning.
· It presents to the general public a clear picture of an open, participatory and accountable organisation.

Currently 44% of charities on the Register (approximately 80,000 charities) have a membership structure that allows voting in order to influence the charity's governance.

However a charity wishing to develop an active and engaged membership should look carefully at its governing document to ensure the role, rights and obligations of members are clearly defined. If they are not, then an alteration to the governing document, or an addendum, needs to be prepared. If there is to be a clear distinction between voting and non-voting members, then that needs to be stated clearly in order to prevent any dispute at an AGM/GM.

Charity Commission research indicates that charities which experience problems with their membership do so for one or more of the following reasons:

· The trustees are unclear about their role/responsibility towards the charity's members.
· Charity members are not clear about their role/ responsibility toward the charity.
· The trustees put up barriers to membership involvement.
· The trustee board is self-perpetuating and/or change-resistant.
· Weak administration resulting in inaccurate membership lists has led to accusations that elections were not validly held.

The Charity Commission estimates that approximately 9,000 charities in the UK now have corporate members (i.e. a commercial body such as a trading company acting as a member). Benefits of corporate membership to the charity include financial support, expertise and influence. Disadvantages include their lack of attendance at an AGM/GM and, perhaps, the potential of a conflict of interest between the corporation's aims and the charity's best interest.

Many corporations are open to membership of a charity, as it gives them a platform to demonstrate their corporate social responsibility, as well as giving them a real voice in the affairs of the charity.

Remember, however, that ultimately the directors/trustees are responsible for the running of the charity. If the charity is intending to strengthen its membership participation then the following suggestions are made:

- The trustees should be clear about their role and legal responsibility towards the charity's members and be clear about the rights of the members themselves.
- The members should be clear about their role and responsibilities towards the charity.
- The membership list should be kept completely up to date as any discrepancies or inaccuracies are a breach of the statutory requirement of the Companies Act 2006.
- The governing document of the charity should clearly set out the respective roles and responsibilities of the members.
- The role of a corporate member is fully understood.
- The trustees should ensure that the membership is truly representative of the group it is designed to serve.

There is a corresponding responsibility on the charity's members to ensure that they exercise their rights to vote in the interest of the charity and abide by decisions that are fairly taken within the provisions of the governing document of the charity.

Church Membership

Churches are a good example of charities that take the issue of membership quite seriously. They tend to fall into three categories:

- "One member: one vote" – these churches tend to maintain an active membership list. Would-be members specifically apply for and are formally admitted to membership, which usually carries voting rights. Membership can be lost if the person subsequently leaves the church or fails to be in regular attendance. Major issues are put to the GM and each member is encouraged to vote. An AGM/GM votes on the appointment of the main officers of the charity (deacons, treasurer, secretary and in some cases the minister).

- "Consensus membership" – the qualification for membership is as above. Although regular meetings are held, no specific voting is undertaken on an issue. Decisions tend to be taken on a consensus which is usually led by the church minister or elders.
- "Informal membership" – this covers scenarios where regular attendees of the church are called members, although there is no formal procedure for admitting people to membership, and members are not given any specific rights. Neither is it clear exactly who the members are at any one time!

Many non-conformist churches draw a clear distinction between the spiritual leadership of the church (the minister, the elders/deacons) and the membership/trustees. While the membership/trustees can and do appoint elders/deacons and in some cases the minister, many churches have disagreed over the years on the question of church government. A fuller discussion of this is contained in Appendix 2 but many church governing documents could benefit by spelling out the difference in responsibility along the following lines:

> "The spiritual government and leadership of the church shall remain with the recognised spiritual leadership of the church fellowship and to the extent to which the trustees are not the same persons as the spiritual leadership, the trustees' power shall be confined to the proper management and administration of the charity in accordance with the provisions of this governing document and charity law, and in so doing they shall have full and proper regard to the spiritual leadership and provided always that they shall not act outside of their powers as conferred by this deed and by the general law"

As an alternative to including provisions with regard to church membership and its officers in the governing document, churches often just refer in the governing document to a separate Constitution, which is something the church can develop itself and which exists alongside the governing document. In that way, changes can be made to the Constitution without the necessity of having to file new documents with the Charity Commission and Companies House each time a change is made. However in such a scenario membership will be regulated under the "Constitution" and people will not become members of the company itself.

The Charity's Meetings

The frequency of other meetings and the procedures for calling them are usually set out in the charity's governing document. The courts have agreed that participants at a meeting should be able to see and hear each other, so telephone conference calls may not be acceptable, unless permitted by the charity's governing document (see section 6). A brief summary of the types of meetings and the methodology for calling them is summarised below:

- **TRUSTEES MEETING**
  See section 6, The Board

- **ANNUAL GENERAL MEETING**
  Not all charities need to hold an AGM. The governing documents of the charity will say whether an AGM is required. Notwithstanding this, it is suggested that it is a good discipline for every charity to hold a meeting annually (GM), maybe as part of a normal trustees meeting. The function of such a meeting would be to approve and sign the accounts, deal with any retirement and appointment of trustees and ensure that annual returns and other compliance issues are dealt with.

  A GM is an opportunity for the trustees of an unincorporated charity, CIO or charitable company to explain their management of the organisation to the members. It is for the board of directors to agree the date of the GM and resolve to call it, although the governing document will state when it should be held.

  A charitable company needs to observe the provisions of the Companies Act in calling a GM, and these require a formal notice that specifies the date, time and place of the meeting (if it is required to hold an AGM then the notice must state that it is an AGM). There is a right for a proxy to be appointed and every notice of a members' meeting must state this.

  The period of notice for a GM is 14 clear days unless the company's Articles specify a longer period of notice. Meetings can be called at shorter notice if it is agreed by a majority (i.e. 90%) of the members. (The charity's governing document may require a higher percentage.) The Companies Act provides that the notice should be in writing and either posted, sent electronically or given to the members personally; (if posted, 48 hours should be allowed within the postal system before the 14 clear days' notice). Notice should also be given to all directors and to the Auditors.

9

The Charities Act does not specify a similar procedure for convening a GM of the members (although the charity's governing document may well lay down a timetable). However, it cannot be wrong for the trustees of an unincorporated charity to follow, as nearly as possible, the procedure observed by a charitable company for convening an AGM/GM. Many churches give notice of the meetings by way of including details in the weekly notice sheet, and also displaying a notice on the church notice board. It is considered that the trustees need to do all they can to be certain that notice has been given to all the members of the charity, particularly if proposals are to be put to the meeting which may be controversial and will require the members to vote.

Again it is considered good practice to circulate the Annual Report and Accounts prior to the meeting, as this enables issues to be raised and dealt with and closed off at the meeting. Charitable companies are required by law to circulate copies of the Annual Report and Accounts prior to the meeting.

There are two main advantages in a charitable organisation holding an AGM/GM. First, it gives the trustees the opportunity to explain their leadership of the charity to the members, and secondly it gives the members the opportunity to ask questions before they vote on any of the business items on the agenda. The trustees are bound to act on decisions taken by members only where the governing document of the charity stipulates that those matters must be decided at such a meeting. It is worth checking the charity's governing document in order to be clear on that point before the meeting and if the trustees are not bound to act on decisions taken by members, then perhaps the point should be made at the outset of the meeting.

The business to be conducted at the meeting will be set out in an agenda which should also be circulated with the notice of the meeting. If any special resolution is to be passed then the agenda must state this, and the exact wording of the resolution itself must be given. If the trustees are to retire or be appointed at the meeting, full details of the new candidates to be appointed should be included in the information send out prior to the meeting.

Minutes of the meeting must be taken. If they are subsequently signed by the chair of the meeting (or of the next meeting), then they are considered to be evidence of those proceedings and unless the contrary is proved, the meeting is deemed to have been properly convened and held, and all the proceedings duly conducted.

Given that a meeting is an open forum where charity trustees and members come together for the purpose of open discussion, the possibility of there being a dispute at such a meeting is probably increased. It is helpful for the trustees to consider in advance of the meeting a procedure for dealing with potential disputes at a meeting and the following points are suggested:

- The chair should make it clear at the outset of the meeting that all members' behaviour is expected to be to a certain standard throughout and that in an instance of unacceptable behaviour the chairman will adjourn the meeting.
- It should be agreed that no new items for the agenda would be received from the membership at the meeting itself; (in that way the trustees have advance notice of the issues that are likely to be raised).

A sample agenda for an AGM/GM is set out below.

Agenda

of the charity . . . .

to be held at . . . .

on the . . . . day of . . . . 20 . . . .

The Chair will be . . . .

1 Apologies for absence
2 Declaration of conflicts of interest
3 Minutes of the previous meeting
4 Matters arising from those Minutes
5 Reports and accounts
6 Appointment of auditors
7 Appointment of charity trustees (including any retirement and reappointment by rotation permitted in the governing document)
8 Proposed resolutions
9 Chief Executive's Annual Report
10 Financial report
11 Any other business

- **GENERAL MEETING (GM) AND SPECIAL GENERAL MEETING (SGM)**

  Any meeting of the members of a charitable organisation, other than an AGM, is known as a GM (sometimes referred to as a Special General Meeting by unincorporated charities). The directors/trustees may call a GM whenever they think fit, subject to proper notice. Members can also ask the trustees to call a GM if they feel the trustees are not fulfilling the charity's aims and Objects or the charity is not being administered effectively. The governing document of the charity may well regulate the procedure for calling a GM.

The members who are qualified to attend a GM are usually those entitled to attend an SGM.

Members of a charitable company holding 5% of the voting rights at a GM, may requisition the calling of a GM by depositing the request at the company's Registered Office. Upon receipt of that, the directors must call the GM within 21 days, and the meeting itself should be held within 28 days after the date of the notice convening the GM. The period of notice required for the GM is 14 clear days' notice. Again the meeting can be held on short notice if this is agreed by a majority of the voting members.

The right to call a GM is one that exists for the members of a charitable company only, as there is, subject to any provisions to the contrary in an unincorporated charity's governing document, no statutory right for the members of an unincorporated charity to call such a meeting.

Proxies

A proxy is a person appointed by a member to attend and speak at a meeting on their behalf. Members have a right to appoint a proxy although the proxy does not have the right to demand a poll.

Proxies must be appointed in writing and a copy of the appointment delivered to the Registered Office of the company 48 hours before the start of the meeting.

Resolutions

A resolution is an agreement or decision made by the directors or members of a charity. When a resolution is passed, the charity is bound by it. The types of formal resolutions that are relevant to a meeting of a charitable company/CIO/unincorporated charity are:

- **ORDINARY RESOLUTION**
  For example, to approve the audited accounts of the organisation. This is passed by a simple majority (i.e. more than 50%) of those members voting in person (or by virtue of a proxy if this permitted). An ordinary resolution requires not less than 14 clear days' notice of the meeting at which it will be considered.

- **SPECIAL RESOLUTION**

  For example, to change the name of the organisation or its Objects. A special resolution is passed by a majority of not less than 75% of those members voting in person (and by proxy if permitted). A special resolution requires at least 14 clear days' notice of the meeting at which it will be considered.

- **WRITTEN RESOLUTIONS IN PLACE OF A MEETING**

  Charitable companies are permitted under the Companies Act 2006, to undertake by a written resolution, anything that may be done by a resolution passed at a GM, providing necessary procedures are completed.

  Written resolutions cannot be used to remove a director or auditor before the expiry of their term of office, as they have a right to make representations to the general meeting. The procedure by which the company undertakes a written resolution (as opposed to convening a GM or SGM)) is as follows:

9

- The board of the charitable company should resolve at a properly convened board meeting to utilise the written resolution procedure to pass (if members think fit) the proposed resolution.
- The form of the written resolution is then prepared and sent with an explanatory letter to each of the members of the charitable company. This letter explains the reasons for the proposed resolution, encloses any supporting documentation and invites the member to sign their agreement (or otherwise) and return the documentation to the secretary of the company by a specified date.
- The company then also sends a letter at the same time to the Auditors enclosing a copy of the resolution.
- The written resolution is passed when the required majority of members have signified their consent to it.
- An appropriate memorandum is then entered in the company's minute books recording the completion of the necessary procedures.
- A copy of the resolution is filed with Companies House where required under the Companies Act 2006.

  A written resolution procedure may therefore be attractive to charitable companies that have a small membership.

Associated Charities

"Daughter" Churches

Many churches, particularly in non-conformist streams, expand their work by planting other churches in different geographical locations ("daughter churches"). The question often arises as to whether daughter churches should be registered as independent charities in their own right, or whether they should continue to function under the charity registration of the parent church. Having worked with both models over many years, I have come to the firm conclusion that it is better to register each daughter church as a separate independent charity. There are several reasons for this.

- Trustees can exercise their governance responsibilities more effectively if they are locally based. They are able to help the charity to adapt to meet local needs and able to observe first-hand the workings of the charity. In my view, it is unwise for a board of trustees of the parent church to try to be responsible for a group that meets in another geographical area, in circumstances where they have little or no first-hand contact or information.
- There would be a simplified accounting treatment – this means that the accounts of the daughter church would be prepared and audited locally, rather than being subsumed into the parent charity's accounts with all the attendant auditing difficulties.
- Strong local leadership is likely to be built up if the leaders are empowered to control and administer their own independent organisation.
- Notwithstanding that the daughter church is set up as an independent charity, it is still possible for at least one trustee to be common to both parent and daughter, provided that the majority of trustees of the daughter are independent of the parent.

The parent church and the daughter church can be linked in vision, mandate and operational style by a written agreement. Such an agreement can be set up as akin to a "licensing agreement", (particularly if the parent church has a specific name that it is prepared to allow the daughter church to use), provided they respect the vision, mandate and operational style of the parent church.

If the daughter church is established as an independent charity, it is vital that the parent church does not seek to control the daughter church in a way that prevents trustees of the daughter church from being able to control their own affairs. Sometimes this can be difficult to achieve, particularly if the parent church is initially underwriting the costs of the daughter church. However it is a fundamental principle of charity law that the trustees of a charity must have free and unhindered discretion to exercise their trustee function without control or undue influence from any outside source. The parent church may, however, prescribe the type and contents of the governing document and seek to have some constitutional influence on the daughter church, including:

- a requirement that no change of purpose or style of operation may take place without the "parent's" consent;
- provisions that would disallow the continued use of the "name" for a specific reason;
- a requirement to approve the disposal of any assets of the "daughter" church upon the winding up of the charity.

If the parent church decides to set up the daughter church without it being an independent charity (i.e. the daughter church will exist under the parent charity's registration), then it is normal to expect the parent church to exert influence and control on the management and function of the daughter church.

"Overseas Cousins"

Some UK charities and mission agencies have been set up by, or closely relate in vision to, an established church or charitable agency registered overseas. While this is perfectly workable, there are some potential pitfalls for the unwary, specifically:

- While the UK charity can include on its board trustees who are ordinarily resident overseas, the simple majority of the trustees should be ordinarily resident in the UK.
- Ultimate control and decision-making must rest with the UK trustees. This is so, even if the overseas body is actually financing the UK one.
- If the overseas body advances money to the UK charity for a special purpose (for example to buy a property), then it is important for the UK trustees to establish in writing whether the asset purchased will:
  - belong to the overseas body – with the UK one having use of it, either for a rental or free of charge;

- be purchased by the UK charity but with a mortgage or obligation back to the overseas one in respect of the monies advanced;
- belong absolutely to the UK charity, in which case the money advanced will be a gift to the UK charity. This means that if the asset is sold for any reason, the money remains with the UK charity.

If the asset is the property of the overseas body, it is important that it is not shown as an asset on the accounts of the UK charity. If it is, then the UK charity trustees will have some explaining to do when they eventually dispose of the asset!

If the UK charity is to send monies back to the overseas organisation at any time, then, unless it is in repayment of a specific loan or liability, the trustees of the UK charity must be convinced that sending the money overseas is exclusively in furtherance of the UK charity's Objects, and complies with HMRC's requirements for sending monies overseas (see section 21).

Some activities that an overseas organisation may undertake may be lawful or "charitable" for them in that overseas country, but not charitable in the UK, for example, political lobbying.

Notwithstanding the need to keep the UK charity and the overseas body "separate", it is still possible to have a legal agreement between the two organisations that defines their shared vision, mandate and operational style.

SECTION 11

Property Issues

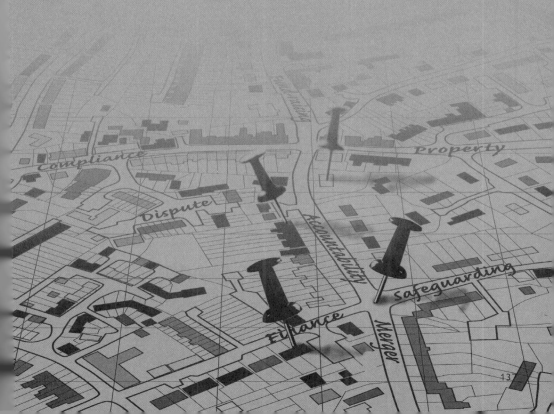

For most charities, a property transaction is likely to be one of the largest, and most demanding, projects that they will undertake. Whether it is the price itself, the complexity of a new build or the sheer emotional drain of the transaction, most charity trustees never forget "the property transaction"!

The Charities Acts do not put any specific constraints on trustees who are purchasing a property whether freehold or leasehold. However it is always wise to check that the charity's governing document permits the charity to hold property and raise money on mortgage. If it does not, the charity will need to obtain Charity Commission approval before purchasing or leasing a property.

Likewise, if the charity is to purchase or rent land from one of the charity's trustees (or a "Connected Person"), or the charity intends to use Permanent Endowment to purchase the property, then again Charity Commission consent will be required.

Before a charity can enter into a mortgage, grant a lease, or otherwise dispose of land or buildings owned by the charity, there are requirements under the Charities Act 2011 that need to be complied with.

In the main, a charity's property issues are as follows:

Acquisition

While a charity does not have to obtain Charity Commission consent before acquiring a property, its trustees have a general duty to act reasonably by exercising such skill and care as they are able and to act in the interests of the charity at all times. This "care and skill" will include ensuring:

- the property is suitable for its intended use and is not, for example, subject to any legal or planning restriction which would prevent the property being used for the charity's purposes;
- any necessary planning permission is obtained;
- the price or rent to be paid is comparable to similar properties on the market;
- the charity can afford the property (including payment of any mortgage that may be arranged as part of the transaction);
- that when they acquire the property on lease they fully understand the terms and potential liabilities under that long-term agreement – see leases (post);
- that they obtain specialist advice from a solicitor and a qualified surveyor.

Trustees of a charity may also wish to acquire land as an income-producing investment. Again the charity needs to have the power in its governing document to do this and the trustees must before purchasing the property take specialist professional property advice, concerning the suitability of this investment to the needs of the charity itself.

Charity trustees would be well advised to consider an independent valuation on the price/rent to ensure the charity is getting good value. The surveyor should be acting solely for the charity and ensure that the valuation will take into account not only the property itself but the permitted planning use and the effect of any restrictive covenants, or likely repairs/improvements on it. The trustees should ensure that the lawyers instructed to act for the charity in the acquisition are specialist property lawyers and are fully briefed as to the intended use of the property. A property subject to a covenant prohibiting the proposed charitable activity or obliging the property to be used only for a specific purpose which is distinctly uncharitable is of little use to the charity. Surprisingly enough, I have seen examples of charities that have acquired such property, subject to such restrictions, and they have had to deal with the consequences.

There are further requirements on charity trustees who are seeking to arrange a mortgage for a charity to assist in the acquisition. These are detailed later in this section.

Registered charities are entitled to relief from Stamp Duty Land Tax (SDLT) on the purchase price. However this relief is only available if all the purchasers are charities or charitable trusts. Therefore, if any of the "purchasers" are not a charity or charitable trust, (for example, a church and its development partner are to be the purchasers jointly), then no SDLT relief is available. Relief is only available if the conditions as to the use of the property are satisfied. There is no such relief from land registration fees which are payable at the appropriate scale on the purchase price.

Trustees of an unincorporated charity need to decide how the property or lease will be held. For example will they hold it in their own names upon trust for the charity? Or will they use a custodian trustee? Or the official custodian of charities? In the case of a charitable company, or CIO, the property is registered in the name of the charitable company or CIO itself and, as discussed in section 8, that avoids the need for constantly changing the registered proprietors when trustees change.

Upon completion of the registration of title, the Land Registry will enter a restriction on the title to the land, effectively preventing a sale by the registered proprietor charity unless the provisions of s117-s121 of the Charities Act 2011 are complied with.

- **LEASES**

  When the charity is considering acquiring a property on lease there are the following specific points to be made:

  - The covenants in the lease need to be carefully reviewed (and interpreted by a property lawyer) to ensure that they are not onerous to the charity.
  - A check should be made to see whether the lease has the provisions of section s24 to s28 of the Landlord and Tenant Act 1954 specifically excluded. Those provisions normally permit a renewal of the lease at the end of the term on substantially the same terms as the original lease was granted (save for an adjustment in rent). It follows that if the provisions of that Act have been excluded, then the charity will have no automatic right to renew the lease at the end of the term.
  - Careful attention should be paid to the rent review provisions that may be contained within the lease. These allow the landlord to negotiate to increase the rent at various times during the lease (usually every three or five years). It is vital to take specialist advice from a chartered surveyor to ensure that any necessary notices are served and the rent review negotiations are properly handled. It is not for the trustees to agree an increase in rent that may be out of proportion to the average market rents in that area, however encouraging the landlord may have been towards the charity!
  - Hidden dangers exist at the end of most leases in the nature of dilapidations. Dilapidations cover the remedial works that the landlord's surveyor calculates will be necessary at the end of the term of the lease, to restore the property to the condition that it was in at the outset. Charities should be careful when taking an assignment of an existing lease, as they could be liable for dilapidations going back to the date that the original lease was granted. Again professional advice from a lawyer or surveyor is essential before a charity enters into the purchase or assignment of a lease.
  - Another potential pitfall for the unwary is the Authorised Guarantee Agreement that features in most modern leases. If the charity takes a new lease then it should regard this as a commitment for the whole

length of the lease, whether or not it sells to a third party before the lease runs out. This is because, if the charity sells the lease to another party, the landlord will require the charity to enter into an Authorised Guarantee Agreement, effectively guaranteeing that the third party to whom it is selling will pay the rent and observe all the covenants for the remainder of the lease term including dilapidations. If that third party defaults, then the charity will have to pay; notwithstanding that it thought it had disposed of its interest.

- **AUCTIONS**

A charity proposing to bid for a property at auction needs to bear the following in mind:

it will need to undertake all preliminary searches, enquiries, investigations and valuations on the property before going to the auction. Furthermore if the charity requires a mortgage this will need to be arranged in place before the auction;

if the charity's bid for a property is successful and the auctioneer's hammer falls, then, at that moment, the charity has entered into a binding contract to acquire the property. This means that the charity cannot pull out if it subsequently changes its mind, or its funding is no longer available;

- A deposit of 10% of the successful purchase price will need to be paid, from cleared funds, on the date of the auction.
- Completion normally takes place 28 days after the date of the auction.
- The purchasing charity will be "on risk" for insurance purposes from the date of the auction.

While some charities have obtained property at a good price from an auction, others have lamented that they became caught up in the excitement in the auction room, and ended up bidding a higher price than the property was probably worth.

Disposal

- **SALES**

Registered charities and charities Excepted from registration, (but not Exempt Charities) may sell or lease land held by or in trust for it, without an order of the court or the Charity Commission, providing certain conditions are complied with and the sale is not to a "connected person, or a trustee or nominee of a connected person". (A "connected person" is defined as a trustee, the donor of any land to the charity, a child/parent/grandchild/grandparent/brother or sister of any trustee or donor, an officer or employee of the charity or any spouse or civil partner of any of the above, or a person carrying on business with any of those people.)

The conditions and the usual procedure for the charity to comply with before it disposes of land (providing it is to a non-connected person) are as follows:

· The charity trustees must obtain and consider a written report on the proposed sale from a qualified surveyor instructed by the trustees and acting exclusively for the charity.
· The trustees should advertise the proposed sale in such manner as the surveyor advises in his report, unless in that report he has said it would not be in the best interest of the charity to advertise the proposed sale, and the trustees decide they are satisfied having considered his report, that the terms of the proposed sale are the best that can reasonably be obtained for the charity.

This procedure covers all "sales" including surrenders or assignments of leases, and the granting of easements. Any proposed disposal of charity land to a connected person cannot take place until a Charity Commission's order has been obtained.

Once the above conditions have been complied with, the sale contract and subsequent transfer document, or lease, will contain specific provisions under the Charities Act 2011, which are in effect statements made by the trustees that they have complied with the provisions of the Act, whereupon the sale can proceed without the consent of the Charity Commission.

(In some instances, the trusts on which the charity hold land, stipulate that it is to be used for the specific purposes of that charity. For example, land may be given to a charity on condition that it is used as a young people's camp ground. In such cases the trustees cannot sell, lease or dispose of the land unless they have given public notice of the proposed transaction, have invited representations to be made within a set period, and have taken into account any representations made to them. This provision does not apply if the purpose of the sale is with a view to acquiring a replacement property, which will be held on the same trusts.)

The provision above does not apply:

- to any sale for which a specific authority has been given (e.g. a Charity Commission Scheme or Order);
- if the disposal is made to another charity for less than its probable value, provided that the disposal is authorised within the Objects of the disposing charity;
- to a lease to a beneficiary of the charity at less than market rent, provided that the property is to be occupied for the purposes of the charity.

- **DISPOSAL AT AN AUCTION**

  This is permissible, provided that the trustees consider it to be in the best interests of the charity. Some suggested recommendations:

- Professional advice on the proposal to use an auction sale for the property, together with a likely valuation, should be obtained beforehand from a suitably qualified surveyor.
- The charity should put a reserve price on the lot in order to achieve at least the value recommended by the surveyor.
- The requirements above for a disposal must be complied with prior to the auction. Failing this, the charity must obtain an order authorising the sale from the Charity Commission between the auction and completion date. In this case it may be wise also to write into the conditions of sale of the auction, that the sale will be subject to obtaining a Charity Commission order, particularly if it turns out that the purchaser is actually a connected person!

- **LEASES**

  If the charity proposes to grant a lease for a period not exceeding seven years, then the charity must:

- obtain and consider the advice on the proposed grant of the lease from a person (not necessarily a qualified surveyor) whom the trustees reasonably believe to have the necessary ability and practical experience to provide them with competent advice on the matter;
- decide that they are satisfied, having considered that person's advice, and that the proposed terms for the transaction are the best that can be reasonably obtained for the charity.

The grant of a lease for a period of more than seven years is dealt with in the same manner as a proposed disposal of property by the charity (set out above).

Mortgages

The Charity Commission's specific consent will not be needed in connection with a loan or mortgage in situations where the charity trustees have, before signing the mortgage, obtained and considered proper advice given to them in writing addressing:

- whether the proposed loan or mortgage is necessary in order for the charity trustees to be able to pursue the particular activity in connection with which the loan is to be taken – for example, to purchase a property;
- whether the terms of the proposed loan or mortgage are reasonable in regard to the status of the charity as the proposed recipient of the loan or mortgage;
- the ability of the charity to repay the loan or mortgage on the terms offered.

The person who provides such advice must be someone who is reasonably believed by the trustees to be qualified by their ability and practical experience of financial matters and who has no financial interest in the making of the loan itself.

The mortgage deed must state the fact that the land is held by or in trust for a charity and contain the appropriate statements under the Charities Act 2011. Furthermore, the mortgage must state that the trustees have power under the governing document of the charity to grant the mortgage and that they have considered the advice that has been given to them.

If the mortgage secures a guarantee that may have been given by the charity, (for example, on behalf of a trading subsidiary) the "proper advice" should address whether or not it is reasonable for the trustees to undertake to discharge that guarantee obligation having regard to the charity's Objects.

There are riders to add to this:

- In some cases, banks and other financial institutions loaning money to charities take the view that the charity's status (i.e. its "risk profile") is perhaps not the same as a commercial company or a purchaser of a residential property, and this results in the interest rate being a little higher than would be paid by a commercial or residential buyer. The "proper advice" that is given to the trustees should address the issue of the interest rate. If it appears to be unreasonably high, then those unusual provisions need to be reported to the trustees. (I have seen some that quote a very high rate of interest, which is then reduced substantially provided loan repayments are regularly made.) If in doubt, the trustees must seek the Charity Commission's specific consent before proceeding with the mortgage, as they could be criticised if the charity subsequently failed to make regular repayments and a loss resulted.

- On occasions a bank lender may require the charity to enter into an interest rate swap as part of the loan arrangement. These are complicated instruments which give the charity the right to move from one type of interest rate to another,.For example, the charity may take out a loan at a variable rate of interest and then swap to a fixed rate of interest. Very often the bank will seek to charge a premium for such an instrument and it is strongly recommended that the Charity Commission's specific consent should be sought before the charity enters into such an instrument, although banks have been less keen to insist on them in recent years.

- The trustees of the charity (whether unincorporated or incorporated) need to check carefully the terms of the mortgage deed, as they may well be liable personally on the direct covenant in the mortgage deed. This means that, if the bank or financial institution need to repossess the property and subsequently sell the same, if there is any loss, the trustees may be liable if the charity has no other assets.

- If the charity needs to arrange an overdraft with its bank, the provisions above concerning "proper advice" will apply. The charity does not need specific Charity Commission consents before setting up the overdraft. However, the trustees need to identify clearly the need for the expenditure to be undertaken. If the bank is reluctant to grant an unsecured overdraft, the trustees are permitted to allow the overdraft to be secured on the charity's assets.

Trustees should be careful before they agree to give any personal guarantees on behalf of the charity. Such personal guarantees can be "called in" by the lender and are not easy to be released from if the trustees' circumstances change.

Currently, no system is in place to register mortgages granted by a CIO with the Charity Commission and this might make it harder for CIOs to borrow money. Monies borrowed by a CIO where the lender is content for it to be secured only on the charity's property would not be affected by this point. See section 2.

Disability

The Equality Act 2010 applies to charities that provide goods, facilities or services to members of the public. In the case of a charity which allows its buildings to be accessible by the general public there are requirements to ensure that access and other facilities for the disabled are provided.

In the case of new buildings these facilities will be provided for in the design specification. Older buildings may need some adaptations to ensure compliance with these provisions. These will include:

- how people enter/leave the premises and find their way around;
- the signs provided;
- counters and checkouts;
- how people communicate with staff;
- accessible toilet facilities;
- emergency evacuation.

For a fuller treatment on this important subject, please see the publications produced by the Equality and Human Rights Commission.

Charity Development Projects

It is not uncommon today for charities to be involved in development schemes. Based upon experience of such schemes over the last 40 years the following points are offered as practical observations:

- It is essential for an independent professional who can advise on the viability and conduct of the whole project to be appointed early on. Such a person should be a qualified surveyor or other property professional with experience in representing charities in such projects.

Many trustee boards have become starry-eyed as to the possibilities and have overlooked some of the down-side and risk that exists in most development projects.

- It is important to appoint a "project manager", if possible one with some experience of property development, but their main role is to be the contact point for the trustees and those that are advising or carrying out the project.

- It is impractical for the entire trustee board to be involved in every detail of the project. By establishing a small working group with appropriate skills (which may also include non-trustees), who are then given appropriate authority to reach decisions quickly and report back to the full board, it will avoid unnecessary frustrations, particularly for professionals involved who are waiting for decisions to be made.

- It is not wise for the minister or spiritual leader to be the project manager or to be intimately involved in leading the project. His role could be neglected as it is all too easy to become intoxicated by the thrill of the project which is going to deliver a sparkling new building to the charity. I have seen instances where the new building has been delivered but the congregation has, meanwhile, gone elsewhere.

- It is essential, particularly in the exploratory/start-up phase of a charity development scheme, that adequate monies are set aside for the charity to obtain good quality legal, accounting and surveyor's advice. If the project is not structured in a way that is legally compliant, financially viable and commercially attainable then it has a limited chance of becoming reality. A further benefit of bringing in these professionals at the outset is that they are often able to help the trustees see the bigger picture, which can make the project more viable and sustainable.

- A feasibility report is essential, together with appropriate tax/VAT advice. The trustees may well turn this into a formal business plan, which is likely to be required by a bank or other funder, as a condition of providing the finance. The funder will, in addition to being convinced of the viability of the project, require to be satisfied that the charity itself represents an acceptable risk for the loan. Charities who have less than three years audited accounts, or who have a history of splits and divisions, are unlikely to be accepted by funders on normal commercial terms.

- Joint venture arrangements with an outside developer need to be carefully negotiated and documented. Within the same project are two conflicting goals – the developer wishes to make a profit and the charity wishes to obtain its facility for little or no money. The charity needs to guard against letting the developer have unfettered use of its asset (for example the land) in

11

circumstances where the charity is left unsecured if the developer fails in any way.

· The use of a limited company as "special purpose vehicle" for a development project is often considered a wise way to proceed. The limited liability (albeit that the shares or a proportion of them will be held by the charity) means that the trustees have another level of protection as they enter into the project. All development projects carry a level of risk that is somewhat higher than the traditional purchase or sale of a property.

Town and Country Planning

Each type of property is given a "use class" by the Town and Country Planning (Use Classes) Order 1987. In the case of a shop it is A1, an office is B1 and a church is D1.

To "change the use" of a property involves obtaining consent from the local planning authority to switch the use from one class to another. For the most part this involves a full planning application. While there are national guiding principles given to local planning authorities, they are also able to impose their own restrictions on building use in the area.

Local planning authorities have shown a marked reluctance to permit a change of use from commercial or retail to a D1 use. On the whole, they are not anxious to see the loss of employment opportunities in areas that are primarily commercial, and they consider that if a property is used by a charity, then it is less likely that employment opportunities will exist as a result. (There is also the small matter of the fact that they will receive a substantially reduced business rate on a property used by a charity.

It is important that charity trustees should not proceed with the purchase of, or the taking of a lease of a property, that will involve the change of use from one class to another, without having some indication from the local planning authority that, in principle, such a change would be accepted. There exists a procedure known as a pre-application (pre-app) whereby the outline proposals can be considered by the local planning officers who will then give an indication as to whether a full planning application on that proposal would be likely to succeed. Of course, this is only the planning officer's views and they cannot speak for the planning committee itself who may make a contrary decision! However, as the planning officers advise the planning committee their response to a pre-app is considered to be worth the fee. It is better to find out at an early stage as to whether the proposal is a non-starter.

If trustees proceed with a purchase or lease of a property in circumstances where they know that the existing planning use would not allow the building to be used for the charity's purposes, then it is considered that they are acting negligently and could be personally liable for the resulting loss to the charity. (I.e. having to pay for a building that it cannot use.)

It is therefore essential to resolve the planning situation before the charity is committed to the transaction. In some cases it may be possible to negotiate to purchase a property or lease, subject to a successful application for change of use. In that case, a contract is exchanged conditionally on the change of use being granted and completion takes place after the planning consent is given. If however the planning consent is refused, then the conditional contract is set aside and the purchaser walks away.

Specialist professional advice on Town and Country Planning issues is, therefore, essential for the trustees before they commit to purchase or lease a property that would require a change of use.

In circumstances where the charity is occupying a property within the permitted use, under the Town and Country Planning (Use Classes) Order 1987 Act, and then desires to set up other operations within the property that involve a different use class (a mixed use), then the trustees need to be very careful that such a mixed use will not put them in breach of the planning laws. For example, a church that has a bookshop or a coffee shop solely for those visiting the church is unlikely to attract the interests of the planning authority. However, contrast that with a church who wishes to rent off specific parts of its building to outside organisations for activities; in these circumstances, the local planning authority may consider this a change of use.

Enforcement action is when the local planning authority decides that the present use to which the building is being put (in whole or in part), is contrary to the permitted planning use for that property. They will usually give the property owner a notice allowing a period of time for the use to be put back to the permitted one. In default of that, they will serve an Enforcement Notice. While it is open for the charity to appeal against the Enforcement Notice, ultimately if that appeal fails, then continued use in contravention is a criminal offence, punishable by imprisonment.

If a person wishes to appeal against either a refusal of a planning permission or service of an Enforcement Notice, then the applicant can request either a public enquiry or an appeal dealt with by way of written representation. In either case, specialist planning and legal advice are vital. The costs involved in a public enquiry are not for the faint-hearted or cost-conscious!

Charities and VAT

In general, charitable registration does not entitle an organisation to receive goods and services free from VAT. In some circumstances, a charity that is involved in activities which may be considered to be in competition with commercial traders would then be required to register for VAT to prevent it getting an unfair trading advantage.

Charities involved in certain areas such as medical research, providing services for the disabled/partially-sighted or the rescue services, may be entitled to VAT relief.

One particular area of possible VAT relief for charities concerns the acquisition of property.

If the seller of property to a charity has elected to charge VAT on either the sale price or (in the case of a Lease) the rent, then it may be possible for the charity to seek either a total or partial relief from VAT on the basis (if indeed it is the case) that all of the property will be used for "relevant charitable purposes", in effect, for non-business activities that do not involve charging fees. It is believed that this relief would not apply to a building used for a charity and head office, and neither would it apply in circumstances where the charity then decided to let out part of the building so acquired at a commercial rent. VAT is a complicated area and specialist advice should always be taken.

Charities undertaking a large building project – e.g. the construction of a new building or church – are likely to find that their main contractors will wish to charge VAT on the cost of construction. Unless the charity is going to have an ongoing "taxable supply" i.e. selling goods or services in excess of £85,000.00 a year, then there is little point in the charity registering for VAT as a way of recovering the VAT it may pay on the construction cost.

Miscellaneous

- S333 of the Charities Act 2011 allows the trustees or unincorporated charities to pass a resolution empowering two or more of their number to sign deeds and documents binding the charity on behalf of all the trustees. This is of assistance when the trustee board is quite large, as it saves documents having to be circulated among a number of trustees for signature. Obviously it applies only to unincorporated charities. All documents for charitable companies and CIOs can be signed by either two directors (trustees), or one director (trustee) and the company secretary or one director (trustee) signing in the presence of an independent witness.

The Charity Commission can make an order to authorise any action where they are satisfied that the action proposed, in the administration of the charity, is in the best interests of the charity. This is a useful provision, as under it, the Charity Commission can make good any apparent defect in the charity's governing document, in order to authorise a particular property transaction. It also extends to general administrative provisions that may need to be specifically authorised and is therefore not limited to authorising property-related matters.

- Compulsory Purchase Orders are binding on a charity in exactly the same way as they would be on an individual or a company. If the charity is the recipient of a CPO, it is essential that professional surveyors are instructed immediately to negotiate on behalf of the charity to get the appropriate level of compensation for the land itself and the costs of relocation.

- Special care needs to be taken where charities use, or occupy, property that belongs to one or more members of its board of trustees. If the use by the charity is entirely "rent free" (i.e. no benefit of any kind is passing from the charity to the trustee in return for the use of the premises), then the situation is permissible. However it is strongly advised that the fact that the use is "rent free", together with any other arrangements as to the length of term and restrictions on use, is documented (preferably in the charity's minute book) so there is no misunderstanding in the future.

- In situations where it is proposed that the charity will make a payment of some kind to the trustee, in connection with the use of a property, then great care needs to be exercised by the charity. As the trustee is a connected person, the negotiations between the charity and the trustee in question should be handled by an independent surveyor/valuer, who should then report to the charity on whether this is in its best interest, and whether the level of rent or other consideration is reasonable for the locality and type of property concerned. This care is necessary, as it is a fundamental principle of charity law that trustees should not benefit directly from the charity that they are serving.

See also section 6 with regard to conflicts of interest.

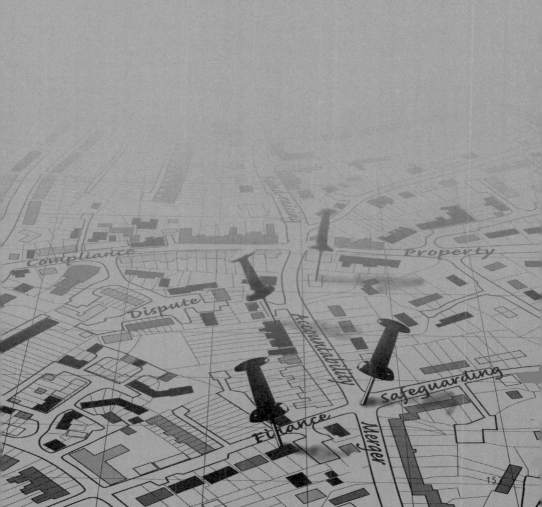

Charity Contracts 12

Contracts bring benefits, but also responsibilities. Charity trustees should take more than a passing interest in the contracts that are signed by and with the charity. In the case of unincorporated charities, the trustees could be personally liable!

For the purpose of this section, we shall consider the charity's contracts in two separate parts: those that benefit the charity; those that benefit others.

Contracts that benefit the charity can include:

· a contract to acquire something for the charity, for example a lease or finance agreement on a vehicle;
· a contract for funding, for example a grant;
· a contracts with the charity's staff;
· contracts with outside suppliers, for example agencies.

Contracts that benefit others can include:

· a contract for the charity to provide services, for example a contract with the local authority for the charity to provide its services;
· a contract with another organisation to provide for the charity and that other organisation to pursue a common purpose, for example a joint venture;

Looking at each of these in turn:

● **CONTRACTS THAT BENEFIT THE CHARITY**
Any such contract, which is in effect a long-term financial commitment, should be entered into only after the trustees have determined that the charity can afford the regular payments. As mentioned above, in the case of an unincorporated charity it is likely that the trustees will be liable personally if the charity defaults. Indeed one or more of the trustees may be asked to stand as guarantor under the agreement.

Grant funding to a charity often comes in an agreement whereby, in return for the payment of money to the charity, the charity is expected to deliver its service to certain standards and pre-agreed timetables. It is important that the charity determines that any such targets are realistic, in order to avoid any claim for repayment. Furthermore, grant-making organisations often reserve the right to conduct an audit to determine the way in which the charity has spent the money and the results of the projects that have been funded. It is not unknown for a charity to be asked to repay all or part of the grant, either because the project could not be completed, or for some error or omission in the way in which the charity accounted for the expenditure.

Furthermore, a worrying trend has developed in recent years, where the grant funders have delayed payments or have altered the terms of the funding during the period of the contract, thereby causing extreme cash flow problems for the recipient charity.

Staff contracts are some of the most important contracts that the charity will sign. (See section 15).

Contracts with outside suppliers need to be reviewed periodically to ensure the charity is getting best value for the services it is purchasing. Such contracts can range from those for office equipment to human resource agencies.

- **CONTRACTS THAT BENEFIT OTHERS**
  Where the charity enters into a contract to provide its services for the benefit of others, care needs to be taken for the following reasons:

  - If the charity is operating under a fixed-price contract, it needs to ensure that it fully understands its cost base and is confident it can provide the service (for the term of the contract), even if it has to buy in outside assistance.
  - Trustees should be alert to the potential loss of independence for the charity. For example, while such contracts could be a useful source of income, there is a risk the charity could become dependent on a particular source and subject to the dictates and agenda of that funding source. As mentioned elsewhere, it is essential that the charity does not compromise its independence and therefore its ability to be innovative and a real force for change in its chosen charitable activities. If the charity is considering entering into a contract jointly with another charity or organisation, then while such an arrangement may spread the financial risk and make the service more effective, the two organisations need to consider:
    - what their individual contributions and duties will be;
    - how they will divide both the income and the expenditure between the two organisations;
    - what happens if the two organisations disagree – who would resolve the dispute? How would liability be apportioned between them? How will the money be divided?

- whether one party has the ability to bind the other into a contract or arrangement.

If the joint venture is between a charity and a commercial concern (for example, where a charity desires to work with a property developer in developing land for the benefit of the charity), care needs to be taken to ensure that the charity is not exposed to unacceptable risk. A special purpose company (a joint venture company) may be preferable.

Potential Risks

Ultimately, trustees are legally responsible for a contract to which the employees of the charity may have committed the charity. (This may be the case even when the trustees have not authorised an employee directly to enter into that contract.) Trustees should therefore ensure that internal controls are in place in the charity so that the charity cannot be committed to significant liabilities under a contract without trustee's prior approval. The Charity Commission has a useful guide (Internal Financial Controls for Charities), which is available on its website.

Charities need to ensure that the proposed activity to be regulated under the contract is, in fact, exclusively in furtherance of the charity's stated Objects. For example, if the charity's specific Object is to provide books to church leaders in Africa, a contract obliging the charity to provide a translator to translate a book for a South American country would be inconsistent. If the contract is within the charity's Objects, then liability that arises under the contract can be settled out of the charity's monies. However, if that contract is for a purpose that is distinct from the charity's Objects, then the trustees are actually in breach of the trusts of the charity and could be personally liable for the performance of that contract and any liabilities that arise under it.

NB: It is wise for a charity to avoid drafting its "Objects" clause too narrowly – see section 1. It is unlikely the Charity Commission would permit the Objects clause of a charity to be changed so that it could enter into a contract, if the subject matter of that contract was quite distinct from the charity's Objects in its governing document.

Specific areas of risk in contractual arrangements include:

- **CANCELLATION OF THE CONTRACT**
  This can result in the loss of income to the charity, damage to its reputation, liability for expenses without the corresponding assurance of income, and possibly a claim on the charity for return of all or part of the monies paid under the contract. If the charity cannot deliver the service or the product contracted, the charity is exposed to a potential claim for damages.

- **LOSS OF INDEPENDENCE**
  A possible compromise of the charity's independence may occur by virtue of it becoming dependent upon one or more major contracts. Reliance upon the contracting parties' terms and conditions for payment could adversely affect the charity's cash flow. Unless the charity has reserves, it may be forced to borrow monies in order to maintain cash flow.

- **POSSIBLE TAX AND VAT IMPLICATIONS**
  There could include the withdrawal of the percentage relief from business rates on the charity's property, if the property is no longer being "wholly or mainly" used for charitable purposes, due to a contract with a commercial concern. This would be the case if the charity leased out part of its office building to a non-charitable entity.

Minimising Risk (See also section 26)

A separate company could be established to provide the service under the contract in question. This would either be a company limited by guarantee (without charitable status), or a commercial trading company or a Community Interest Company. Other steps to minimise risk could include:

- **INSURANCE**
  There are three kinds of policy that could be applicable:

- A commercial insurance policy to cover fire, theft, occupier's liability, or third party liability.
- public liability insurance. (This provides indemnity if someone is injured as a result of the negligence of one of the charity's employees.)
- indemnity insurance. (This would indemnify the contracting party as a result of losses that may come from the failure of the charity; or be a policy to indemnify the trustees of the charity against contractual liabilities, which they may have to pay out of their own pocket.)

- **INDEPENDENT LEGAL ADVICE**

  This would cover areas such as whether or not the charity's Objects allow it to enter into the contract, the contract itself, and any resultant liability (for example, if the contract obliged the charity to take on a lease of a property). In addition, wording may need to be written into the contract to limit the liability under the contract to the value of the assets that the charity has legally available to meet such liability.

Data Protection

Jennifer O'Brien,
Wellers Law Group

13

"… when it comes to privacy and accountability, people always demand the former for themselves and the latter for everyone else …"*

We live in an information age the like of which we have never seen before. This has come about because of the dizzying range of new technologies, available to us at an unprecedented rate of advancement. Who could have imagined the internet 50 years ago with information on almost any subject available with little more than a click?

Yet while these developments undoubtedly give rise to huge benefits, their result is the processing by businesses, charities and individuals of ever-growing volumes of information, allegedly increasing at the rate of ten times every five years! In response to that, governments around the world have recognised the need to regulate the use of data to reduce the risk of its misuse, while at the same time seeking not to unnecessarily stymie the evolution of new technologies.

New Europe-wide Data Protection rules are due to be implemented in 2018 called the General Data Protection Regulation (GDPR). Broadly, the new rules will impose a significantly stricter regime on all organisations including levying much higher financial penalties for failure to comply, as well as a requirement for charities to establish and resource higher compliance standards. Further information about GDPR is contained below. Although the UK is now intending to leave membership of the European Union (EU), its data protection regulator has already indicated that it is likely to continue to require compliance with EU equivalent standards to the processing of data by UK-based entities so that they are able to effectively operate and compete within the EU. Therefore organisations will need to take account of the GDPR as compliance with it is likely to be necessary. However as there are still many "unknowns" about how compliance with GDPR will be achieved this section will refer to anticipated changes to current law where applicable, but without detail on necessary compliance steps as there is still some detail to be "worked out" in terms achieving that. What is clear however is that charities need to take implementation of GDPR extremely seriously given its rigorous provisions, and begin to plan compliance with it well ahead of time.

* David Brin http://davidbrin.blogspot.co.uk/

The Data Protection Act 1998

Data Protection rules in the UK are contained in a number of laws the primary one of which is the Data Protection Act 1998 (Act), which will be replaced by the GDPR in mid 2018. The underlying principle of the Act and GDPR is transparency re data, that:

· individuals have a right to know what information organisations hold on them;
· what the organisations do with it;
· crucially individuals have the ability to grant or withhold consent to those uses.

Charities therefore need to understand what the Act says and what they need to do to comply with it as well as other data privacy laws (generally called "privacy laws").

The Act applies to "personal data" which is information which identifies an individual such as name, contact details and even just an email address. It also includes information which when put together with other information enables an individual to be identified. Note that personal data relates to living individuals and not the deceased. There is also another class of data called "Sensitive Personal Data" which applies to other categories of data such as physical or mental health, ethnicity, religious or other similar beliefs, sexual life and trade union membership. This will be called "special category personal data" under the GDPR which will be expanded to include genetic data, biometric data and data concerning sexual orientation.

Anyone who "processes" or handles personal data must comply with eight core principles to ensure that information is:

· fairly and lawfully processed;
· processed for limited purposes (i.e. only as necessary);
· adequate, relevant and not excessive;
· accurate and up-to-date;
· not kept for longer than is necessary;
· processed in line with individuals' rights;
· secure; and
· not transferred to other countries without adequate protection.

The first two principles essentially require charities to tell all individuals whose information they hold what they hold and what they do with it. All organisations hold information on a number of categories of individuals. For example charities will generally process data relating to employees (if they have any), donors, members, volunteers and suppliers (for example those providing cleaning or waste disposal services to the charity). All of these classes of individuals need to be notified about all the information which has been collected about them. The process for doing this is outlined below under "Charity Priority Areas".

The third and fourth principles relate to the nature of information collected by charities and its ongoing accuracy. Charities should only collect information they need for the purpose for which they intend to use it. For example to process donor contributions it is unlikely that a donor's date of birth would be required. Therefore charities should not ask for any unnecessary information even if they would like to have it to build up a better profile of their donor base. Similarly efforts must be made to ensure that information is up-to-date. Employees for instance can be reminded to notify Human Resources (HR) if there is a change to their contact details which achieves compliance with this obligation. Note however that charities will need to think about how to comply with this principle for every other class of data they hold.

Retention of data is the fifth principle and another important area under the Act. The rule is that an organisation must not keep personal data for longer than is necessary. This means that every charity should have a data retention policy outlining the different kinds of data it holds and the different periods for which it intends to keep it. For example if a charity interviews a number of candidates for a prospective role it should not retain the data of the unsuccessful candidates after notifying them that they were unsuccessful, unless it has asked their permission to do so (e.g. in case another position arises); but it may keep employee data for six years after an employee leaves employment in case the ex-employee brings a legal claim at a later stage (generally legal claims cannot be brought after six years).

The sixth data protection principle grants individuals a number of particular rights in relation to their data which charities need to be aware of and responsive to. These include the right for an individual to ask a charity for a complete copy of all the personal data it holds on that person and the right to ask it to stop marketing him/her if asked (discussed further at "Marketing" below).

A major focus under the Act (and GDPR) is security of data which is the seventh principle. This applies to manually as well as electronically held data. As technology develops and threats to electronic security increase (such as cyber attacks, proliferation of electronic devices etc.) the steps a charity needs to take to ensure security of its information will be constantly changing. However it is crucial that organisations take this issue seriously as the loss or leaking of data can result in large fines by the UK and overseas regulators and claims by individuals for compensation against the charity for damage and/ or distress; it can also result in severe reputational damage as these issues are increasingly reported in the press. Remember too that fines under the GDPR can be considerable (see Enforcement below).

Enforcement

The Information Commissioner is the UK's independent authority who upholds information rights promoting openness particularly by public bodies, and data privacy for individuals. The Information Commissioner (www. ico.org) acts to:

- promote good practice in handling personal data giving advice and guidance;
- keep a register of organisations that are required to "notify" him about their information-processing activities (see "Notification" below);
- help to resolve disputes in deciding whether an organisation has complied with privacy laws or not;
- take action to enforce compliance where appropriate;
- bring prosecutions for offences committed under UK privacy laws.

The ICO will become a "supervisory authority" under the GDPR as will regulators across the EU.

The Information Commissioner's Office (ICO) can take action to change the behaviour of organisations and individuals that collect, use and keep personal data. It can do so in three ways, namely:

- auditing organisations (inspecting levels of compliance),
- issuing non-criminal enforcement notices (telling organisations what they need to do to correct failures) and
- bringing criminal prosecutions.

The ICO also has power to impose fines of up to £500,000.00 on an organisation, but under the new rules fines can be the greater of Euro 20m or 4% of global turnover!

Fines are imposed if a breach was deliberate or, more importantly for charities, if the organisation knew (or should have known) that there was a risk of a breach which was likely to cause substantial damage or distress but failed to take reasonable steps to prevent it. Therefore it is critical that all charities take compliance with privacy laws seriously – poor security systems expose a charity to the risk of individuals' personal details being carelessly lost/leaked with resultant large fines.

Not every breach of the Act is a criminal offence but examples of criminal offences under the Act are:

- selling or offering to sell personal data which has been unlawfully obtained;
- failing to comply with an ICO Enforcement Notice.

Fines can be imposed as a result of successful criminal prosecutions and trustees/directors can be personally liable as well as the charity they act for where an offence under the Act has been committed with their consent or is attributable to neglect on their part. Trustees need to be aware therefore data privacy compliance needs to be on the Board agenda!

Priority Areas for Charities

Helpfully the ICO has highlighted five "Charity Priority Areas". These areas do not cover every obligation of a charity under privacy laws but are a good indicator of some priority areas with which at a minimum charities should ensure compliance. They will also be issuing bulletins on how to comply with the GDPR so charities should refer to their website periodically to prepare for the GDPR.

- **TELL PEOPLE WHAT A CHARITY IS DOING WITH THEIR DATA**
  As previously stated the first two data protection principles require a charity to tell individuals what information they hold on them, what they want to do with their information and to obtain their consent to each intended use.

  To be valid this "consent" must amount to a positive act of some kind such as completing a paper form or clicking submit on a website. Under the GDPR the standard is higher – it must be "unambiguous", so asking people to un-tick pre-ticked boxes will not be acceptable. Note that sensitive data requires "explicit consent" – the Act doesn't explain how that differs from "consent" but consent must also be unequivocal.

The easiest way to comply with these requirements is to make sure that a charity tells people what it is going to do with their information at the point at which it collects it from them. In many cases this will be the first contact point between an individual and a charity, for example a donor filling out a form with contact and financial information in order to make a donation. It is important that the form includes clear statements about all proposed uses of the donor's information.

The importance of obtaining consent from an individual at this initial point of contact is clear – the individual is more likely to respond to a request for consent while providing information at the same time. It is generally far more difficult to obtain consent at a later stage of relationship. The same approach should be taken to any forms individuals submit via a charity's website i.e. clear statements about all uses of data should be included in understandable and prominent wording. Note also that if information may be transferred outside the European Economic Area (EEA) then this also needs to be stated.

Full information about use of data should be included in Privacy Policies. They should be posted on every page of a charity's website and hard-copy forms which individuals fill out should also refer to the relevant website and Privacy policy. Importantly under the GPDR additional information is required to be given in information notices which means that organisations need to review their privacy policies and other documents to ensure compliance – that work should begin well before 2018.

Note that statements about intended use of data must only state what a charity envisages doing in the relatively short-term. It is not acceptable to include a list of possible uses of data which are merely theoretical and/or may be carried out in the distant future.

- **ASKING FOR A COPY OF DATA**
The right for an individual to request a copy of his/her personal data is an important one and called a "Subject Access Request" (SAR). The general rule is that the individual is entitled to a copy of all their own personal data. In terms of procedure on receipt of a SAR a charity can charge a fee of £10.00 for complying with the request but once the fee is received then the

charity has 40 calendar days within which to supply the information. Note that under the GDPR organisations will only have a month to comply and in most cases will not be able to charge a fee so policies and procedure should be amended to take this into account.

Charities are expected to search all their information sources for relevant data including databases, archived material and manual files unless it involves disproportionate effort (see "Exemptions" below).

Valid Requests

Requests need to be in writing but note that requests may be validly made by email or even on social media.

A charity may ask for identification of the person who requests the information if there is doubt about it. Furthermore it can ask for some information to help in the search for the data which may be helpful if there are large amounts of data to search through. However if the individual does not provide any information to narrow the search then all data must be searched to comply with the request.

Exemptions

A charity is not required to comply with a SAR if it would involve "disproportionate effort", but increasingly the ICO's view is that it would be rare for this to be a justification for not complying. However if there are references to third parties in an individual's personal data then the data can only be disclosed if the third party consents to disclosure or it is reasonable in all the circumstances to comply without the individual's consent. To make this assessment further legal advice should be sought.

Repeated or Unreasonable Requests

If an individual submits SARs at unreasonable intervals (i.e. in close succession) a charity is not required to provide information unless a reasonable interval has elapsed since the previous request. Very importantly on this issue (as with others) staff must be trained to understand what a SAR is and to be able to respond appropriately (see "Training" below).

- ### SECURITY

A key principle is the requirement for organisations to keep data secure by means of "technical and organisational measures". The purpose of the measures is to prevent both unauthorised or unlawful processing of data and accidental loss or destruction of or damage to personal data.

In 2014 the ICO found serious failings in the way volunteers at a charity handled sensitive personal data - they were using personal email addresses to receive/share information about people using the charity, unencrypted data was stored on home computers and there was a failure to lock papers away. The ICO made corrective recommendations. When the charity's website was subsequently hacked in 2015 putting at risk a large amount of personal data the ICO made further recommendations. However because the charity did not implement them all the ICO served an enforcement notice on it – a serious step and generally only taken after a charity has failed to implement earlier recommendations. Compliance in the first instance should be the priority of every organisation to avoid the damaging publicity which this charity received. Note too that failure to comply with an enforcement notice can lead to prosecution.

So what does a charity need to do? Each charity needs to assess its own security practices to address the security risks to which its information could be exposed. Remember also that as technology develops practices should be subject to regular review to ensure they are adequate.

Technical Measures
Technical measures refers to IT security so even the smallest charities need to ensure that they source adequate technical advice to satisfy this obligation. While the ICO does take into account the size of an organisation in considering whether its security measures are adequate, its expectations are likely to change over time taking into account technological developments with reference to market practice and cost. For example in the early years of the Act small organisations were not expected to encrypt data but the ICO now advises that all portable devices be encrypted (see below for comments on "Personal use of Portable Devices").

Organisational Measures
Organisational measures relate to how an organisation handles data in terms of people access and physical security. For example HR records will inevitably contain sensitive personal data (e.g. sickness records) which should only be viewed by those who are required to have access to it. Therefore a security policy should specifically limit access to data to specified individuals depending on the type of information in question.

Similarly organisational security should be considered for example in relation to locked doors/cabinets/access to buildings. Surprisingly perhaps loss or theft of paperwork accounted for the most common form of data security breach in the UK in the last quarter of 2015! This represents a serious risk to organisations, as individuals can make claims against them for compensation for damage and distress yet the risk of these kinds of breaches could be hugely reduced with appropriate physical security.

The next most common data security breaches in 2015 were data being posted, faxed or sent by email to the incorrect recipient, insecure web pages (including hacking), loss or theft of unencrypted devices and insecure disposal of paperwork.

ICO Security Top Tips
The ICO has published informative guidance on its IT security top tips, accessible at its website. Some of these are:

Computer Security
- Install a Fire Wall and virus checking on computers.
- Only allow staff access to information they need to do their job.
- Encrypt any personal information held electronically that will cause damage or distress if it were lost or stolen.
- Take regular back-ups of the information on computer systems and keep them in a separate place.
- Consider whether the content of an email should be encrypted to password protect.

Other Security Measures
- Shred all confidential paper waste.
- Check the physical security of premises.
- Train staff to know that they can be prosecuted if they deliberately give out personal details without permission.
- Train staff to use strong passwords.

• THE CLOUD
Cyber-attacks are increasing at an unprecedented rate. Although large scale criminal attacks tend to hit the press, the most common instances of data theft and hacking apparently are disgruntled employees. Increasingly charities put their data in the "Cloud" and assume that it is therefore "safe". Essentially the Cloud is a means of having a charity's data stored and accessed remotely in a data centre belonging to a third party rather than on a charity's own system. The servers might be in the UK or overseas. However companies

providing Cloud services don't necessarily offer levels of security that are appropriate so charities need to read their terms of business very carefully before choosing to place their data on the Cloud.

Charities should also be prepared to negotiate their contracts with Cloud providers to ensure that the data is appropriately backed-up and that they have commitment from the Cloud providers to fully comply with data privacy laws.

- **PERSONAL USE OF PORTABLE DEVICES**
The use of electronic devices such as smart phones and tablet computers is increasingly popular. Many charities are faced with demands from employees, board members and even clients to use these devices to process charity information in the course of performing their roles. The ICO calls this practice "Bring Your Own Device" or BYOD.

Although this may be convenient for owners of these devices it raises its own significant security problems. The safest course of action is for charities to provide their own portable devices to employees, volunteers, members etc. so that it is able to process information on these devices in the knowledge that it has ownership of them and not the individual. However in reality the trend towards individuals using their own devices in the course of their work/volunteering is almost unstoppable. This means that organisations need to put an appropriate BYOD policy in place governing use of private personal devices to the extent that they process a charity's personal data.

The main risk of BYOD is that because the individual owns, maintains and supports their device(s) the charity has significantly less control over it than it would over its own devices. However under the Act the charity must still take appropriate security measures to protect its data.

Each charity will need to assess the risks which BYOD presents to its organisation. Having done that it should develop an Acceptable Use policy outlining what types of data can be held on personal devices, the responsibilities of the individual/employee in ensuring the safety of that information as well as the rights of the charity in relation to the data and device. The ICO has produced very helpful guidance called "Bring Your Own Device (BYOD)" which charities should read when designing their policies. Some key considerations are:

- Identify what data can be held on a personal device and what must be held in a more restricted environment, e.g. sensitive HR data.

- Insist on use of strong passwords to secure devices.
- Use encryption to store data on devices securely.
- Ensure that access to devices is locked or data deleted if an incorrect password is entered too many times.
- Consider using different "Apps" for business and personal use so that there is a clear separation between the personal data processed on behalf of the charity and that processed for the device owner's own purposes.
- Make sure there is a process in place for quickly revoking access to a device if a user reports loss or theft.

Bear in mind use of personal devices requires compliance with other aspects of the Act as well as the security principle. So for example if data is located on the personal device there is a risk that it would be retained for longer than the charity retention policy prescribes or that a SAR would be more difficult to comply with if data concerning an individual is contained on the personal device.

The increasing trend towards use of personal devices is unlikely to diminish so organisations need to be proactive about tackling the risks practically and in policy form rather than do nothing and find themselves dealing with serious security breaches simply for failure to put some basic preventative steps in place.

- **MANAGING SECURITY BREACHES**

Charities should have a plan in place for managing security breaches. Under the GDPR significant new obligations are imposed. Each charity should have a data-breach response plan which enables it to react quickly in the event of a data breach. Generally breaches will need to be reported to the relevant Supervisory Authority as well as to affected individuals if the breach is likely to result in a high risk to their rights and freedoms. Breaches must be reported to the Supervisory Authority no later than 72 hours after being discovered and to affected individuals without undue delay if that is necessary. A failure to comply can result in a fine of up to €10 million or 2% of annual worldwide turnover, whichever is greater, so this issue needs to be taken extremely seriously by charities! Any breach opens the door to reputational damage so all the more reason for security to be taken extremely seriously.

· **What Are Data Contollers and Data Processors?**

A data controller (DC) is an individual/organisation which controls use of data and is subject to data privacy laws. A data processor (DP) is an individual/organisation which processes data on the instructions of the DC. Most charities will be DCs in relation to the data they process but are likely to use DPs to handle at least some of their data e.g. companies which deal with paper disposal on their behalf. The Act currently requires DCs to have written contracts in place with DPs specifying that they can only deal with the data on the instructions of the DC and with appropriate security measures in place. The GDPR however introduces a significant change in that it applies to DPs directly as well as DCs. It also specifies that contracts between DCs and DPs need to contain additional information. Currently many organisations include additional information such as an obligation on the DP to impose a duty of confidentiality on its staff and a right for the DC to audit the premises of the DP from time-to-time to check compliance. However all such contracts will need to be reviewed to ensure conformity to the GDPR.

● **DIRECT MARKETING**

For many charities marketing is an important tool in raising awareness of its activities, as a means to raising funds and in some cases to sell products and services. The law does not prohibit marketing - there is no restriction on sending marketing material to people who have requested it. However there are rules which apply to unsolicited direct marketing. Therefore in these days of ever-increasing and arguably aggressive marketing of individuals, it is critical that charities understand the rules and adhere to them – failure to do so can have serious consequences with loss of public confidence and reduction in donations/support.

· **What Is Direct Marketing?**

Direct marketing is "communication (by whatever means) of any advertising or marketing material which is directed to particular individuals".

Forms of marketing which are covered by this definition include mailshots, online marketing (emails), texts, social networking and other emerging channels of communication. This means that marketing applies to charities promoting their aims and appealing for funds as well as to the commercial sector which is typically associated with marketing. (Note that general marketing is not covered by these rules i.e. a leaflet drop to every house in a particular area.)

Marketing is necessary for charities to flourish and it is unfortunate that the poor practice of a few has led to some public disenchantment. Although people do like to support and donate to charities it is clear that they generally need to be asked in order to do so – so marketing is as appropriate and important to the charitable sector as to any other.

· **What Are the Rules?**
A wider range of rules applies to direct marketing than just the Act. The Privacy and Electronic Communications Regulations 2003 (PECR) contain detailed rules around marketing using electronic communications and even apply to marketing by a charity which doesn't involve using personal data. In addition there are other rules and industry codes of practice which affect marketing such as the Direct Marketing Code of Practice and UK Code of Non-broadcast Advertising, Sales Promotion and Direct Marketing (CAP Code) which are outside the scope of this book but of which charities ought also to be aware.

· **How to Market**
Obtain clear consent from the individual to market him/her – this is the golden rule for marketing!

Generally charities will need an individual's consent before they can send marketing texts, emails or faxes, make calls to a number registered with the Telephone Preference Service (TPS) or make any automated marketing calls to him/her. (The TPS is a service [www.tpsonline.org.uk] which allows individuals to list themselves on it to indicate they do not want to receive marketing telephone calls.)

If a charity wants to pass personal data on to another organisation then it will also need consent from individuals to do so. This derives from the first two principles of the Act which require data to be used lawfully (i.e. legitimately provided to another organisation) and all its proposed uses made clear.

Consent itself must be clear and specific with the necessary positive action like clicking on a button or subscribing to a service. Charities must keep clear records of exactly when and what an individual has consented to and how that consent was obtained. This will be important if there is an enquiry into the marketing practices of a charity. Consent must also be specific to each type of marketing which means that separate consent needs to be obtained for marketing by post, by email, by telephone, by text or by recorded call (see "Forms of Marketing" below). All consent statements must be clear and in prominent writing so that it is easy for the individual to understand what they are giving and not to miss any descriptive wording.

Note that the PECR sets a higher standard for what amounts to adequate consent than the Act – this therefore affects how charities can market by email/fax/automated calls. The effect of these rules is that a charity cannot rely on consent passed on from another organisation to market individuals – see "Indirect Marketing" below for further discussion of that point.

· **Forms of Marketing**

As stated above there are different rules for different types of marketing. For best practice the ICO recommends opt-in boxes on forms/online to obtain explicit consent.

Opt-in and Opt-out Boxes

Opt-in boxes are boxes where a tick indicates that the person agrees to receiving the specified marketing. Best practice is to provide an un-ticked opt-in box and invite the person to indicate their agreement to marketing by ticking it.

Pre-ticked boxes require the individual to untick the box if they don't want to consent to the marketing described. This is more like an opt-out box as it assumes consent unless the individual ticks the box, although the weakness of this approach is that a failure to untick the box is arguably not clear evidence of consent.

Opt-out boxes are boxes where an individual is invited to tick to object to or opt-out of receiving marketing messages.

The fact that an individual fails to tick the box only means that he/she has not objected so there is an argument that this approach does not indicate valid consent. However if this approach is adopted with clear and prominent wording then charities may take the view that this is adequate.

Soft opt-in is when an organisation that already provides products or services to an individual obtains their consent to marketing by opt-out only. The ICO accepts this because there is a presumption that those individuals are unlikely to object to receiving marketing material about similar products and services given that they are existing customers although they must be given the opportunity to opt-out at any time. This does not apply to charities unless they provide commercial products or services.

Note that the above complies with the PECR rules on marketing. However the standard of consent required by GDPR if it is applied to marketing would arguably not be satisfied by some of the methods referenced above e.g. pre-ticked boxes, opt-out boxes etc. Currently the impact of the GDPR on the PECR is unclear. Charities should therefore keep an eye on ICO notices/ guidance issued on the subject before mid-2018 to ensure that their marketing practices comply with consent standards.

· **Indirect marketing**

Indirect consent is when a person tells one organisation that they consent to receiving marketing material from another/other organisations. This could arise if a charity is given/buys a list of contacts for email marketing purposes from another organisation in an effort to increase its donor base and/or profile.

However charities need to be extremely cautious in using data received from third parties in these circumstances because the PECR require consent for email marketing to have been notified by the recipient of the email direct to the sender – this would not be the case if the list has come via a third party. If those third parties have clear evidence that the individuals have consented to their information being passed on to the named third party then a charity may take the view that that is adequate, but it is important to examine the extent of consent given and evidenced in each circumstance and to be aware of the risks of breaching privacy law with this approach (further advice will generally need to be sought).

Note that the same standard for consent under PECR applies to text and automated call marketing.

Calls
· Before making a list of marketing calls always screen numbers with the TPS unless the individual has specifically given consent to receiving calls.
· For automated calls individuals must have specifically given consent to receiving those calls so there is no need to screen against the TPS.
· For non-automated calls ensure your charity has opt-in consent or, failing that, make sure that your opt-out consent is very clear as per below.

Texts
· Opt-in consent is required except where "soft opt-in" consent is permitted (but note that this generally does not apply to charities).

Emails

- Opt-in consent is required (except where "soft opt-in" consent is permitted which generally does not apply to charities).
- Note that with reference to text and emails a charity should take its own view regarding the use of opt-out as adequate consent with reference to the ICO's preference for opt-in consent and other factors outlined above.

Business-To-Business Texts and Emails

- The rules on consent (and opt-in/opt-out) do not apply to emails sent to companies and other corporate bodies - the only requirement is that the sender identify themselves and provide contact details. However this does not apply to email addresses which contain a personal name e.g. firstname.lastname@org.co.uk.

Faxes

- Opt-in consent is required.

Mail

- Best practice is to obtain opt-in consent.
- Individuals can register their address with the Mail Preference Service (MPS, www.mpsonline.com) to avoid being marketed by mail but the Act does not require organisations to screen against the MPS before mailing individuals although it is good practice to do so.

- ### Marketing and Fundraising – Why the Controversy?

  Fundraising for charities is dealt with at section 23 which outlines new developments in this area. Considerable controversy arose in 2015 regarding the perceived aggressive fundraising tactics adopted by some charities as well as their flouting of privacy laws by selling their donor lists without the knowledge or consent of donors. The damage which has resulted in terms of loss of public confidence in this sector cannot be overstated. Charities are believed to exist for altruistic purposes and the public does not expect them to engage in some of the more "cut-throat" kinds of activities associated with the general commercial sector. The fall-out from the exposure of these practices has been significant, such that the charity sector needs in a sense to "rediscover" itself to regain public trust.

  However for the purposes of this section we are concerned with data privacy breaches only. Therefore if a charity buys databases from other organisations for the purpose of marketing/fundraising it needs to satisfy itself that it has adequate consent to use the data in this way and, as previously stated, the standard of consent for email marketing under the PECR is high as it requires consent to have been received by the sender of the email from the recipient (see "Indirect Marketing" above). Similarly a charity should not pass on or sell its customer/donor lists to any other organisation unless it has express consent from its donors to do so.

These latest controversies all highlight the importance for charities to ensure that their marketing practices are in accordance with privacy law. If charities fail to do so they risk loss of support and donations which will cause them to fail but most importantly ultimately harm the intended beneficiaries.

· **Breach of Marketing Rules**
The ICO increasingly receives complaints about unwanted direct marketing particularly in relation to calls and texts. It can impose high fines for breaches of rules. In 2012 it fined a Telecoms company £440,000.00 for sending millions of texts without prior consent and issued numerous significant fines against other companies for making marketing calls to numbers listed on the TPS without prior consent. All the indications are that the ICO will increasingly adopt a robust enforcement approach to failure to comply with marketing rules, given that the rules have been in place now for some time and that breach of them has attracted wide-spread publicity. Charities therefore need to prioritise ensuring that all their marketing practices comply with legal requirements. As, at the time of going to print it is unclear whether the GDPR will affect the PECR in terms of levels of fines for marketing breaches, organisations should ensure at a minimum that their existing practice complies with current rules and keep an eye on any guidance issued to ensure compliance going forwards.

· **What If an Individual Objects to Being Marketed?**
Under the Act and GDPR individuals can prevent their personal data being processed for direct marketing. At any time an individual can give a charity written notice to stop (or not begin) using their personal data for marketing. If a charity receives a notice it must comply within a reasonable period - the ICO recommends 28 days. Individuals will often ask a charity to remove or delete their details entirely from a database or marketing list. However it is generally not appropriate to do so but rather to "suppress"

the details. This means that a charity can retain enough information about them to ensure that their preferences are respected - if it deletes their details it will have no way of ensuring that they will not be put back on the database again.

A legitimate question is whether it is possible to subsequently ask people if they want to opt back in to receiving direct marketing. ICO guidance is cautious about this although accepts that individuals can be reminded of their ability to change their marketing preferences if the reminder is a minor and incidental addition to a message a charity is sending anyway.

Importantly the GDPR introduces a "right to be forgotten" as part of the new "right to erasure" for individuals. Individuals can ask for the right to erasure for a number of reasons including that the data are no longer needed for their original purpose, the individual withdraws consent, the processing is unlawful etc. Charities will need to plan to be able to respond to these kinds of requests and to conduct the appropriate analysis to know whether they are required to. Further advice should generally be sought.

As an aside individuals will also have a right to "data portability" under the GDPR. This means that they can ask a DC to send their personal data to another DC in a commonly-used and machine-readable format. Again charities need to take steps to ensure that their systems can accommodate these kinds of requests.

- **KEEPING INFORMATION**

Every organisation needs to have a "Data Retention Policy" outlining the length of time for which they will keep different types of data. This is because one of the principles under the Act is that information can only be kept as long necessary. The ICO will expect organisations to have considered this and have a written policy in place. In deciding what policy to apply charities need to consider each type of information separately. For example for as long as a donor is an active donor their information can be kept. However if they cease to be a donor then a charity should have a set timeframe within which it stops processing their information. One common approach is to write to that individual stating that a charity has not had contact with them for some time and that it will assume unless a charity hears otherwise from them that they do not want to be involved in the charity going forwards. Although charities understandably are keen to hold on to information about donors the current rules prohibit information being kept indefinitely.

Charities need to go through every type of data they hold to establish practice in terms of keeping the data.

- MISCELLANEOUS

· **Training**
Compliance with privacy laws will only be achieved if staff and participants are given some training in the importance of data privacy. Mishandled data can have serious consequences for organisations as well as their employees and supporters. Privacy law breaches can lead to very high financial penalties, seriously damaged reputation together with bad press, loss of trust from supporters and the public as well as loss of revenue as a result.

In terms of staff it is important that all employees are made aware of the fundamentals of data privacy so that they treat information in line with their obligations. So in practical terms all new employees and volunteers should receive some initial training on the rules around data privacy especially the need to keep data secure.

Depending on the role of employees some additional training may be required for those with access to sensitive information such as those working in HR. However it is important that refresher training is put in place every year for employees not only to reinforce the need for compliance but also because an organisation's policies are likely to evolve and change over time. In addition privacy law itself is likely to develop so that there will be a need to train people on an ongoing basis.

As well as being security aware all employees should be given an understanding of:

· What a SAR is and how to respond.
· What to do in the event of a security breach.

Alongside data privacy training it will also be appropriate to train employees on their obligations under the Freedom of Information Act 2003 and the Environmental Information Regulations 2004. For most charities these pieces of legislation will not apply but employees should be given a basic understanding of their substance as the public often confuses them with data privacy laws and makes requests to organisations which do not apply.

· **Register with the ICO?**
Under the Act most charities have to register (called "notify") with the ICO

outlining their data processing activities which can be viewed publicly on its website (there are limited grounds for exemption). Note that a failure to notify is a criminal offence. However under the new GDPR, there is no requirement to notify, although charities need to continue to do so until the new rules are in place.

- **Transferring Information Outside Europe**

The basic rule is that personal information cannot be transferred outside the European Economic Area (EU, Norway, Iceland and Lichtenstein) (EEA) unless the recipient of the information agrees to ensure it is handled in accordance with European privacy standards. Most countries outside the EEA are not deemed by European authorities to provide adequate protection for personal data.

13

This is a complex area and there are a number of different solutions to the problem. One way of dealing with it is to enter into a contract with the recipient of the data in which the recipient agrees to comply with European standards. The European authorities have produced "model contracts" for these transfers although there is no obligation to use them. Remember that even sending an email containing a name (firstname.surname@ charityname.org. uk) amounts to a "transfer of data" outside the EEA which means that almost every charity will be affected by these rules. In addition if an organisation's server is located outside the EEA then all of the organisation's data held on that server is deemed to have transferred. Another option particularly for global organisations which need to transfer data internally is to adopt "Binding Corporate Rules", effectively an agreement within an entity worldwide to adhere to European data privacy standards in relation to European data. As this is a complex area advice should be sought in each case.

Organisations need to conduct an audit on the pathway of their data so that they can ensure that they have appropriate contracts and protections in place. In addition Privacy Policies need to clearly tell individuals if their data may be transferred explaining that there may be risks to the security of data.

· **The New Rules**

> "Privacy – like eating and breathing is one of life's basic requirements."*

As stated throughout, the GDPR introduces a more rigorous regime in some regards. In addition to aspects already referenced some new areas which charities should be aware of and begin to prepare for are the following:

· An obligation to obtain parental consent to the processing of personal data relating to a child under 16 years of age or lower depending on the law of each European Member State but which can't be below 13 years. It will be important for organisations to consider how to comply with this particularly in an online context where identities can be difficult to verify.
· Extra-territorial scope of the GDPR. This means that organisations based outside the EU which process data relating to individuals in the EU are subject to European rules. They will have to appoint a representative in a single country in the EU. This aspect of the GDPR is controversial but nevertheless needs to be taken into account.
· Individuals will have the right to obtain compensation for breach not only from a DC but also from a DP for damage suffered.
· Accountability is a strong theme in the GDPR. It requires DCs to be able to demonstrate their compliance with the regime such as by appointing a Data Protection Officer (DPO), maintaining internal records of compliance, implementing robust security measures and privacy by Design/Data Privacy Impact Assessments (see below for explanations).
· Consent for "Profiling" will need to be obtained. Profiling is any automated processing of personal data to evaluate any feature of the behaviour/ preferences/location of an individual which may be used to track customer behaviour.
· Data Protection by Design is a new concept which requires a business when adopting a new technology/product/service to plan for data protection compliance when doing so. Charities therefore need to consider data protection obligations at the outset of projects.
· Data Privacy Impact Assessments (DPIAs) will be required for high risk processing to identify steps to mitigate against those risks.

---

* Katherine Neville http://www.katherineneville.com

The GDPR not only aims to address technological advancements but also to harmonise privacy laws throughout Europe. Under the existing European Data Protection, Directive Member States have implemented aspects of the rules differently which has resulted in organisations being subject to different rules in different countries. The GDPR will reduce that and will require an entity with presences in different European countries to be subject to a main Supervisory Authority which will have conduct of all privacy issues which arise in relation to that organisation. This may result in an entity for example with a small operation in the UK being subject to the Supervisory Authority in Germany where its headquarters are located but with the aim of having a "one-stop shop" approach to privacy law.

· **Freedom of Information Requests**

The Freedom of Information Act 2003 (FOI) gives individuals a right of access to information held by public authorities. It does not therefore generally apply to the not-for-profit sector as charities are not public authorities (with some limited exceptions for charities which receive significant Government funding). An FOI request is different from a SAR which only applies to personal information. FOI requests can cover a wider range of information such as commercial, strategic and financial information.

Charities should be aware however that the Charity Commission (Commission) is a public authority which is subject to the FOI. This means that any correspondence between a charity and the Commission could be disclosed to an individual who makes an FOI request for information about the charity to the Commission. There are various grounds under the FOI which may enable the Commission to withhold some information but charities should nevertheless be aware in communication with the Commission that the content of the communications could be disclosed to an enquiring individual under the FOI.

Although the means to compliance with many aspects of the GDPR is unclear, Regulators have made clear that that is no excuse for organisations failing to plan for compliance.

· Help!

There are 3 obvious steps for a charity to take to fulfil its responsibilities under current data protection laws and with the GDPR in mind:

- Arrange for a data protection audit to be carried out by a lawyer experienced in the area.
- Arrange for training for staff.
- Begin to plan for the GDPR in light of the information available on it.

SECTION 14

Intellectual Property

Intellectual Property is the collective name given to items that are intangible (i.e. do not physically exist) but that are nevertheless assets of a charity, for example a name, a logo, a publication or a recording. Although initially the worth of those items may be difficult to calculate, nevertheless they have a certain value to an organisation and can be worth protecting. Such protection can come in the following ways:

Copyright

It is not an idea that is copyrighted, but the way in which that idea is expressed. Copyright can cover written, artistic, musical and dramatic works. For example, once a book has been written or a song composed, then providing it is an original work, then it is capable of being copyrighted.

Generally speaking, copyright lasts for the life of the author of the work, plus an additional 70 years. The copyright owner has the right to prevent another person from copying or publishing that work. In fact, it is not necessarily for the copyright itself to be registered formally, although the person entitled to the copyright would usually affix a legend ("copyright © Paul Martin 2016") on any works they wish to protect. This action both establishes their claim to the copyright and warns the public at large not to infringe it.

Charities involved in publishing and/or the production of music and dramatic works should take care to research the issue of copyright carefully and understand how it applies to the charity's activities. For further information on this important subject, specialist advice should be taken.

Trademark

A trademark is a sign (usually shown as "TM") which distinguishes the goods and services of one organisation from another, for example a logo or a brand name.

There are 45 different classes of trademark registration. Each class lists distinct products, processes or services and it is possible to register a trademark in more than one class. For example, a trademark protecting a particular design is likely to be registered in several classes to cover the reproduction of that design in print, media, and electronic formats.

If a charity wishes to register a trademark, the successful registration will give it the exclusive right to use that mark for the particular goods or services for which it is has been registered. Clearly, before a mark can be registered, it has to be distinguishable from any other registered marks.

Some charities have trademarked their logo and formally licenced it to other charities and organisations in order to build a common brand yet retain influence on the way in which the particular activity of the charity is to be carried out.

Patent

Patents cover new inventions which have the potential for a commercial application. Once granted, a patent gives the inventor an exclusive period (currently 20 years in the UK), during which he can stop others using the invention. Patents are often granted for new drug compounds or methods of manufacture. They are granted by the UK Patent Office and before one is granted the invention is carefully examined. The process can take several years and be very expensive.

The main areas of intellectual property which might affect charities include:

14

- **PUBLICATIONS**

The charity, or those employed by it, may write manuals, books and other documentation that may have some commercial value at the time they are written. In such circumstances, the charity would be wise to affix the © to the works they have produced. However before doing so, the issue of ownership may need to be clarified. For example the minister of a church might write a book that subsequently is marketed. Who can rightfully claim the copyright in the authorship? The church may claim the authorship of the work, on the basis that the minister is employed by the church and wrote the book during the period of his employment. Alternatively the minister may claim the copyright and authorship, on the basis that he wrote the book in his spare time.

To save such a dispute arising, the minister's contract of employment should make clear the issue of ownership in any works (written or recorded) that the minister may produce during his employment. If it is not made clear, then the strong presumption is that the copyright and the ownership rests with the church as the employer. If the minister wishes to be able to claim the copyright (and therefore receive the royalties), then his employment contract must make that point clear.

- **RECORDINGS**

Copyright in any new music or songs written by a member of the church or charity will belong to the individual, and if the church wishes to use the songs on a regular basis, they will need to come to an appropriate arrangement.

If there is to be a live music performance in the church, then ordinarily the consent of the owner of the copyright in the music, (provided the music is still in copyright), will be required. This is often dealt with by paying a licence fee to the Performing Rights Society. However there is an exception to this rule where music is played in a church or other worship service.

If the performance is to be of pre-recorded music then ordinarily consent is required from both the Performing Rights Society (copyright) and the Phonographic Performance Ltd (Public Performance). However, again there is an exception where the playing of the sound recording is heard in public as part of the activities of, or for the benefit of, a charity. In this example, if the public are charged an admission price for the performance, then the exception can only be claimed if the admission charge is applied exclusively for the benefit of the charity itself.

Churches and Christian organisations seeking to reproduce songs for public worship, photocopy from a wide range of publications, show films, play or perform music or download songs or sheet music from the internet, are advised to take advantage of the copyright scheme administered by Christian Copyright Licensing International. For a small annual fee, the church or Christian organisation is given the freedom to reproduce many of these items, without the necessity of having to contact many different copyright owners. In turn CCLI ensures that the owners of the copyright are properly rewarded for their work.

CCLI has a helpful website which explains its service in greater detail and clarifies the licences available.

Care should be taken when a church or other organisation uses visuals that may have been taken from another organisation which would hold the rights to it. For example:

- Photographs/images taken from the web will usually belong to a third party. I am aware of instances where an agency that owns the copyright has seen an image that a charity has downloaded and reproduced on its publicity or website and has demanded a sum for the use of the photograph/image in question.

- Likewise videos produced by a church may well use some standard images that are the property of a third party. In instances where a video contains an interview with an individual, that individual should be asked to sign a written consent allowing the church to reproduce the interview in whatever medium it may choose.

- **WEBSITES**

  Any written material or music included in a charity's web site is legal only when permission has been obtained in writing from the copyright owner.

- **NAME**

  A charity's name may become increasingly valuable over a period of time, particularly if the charity has become well known for innovative and unique work. To defend a charity's name successfully against any party seeking to use it, or a name that is remarkably close to it, would require the charity to show that is has built up goodwill or reputation in that name over many years.

Protection

A charity can consider protecting its Intellectual Property in one of the following ways:

- **PASSING OFF**

  A "passing off" action can protect goodwill, a name, copyright and even the product itself. To succeed in an action for passing off, the charity will need to show that the third party, whose action is adopting the name, style or appearance of the organisation, is likely to confuse the public and lead them to believe that the organisation's goods and services and the third party, are one and the same. However it is necessary to also show that the charity is likely to suffer damage to its reputation and/or lose out financially. Passing off actions are usually very expensive, mainly because they are difficult to prove.

- **TRADE MARK ACTION**

  If the charity has a registered trademark, then action can be commenced based on that trademark against any third party that is infringing the same.

- **CONFIDENTIALITY**

  Before disclosing any information owned by the charity, which could cause the charity damage if such information were supplied to a third party (confidential information), the use of a Confidentiality and Non-disclosure Agreement mshould be employed. Such an agreement puts the third party to whom this information is disclosed (for example, a marketing company who may be retained by the charity to advise on the marketing and promotion of a particular issue), on notice that, if they allow the confidential information to be communicated to the public at large, or to a competitor, then they could be liable in damages to the charity.

- **ASSIGNMENT**

  If the charity has ordered and paid for a unique piece of work, for example an architect's design for a building or a particular piece of music to be written for it, then it should request the originator of the work or licence to assign the copyright specifically to the charity. This would then allow the charity to utilise that design and exploit it commercially, although the originator may ask for royalties in return for either assigning or licensing the use of the work.

  For further information on Intellectual Property, please look at the websites of the Intellectual Property Office and the Christian Copyright Licensing International.

SECTION 15

Employment

Mark Bainbridge,
Wellers Law Group

15

When employee relations go wrong, operations and individuals suffer, causing lasting hurt, and often hitting a charity's reputation as well as its pocket.

Laying the Foundations

The key to successful employee relations is laying the right foundations. This involves thinking strategically about the charity's staffing requirements, and recording this in writing so that it is clear how each worker's role enables it to achieve its purposes.

Role

When defining role, the charity is trying to work out the scope of the job required, and the type of person required to do this work. This is normally done by way of a Job Description and Person Specification. All too often Job Descriptions and Person Specifications are reactive documents – what a person is doing, rather than what should they be doing. In many cases these documents are completely overlooked, and workers have no clear sense of what they are required to do.

Legally, a Job Description and Person Specification are key to a fair and objective recruitment process and to performance management. Without them, the role will not appear thought through, and recruitment is likely to be subjective ("do we like this person, and can we get on with them?" rather than assessingtheir ability to do what is required by the job) opening up the potential for complaints of unfairness and discrimination, and making it difficult for the charity to challenge a worker who is not doing the job expected of them.

- **JOB DESCRIPTION**

  The Job Description is simply about describing the job to be done. Remember that the document will be used:

  By job applicants
  To understand the job and to decide whether to apply for it.
  To check what they are required to do.

  By the charity
  In advertising a job.
  In assessing applicants for a job.

In work planning and supervision.

To manage performance and conduct issues.

To defend Tribunal claims.

- ## PERSON SPECIFICATIONS

The Person Specification follows from the Job Description, and says what skills, qualifications, and experience are essential and desirable in order to do this job. It can be part of the Job Description or a separate document.

There is a very real potential for Person Specifications to be discriminatory. As a general rule, protected characteristics (age, disability, etc) must not be used as a person specification because this would amount to direct discrimination which cannot be justified. A requirement for relevant experience may amount to indirect discrimination on the grounds of age and gender. Always check whether each criterion in a person specification is relevant to the Job Description tasks.

Notes made as part of this process should be kept as they can help to show rationale, which may be important in justifying the inclusion of any criteria.

Status

- ## EMPLOYEE, WORKER, OR SELF-EMPLOYED?

Fundamentally, status defines the relationship between the charity and those who work for it. Status distinguishes between a contract of employment (the relationship between an employer and an employee), and a contract for services (made between an organisation and an independent contractor). The law is not straightforward, and many employers have been surprised at how an Employment Tribunal has viewed their working relationship. Distinctions are often assumed between casual workers, agency workers, zero-hours workers, temporary workers on the one hand, and employees on the other, when there may be no distinction at all.

- ## EMPLOYEES

Most organisations do not want to invest time and money in individuals who may be here today and gone tomorrow. They want personal service, effective management control, workforce stability, and a long-term return on their investment of time and money in the people who work for them.

Some of the main reasons why charities sometimes do not employ staff include:

Fear of the Law

Much is said about the difficulties which businesses have managing red tape and regulations, and the cost if they get it wrong. Employment rights are extensive, but using up-to-date employment contracts and staff policies and procedures will provide employers with an easy framework to follow. An employer, when making decisions, can then check:

· Is there a policy and procedure covering this point? If so, what does it say that I should do?
· Does the employment contract say anything about this situation? If so, what does it say that I should do?

Most employment problems can be resolved by this simple 2 stage check, and then by doing what has been agreed. Additionally, there are Employment Lawyers, who provide an advice service allowing issues to be referred to them.

Employees also have legally binding rights in the employment relationship, such as loyalty, trustworthiness, and confidentiality.

Administration of payroll, National Insurance, and taxation.
Employment of staff involves management of their pay, national insurance, and tax. All of this is regulated by law and includes:

· Pay slips
On or before pay date an employer must provide its employees with an itemised pay slip containing:
   · The amount before deductions
   · The amounts of and reasons for each deduction
   · The actual (net) amount of wages or salary paid

· National Insurance
The amount which each individual pays depends on their employment status and how much they earn. Employees pay Class 1 which is deducted by the employer at source, and paid with their tax. Contribution rates are available on line.

· Taxation
Employers use a tax code provided by HM Revenue and Customs to work our how much Income Tax to deduct from pay.

All of this may be easily managed by:

- Outsourcing payroll to an accountant, bookkeeper, or payroll firm;
- Using payroll software which will do the calculations for deductions such as tax, NI, student loans, sick pay and maternity pay.

Lack of flexibility

While charities using workers and self-employed contractors have more choice about the terms on which they engage someone, workers who are not employees have many legal rights (see below), and commercial agreements with contractors often have strict requirements.

Ultimately, parties in a working agreement are concerned about control, and protecting their rights. Using self-employed contractors may offer flexibility over employing staff, but the price may be a loss of control, particularly about who does the work when, and how, and therefore the absence of certainty. For many charities, control and certainty may be vital to the effective administration of their operations.

Cost

There are employee costs which do not apply to workers and contractors, which include NI employer contributions, and employer pension contributions. If the work required to be done is variable in nature, these additional costs may not be worthwhile. However, before deciding which is most cost-effective, a charity should consider the comparable cost of using a worker or contractor (in some cases, an employee is cheaper, even with their on-costs), and negative cost implications (an employee who is familiar with and trained in a charity's systems may be more efficient than a non-employee, avoid costly mistakes, and develop the charity in a way which leads to increased revenue). Sometimes, a worker or contractor can be an expensive option.

To summarise

Status	Key reasons for	Key reasons against
Employee	Personal service Control Stability	Administration of payroll and taxation Legal obligations Lack of flexibility More administrative and legal obligations than for non-employees
Self-employed contractor	Flexibility Less admistrative and legal obligations than for employees	Less control and stability than an employee

15

- **VOLUNTEERS**

Most charities depend upon willing unpaid volunteers to do their work. Their status is sometimes unclear, which can leave a charity open to a claim for backdated wages and other employment claims if it is later decided that the supposed volunteer is in fact an employee of the charity.

Charities should be clear about the role and responsibilities that volunteers have. Essentially, volunteers do not have a contract, they are not obliged to work, and they can come and go as they please. The fact that they do not do so is voluntary. Volunteers are not paid, although they can be reimbursed for any reasonable expenses that they incur. It can be helpful to clarify all of this in a clearly labelled volunteer agreement. Volunteer work relationships should be reviewed regularly to check that they are not in practice an employee, by virtue of the expectations put upon them and the way that they are managed. If volunteers are regularly receiving payment from the charity (sometimes called an "honorarium"), this may lead to a conclusion that they are employed.

- **CHURCH PASTORS/MINISTERS**

Prior to 2006 church pastors and ministers of religion were generally regarded as office holders rather than employees. The reasons for this included:

- the spiritual nature of the work;
- a presumption against any intention to create a legal relationship, required by a contract;
- an understanding that their duties arose from the church's constitution and rules, rather than an employment contract;
- the lack of control and mutuality of obligation;
- difficulties identifying the employer (particularly in large denominations, where an individual church may not be a separate legal entity).

The status of ministers of religion determines their legal rights, including whether they can claim unfair dismissal.

The law now is quite clear. The spiritual character of a minister's duties does not prevent them from being an employee, and there is no longer a general presumption against a contractual relationship.

Practically, an Employment Tribunal will look at the rules and terms which govern the service which a minister of religion provides to assess whether they are an employee or not. This will normally involve an assessment of written documents (letter of appointment, contract, the church/denomination rules, etc.) plus verbal evidence (particularly what was said to the minister of religion in relation to their appointment). Not every minister of religion will be an employee, but many are. This can be seen positively, but needs to be managed to ensure that a minister of religion's employment rights are recognised and complied with.

Recruitment Process

Recruitment requires a careful process, particularly to ensure equal opportunities. Appointment by word-of-mouth, or on the basis of an informal meeting, can cause resentment among existing employees, and lead to discrimination claims. The best way to ensure fairness and equal opportunity is to follow an agreed recruitment policy and procedure, which should provide the appropriate checks and balances, as well as the necessary authorisation for each stage.

Those involved in recruitment should be familiar with the recruitment policy and follow it carefully to ensure consistency. Notes should be made of each stage, together with other relevant documents including copies of adverts, job descriptions/person specifications, application forms, CVs, letters and emails from and to job candidates, email correspondence and short-listing forms.

The job advert should be checked to ensure that it is not discriminatory, and that the person specification identifies what, objectively, is essential and desirable for the job. Application forms, short-listing forms, and interview questions should each be based on this document. The purpose of the application form is to ensure that job applicants provide the information that the charity requires to assess whether they meet the person specification. The short-listing form should, in a simple table format, allow those short listing to confirm whether the job applicant does or doesn't meet the person specification. If a candidate doesn't meet the essential criteria, they shouldn't ordinarily be invited to an interview. The interview is about asking set questions to each interviewee to enable an assessment about which candidate is best able to do what is required by the job. Provided the person specification is objectively measurable and not discriminatory, getting this document right will assist enormously in choosing the right candidate.

Generally, an interview should be conducted by at least two people.

15

Decisions and reasons for appointing or rejecting candidates should be recorded and checked.

Any offer should be made subject to receipt of at least two satisfactory references from previous employers or from someone able to comment on the candidate's suitability from a professional capacity. The work of many charities can be sensitive in nature. In addition to standard pre-employment checks (which should include references, and proof of right to live and work in the UK), a Disclosure and Barring Service (DBS) check is a must for those working with children, young people, and vulnerable adults. Employers must do this check as job applicants are unable to check on themselves.

Following receipt of satisfactory references and other pre-employment checks the job offer can be agreed and a start date given. Normally this will involve a probationary period to assess suitability and performance in the job.

Prior to the employee starting, it is helpful to plan an induction programme to introduce the new recruit to the organisation, other staff and volunteers, and to the role. This is an important exercise which will accelerate an individual's ability to do the job that they are being hired to do. Time spent thinking about what and who the employee will need to know to do their job effectively, and a plan for how the charity wants them to learn this and when, will be important. It is good to have a checklist with review meetings with the line manager each day during the first week, at the end of each week during the first month, and then at the end of each month until the end of the probationary period. If problems arise during the probationary period, ensure that these are dealt with promptly by the employee's manager, who should offer support and training as appropriate. It is wise to extend the probationary period if there is uncertainty as to the employee's suitability. If an employee passes their probationary period, it should be confirmed in writing.

Contractual terms

An employment contract is made up of express terms (those stated and accepted verbally and/or in writing), imposed and implied terms (matters not stated and accepted, but which are required by law, by custom and practice, and by necessity), and statutory terms (rights guaranteed to employees by UK and EU law).

The employment contract should be carefully thought through in advance of employment starting. The key matters for agreement are:

- Defining what is expected of the employee.
- Confirming the benefits the employee will receive in return for their work.
- Management.

EXPRESS TERMS

At the start of an employment relationship, the law requires an employer to give to the employee a written statement of the main particulars of employment. The main particulars of employment cover:

- The names of the employer and the employee.
- The date when the employment began.
- The date on which the employee's period of continuous employment began (if their employment was transferred, employment with a previous employer may count).
- Pay or method of calculating pay.
- Pay dates (weekly, monthly, or other intervals).
- Hours of work.

- Holiday (including pay).
- Sick leave (including pay).
- Pension.
- Notice periods.
- Job title or job description.
- Job duration (if not permanent).
- Place of work or, if the employee is required or permitted to work at different places, an indication of that and of the employer's address.
- Collective agreements.
- Working outside the UK.
- Disciplinary rules.

15

A written statement of main particulars is a starting point, but is rarely comprehensive. Many employers assume that if an employee has signed a Statement of Main Particulars, that they have an adequate contract. They do not. A written Statement of Main Particulars can amount to an Employment Contract, but this is not the intended purpose of this document. The Main Particulars do not cover important matters such as: probationary periods; confidentiality; data processing consent; garden leave; and post termination restrictions. It is therefore better to discuss and agree a single comprehensive Employment Contract which includes the main particulars.

IMPOSED TERMS

Some terms are implied by law and they cannot be signed away by the employee.

These include common law terms (terms which result from court decisions) such as:

- A duty of mutual trust and confidence. This is positive (treating each other with respect and civility) and negative (not treating each other in an unreasonable manner). It applies to how the employer and the employee behave towards each other. An employer who fails to follow their procedures, or who doesn't comply with their legal duties towards an employee may breach this implied term, as might an employee who steals from their employer.
- An employee's duty to serve their employer faithfully and loyally (the duty of fidelity). Again, this is a broad duty, requiring an employee to act honestly for their employer, and not to behave in a way that conflicts or is to the detriment of their employer, such as by making a secret profit from them, by acting in competition, or by misusing confidential information.
- An employer's duty to provide a safe place and system of work. Where an employee suffers a workplace injury or work-related ill health they will generally say that their employer has breached this implied term. This is more than compliance with Health and Safety law; it is about implementing procedure, policies, and practices that protect employees from harm. An employer who receives a complaint about bullying and harassment by a manager at work, for example, but does nothing about it could be in breach of this implied term.

Imposed terms include terms imposed by UK or EU legislation, such as:

- A minimum notice period.
- Payment of the National Minimum Wage.
- A right to a minimum 5.6 weeks' paid holiday (therefore an employee working 5 days per week should receive 28 days paid leave per year, which includes the usual 8 public holidays).
- An equality clause that a woman doing equal work to a man should not be paid less.

- **IMPLIED TERMS**
  In addition to terms agreed verbally or in writing, and terms imposed by law, there are other contractual terms which the parties are taken to have agreed, for example:

- Where it is obvious from the parties' conduct. For example, if an employer pays their employees on the same date every month, an employee might argue that it is implied that this date is the agreed pay date.

· Where it is "reasonable, notorious, and certain" custom and practice, in a particular industry or individual organisation.
· Where it is genuinely necessary to make the employment contract work.
· Where it is so obvious that the parties intended to include it and would have agreed it if it had been suggested to them.

Implied terms include:

· Confidential information: During employment an employee is bound by an implied term not to disclose trade secrets and/or confidential information to a third party. If information is sensitive and important to the charity's work, then it should be covered by a specific confidentiality clause.
· Intellectual property: During the course of employment employees may create a wide variety of material such as software, videos, written articles, design logos. This is known as "Intellectual Property". Unless there is specific agreement to the contrary, it is implied that the employer will own any intellectual property that an employee creates in the course of their normal duties, or specific work that is given to them. See section 14.

● **CHANGING TERMS AND CONDITIONS OF EMPLOYMENT**
There is a number of different ways that employment contracts can change or be changed. The key principle is agreement:

· Has the change be agreed verbally or in writing?
· Can agreement be implied by the employee's acquiescence to a change?
· Has the employee effectively been dismissed and re employed on new terms?
· Is the employee bound by an incorporated collective agreement?

In every case, changes should be consulted upon with the individual and any representative organisation, and reasonable attempts should be made to agree new terms and conditions. Negotiations may end up being protracted, but are preferable to a breakdown in employee relations, good will, and the possibility of legal claims. Fundamental unilateral changes, i.e. those imposed by the employer to an employment contract can lead to the employee suing the

15

employer for breach of contract, claiming they have been effectively dismissed and re-employed, or even resigning and claiming constructive dismissal. The bottom line is that employers can change terms and conditions of employment where they have a good business reason for doing so, but they should do so carefully, and only after taking legal advice.

Statutory Rights

Statutory rights are legal rights based on laws passed by Parliament. A charity needs to be clear about the legal status of someone who works for them, so that it can meet its legal obligations towards them, and not be liable for a legal claim.

- **EMPLOYEES**
  Employees have the most protection at work. Their most important statutory rights include:

  ### Pay and Employment Condition Rights
  The right to a written statement of main terms (see above), as well as to a Statement of Changes if these change.
  · The right to an itemised pay slip (see above).
  · The right to be paid at least the national minimum wage (the "NMW"). The NMW rate depends on the worker's age and whether they are an apprentice or not.
  · The right not to have unauthorised deductions from wages. The law authorises certain types of deductions (such as when an employer is trying to claw back an overpayment of wages or expenses).
  · Pension.
  Employers are required by law to automatic enroll workers into a workplace pension scheme if they are at least 22 years of age but under state pension age, working or ordinarily working in the UK, earning a qualifying amount of earnings. All charities that employ 1 or more workers, regardless of their age, have to declare their compliance with auto-enrolment with the Pensions Regulator and adhere to a number of safeguards to protect the rights of individuals to have access to pension savings. See section 17.

  ### Reporting Wrongdoing
  Reporting wrongdoing in the workplace is commonly known as

"whistle-blowing". It is about making a protected disclosure. Not all whistle blowing amounts to protected disclosure. It depends on what is disclosed, how and when, and to whom. In principle, workers reporting wrongdoing in the workplace in good faith are protected from suffering a detriment and from dismissal.

Health and Safety Rights

· The right to paid holiday.
There is no right to carry forward holiday from one leave year to the next. However, if a worker is unable to take holiday because they are off sick, they can carry forward unused holiday.

· The right to daily and weekly rest breaks/limit on working hours.
If an employee/worker works more than 6 hours in a day, he is entitled to an uninterrupted but unpaid rest break of at least 20 minutes. Significantly for charities, the right to a limit on the working week and rest breaks during the working day do not apply to those whose working time is not measured (such as charity directors and those with autonomous decision-taking powers, and ministers of religion). If a worker's time is not measured, best practice is to agree this in an employment contract.

Training Rights

The right to time off for study or training for 16-17 year olds.

Family Friendly/Carer Rights

· **The right to paid time off for ante-natal care or adoption appointments**
A pregnant employee, on the advice of a registered medical practitioner, midwife or nurse, is entitled to reasonable paid time off work for antenatal care. An employer is entitled to ask for evidence of this before they agree to it.

· **The right to paid maternity/adoption leave**
Statutory maternity and adoption leave are both 52 weeks. The first 26 weeks of leave are called Ordinary Maternity/Adoption Leave ("OML" and "OAL"). The last 26 weeks of leave are called Additional Maternity/Adoption Leave ("AML" and "AAL").

During maternity and adoption leave all of an employee's contractual rights continue, except the right to normal pay. At the end of OML and

OAL employees have the right to return to the same job on the same terms and conditions. At the end of AML and AAL employees have the right to return to the same job unless that is not reasonably practicable, in which case an employer must offer them a suitable alternative job on similar terms and conditions.

Employees taking maternity/adoption leave are protected from unfair treatment and dismissal for reasons relating to maternity/adoption leave. In the event of redundancy, employees on maternity/adoption leave have priority rights to suitable alternative vacancies.

- **The right to paid Shared Parental Leave (SPL)**
  Since April 2015 eligible employees have been able to cut short their maternity or adoption leave to share the balance of their statutory leave with their partner. The law is quite complex. In broad terms:
- The mother/main adopter curtails their right to maternity/adoption leave.
- At least 8 weeks before they intend to take SPL, the mother/main adopter and their partner give their employers notice of entitlement with a declaration of eligibility for the right to take SPL.
- Employees can submit 3 requests (notices) of taking SPL. They can choose to take their leave in a continuous (unbroken) block or in a discontinuous block (leave over a period of time with breaks when the employee returns to work).
- Following SPL they are entitled to return to the same job if their combined leave period (Maternity/Adoption + SPL) totals 26 weeks or fewer. If it exceeds 26 weeks, an employer must allow an employee to return to the same job unless it is not reasonably practicable, in which case they must offer an alternative job on similar terms and conditions.

- **The right to paternity leave**
  Employees are entitled to 2 weeks' paid paternity leave if they:
- are the father, the husband or partner of the mother, the child's adopter, or the intended parent (if the employee is having a baby through a surrogacy arrangement);
- have been employed by the charity continuously for at least 26 weeks by the end of the 15th week before the expected week of childbirth, or the adoption-matching week;
- have given the correct notice.
  Employment rights are protected during paternity leave.

- **The right to unpaid parental leave for men and women**
  Up to 18 weeks' unpaid leave for each child can be taken up to their child's 18th birthday, in whole week blocks up to 4 weeks for each child each year.

- **The right to ask for flexible working**
  Employees have the right to ask for flexible working. It can include a request for flexibility such as home-working, job-sharing, flexi-time, and compressed hours. When someone applies for flexible working in writing, an employer must follow a statutory procedure and meet statutory timescales. If the employer refuses a flexible working request, there is a limited number of specific reasons which they can rely upon. If the employer agrees to a flexible working request it changes the employment contract. Employees can only make one flexible working request per year. A refusal of flexible working can also amount to indirect sex discrimination, and legal advice should be sought before refusing a request.

- **The right to time off for family and dependents.**
  There is a right to reasonable unpaid time off work to deal with an emergency involving a dependant. This is different from compassionate leave.

Dismissal rights

- **Protection against retirement dismissal**
  It is not lawful to dismiss someone because they have reached what an employer believes to be the retirement age. It is sometimes possible to justify retirement dismissals, but legal advice should be taken.

- **The right to minimum notice of the termination of employment**
  After 1 month's employment an employee is entitled to 1 week's minimum notice, increasing to 2 weeks after 2 years' service, and then an extra week for each additional year's service up to 12 weeks after 12 years' service. If someone is off sick during their statutory notice period, in most cases they should be paid their normal salary.

- **The right to written reasons for dismissal**
  If an employee is dismissed they are entitled to a written statement of the reasons for their dismissal if they request it. If an employee is pregnant or on maternity or adoption leave when they are dismissed,

they are automatically entitled to such a statement, without asking for it. If an employer fails to provide the statement, an employee can complain to an Employment Tribunal who may award them up to 2 weeks' pay.

- **The right not to be unfairly dismissed**
  See below.

- **The right to a redundancy payment**
  Employees with 2 years' service are entitled to be paid a redundancy payment if they are dismissed for this reason. A redundancy payment is calculated on the basis of length of service, a week's pay (capped), and their age.

- **The right to paid time off to look for work if being made redundant**
  An employee who has received notice of a redundancy dismissal is entitled to reasonable time off during their notice period to look for another job, or to arrange training to help them obtain another job.

Reliance on Statutory Rights
It is important that employees and workers are able to rely on their statutory rights without fear of being victimised for doing so. The law protects them against suffering detriment or being dismissed for using or helping someone else to use their statutory rights.

Workers

Workers (such as agency workers, but not the self-employed) have less protection than employees, but share some significant rights in law, including:

- National Minimum Wage.
- Paid holiday.
- Workplace pension.
- A cap on working hours (unless they opt out).
- Statutory rest breaks.
- Protection for whistle blowing.
- Protection against unlawful discrimination.

They are not normally entitled to:

- Minimum notice periods.
- Protection against ordinary unfair dismissal.

- Request flexible working.
- Time off for emergencies.
- Statutory redundancy pay.

They may be entitled to:

- Statutory Sick Pay.
- Statutory Maternity Pay.
- Statutory Paternity Pay.
- Statutory Adoption Pay.
- Statutory Shared Parental Leave Pay.

Others

The Equality Act 2010 covers a wide range of workers, including those who are applying for work, the self-employed who are personally engaged to do work, contract workers, business partners, and office-holders (e.g. police officer). Former employees are also protected under the Equality Act from victimisation. For more information about this, please see Chapter 16.

Staff Handbook, Policies and Procedures

The complexity of Employment Law and the challenge of managing the employment relationships are a substantial consideration for any charity. A staff handbook with a set of policies and procedures will:

- Provide a single reference point for staff and management.
- Spell out expectations and procedures.
- Provide a consistent response to staff questions.
- Help ensure fairness and equal opportunities at work.
- Help to create a positive and open culture at work.

Unless the contract says that they are contractual, policies and procedures can be reviewed, amended, and reissued to staff as the charity's requirements and the law changes.

The Staff Handbook is an introduction and summary guide to working for the organisation. Many employers publish their Staff Handbook on the intranet.

Every employee should be required to read certain policies and procedures (such as the Code of Conduct, Equal Opportunities policy, Internet, Email and Telecommunications policy and expenses policy), and to confirm that they have done so in writing. Other policies and procedures are relevant to specific employee circumstances and legal advice, e.g. maternity leave.

Policies and Procedures

A charity wishing to develop policies and procedures should take specialist legal advice. Once written there are five suggestions for introducing policies and procedures:

- **Adapt**. Make sure each policy is adapted to the specific circumstances of the charity.

- **Circulate**. Once the policy has been written, circulate it to staff and management, and ask them to confirm receipt by email or by a signed acknowledgement.

- **Implement**. Implementation often requires some degree of training. When reviewing training and development needs with staff, ask if there are any policies and procedures for which they require training.

- **Monitor**. Review how the policy works in practice.

- **Amend**. Employment relations and the law are changing. A charity should check on a regular basis whether their policies and procedures need to be amended, so that they are legally compliant.

- ## USE OF THE INTERNET, EMAIL, SOCIAL MEDIA AND ELECTRONIC DEVICES

The use of electronic devices, the internet and social media are critical to the daily operations of the charity. The website is the shop window; the Internet is how the charity explores and deals with the real world; social media are the means by which it communicates (or fails to communicate) its message; employees are more likely to speak to each other and others by email than face to face.

Our dependence on IT systems means that a charity is vulnerable if its systems break down, or are abused, or attacked.

The following example illustrates some of the many ways a charity can find itself in difficulties:

William is employed as a manager for a charity that provides confidential debt advice. When he commenced employment he was provided with a laptop for his work. It is the only laptop at William's place of work. William has basic IT knowledge, and uses the laptop to

Some important questions for charity managers to ask include:

- Is there someone who manages your IT systems?
- Do they have up-to-date knowledge and qualifications for this task?
- Is there automated scheduling for IT security software updates?
- Is there a policy for permitted use of the Charity's electronic equipment?
- Are the workers able to download software and modify the settings on the Charity's electronic devices?
- Is there a policy for the use of social media?
- Is there a policy for the use of the internet?
- Is there a policy about intercepting communications, and is this reissued to all workers at least every 12 months?
- Is electronic data contained in a secure hosting environment, and is this backed up at least daily?
- Are emails encrypted and/ or does the charity password protect documents that are sent electronically?
- Is there a policy about employees' use of their own electronic devices?
- Does the charity record whether every new worker receives training in each of the policies, and is training refreshed at least every 12 months?
- Are the policies renewed in view of legal and technological changes, and is this done at least every 12 months?
- Does the charity have a procedure for checking the electronic devices of outgoing employees to ensure that they do not contain confidential information?

15

receive and send emails, to record interviews with service users, and to type letters of advice. Confidential data is stored on the laptop. The laptop is also configured to provide William with remote access.

When William is given the laptop it is installed with the latest security software, which is free for an initial 3-month trial period. The trial license lapses after 3 months and is not renewed. William is not informed that this is his responsibility.

The laptop does not have an administrator account. William is able to download software onto his laptop. As a security measure, William decides to password-protect his laptop. He chooses to use the following password: "Password".

The charity does not have a policy for the use of electronic devices.

The laptop is used by William from home, to access data, manage emails, prepare for charity meetings, draft advice letters to service users, and correspond with third parties on behalf of his service users. William also uses the laptop for his private purposes, for internet shopping, Facebook, and for private emails. William does not routinely check whether the websites that he uses have security certificates.

In addition to his work laptop, William uses his mobile phone for receiving and sending emails, and for making phone calls relating to the charity and its service users. His mobile phone is an android device. It is not password protected. It does not have security software. The emails which it sends and receives are not encrypted.

Other employees and volunteer workers do not have laptops provided by the charity. If they are doing presentations, or providing external training, they will borrow William's laptop. Sometimes during coffee and lunch breaks the laptop is left in the training room, unsupervised.

Consider the implication for William and the charity if:

- The laptop or mobile phone is lost or stolen.
- The laptop's hard drive is corrupted or the charity's network is infected with a virus.
- Pornographic images are downloaded on to the laptop.
- Sensitive information about the charity's donors is leaked.
- A prank comment is posted on to William's Facebook page about the work of the charity.
- William is dismissed from the charity, but is allowed to retain his laptop as part of a severance package provided he agrees to delete charity data, but this is never checked.

The implications for William and the charity are potentially far-reaching. If data is lost or compromised, it could lead to a fine by the Information Commissioner's Office. The fact that it is on a personal device does not provide a defence to breach of the Data Protection Act. If pornographic images are downloaded or a prank Facebook comment is posted it could lead to reputational damage. It is for these reasons that every charity should think through how they manage and secure the use of the internet, social media, and electronic devices. Given the risks, the charity should consider:

- Preparing a specific policy.
- Circulating the policy and asking staff to sign an acknowledgement form confirming that they have read the appropriate staff policy, and that they agree to its contents, and consent to the monitoring of emails, etc for purposes relating to the charity's business.
- Monitoring use of the internet, emails, and social media. The law permits monitoring or recording communications relevant to a charity's business. Employers may do this to prevent or detect crime, to check that their phone systems are being used for proper and authorised purposes, and to check compliance with regulatory and self-regulatory practices and procedures, or for quality control and training.

Dismissal and Termination

Generally dismissals take one of the following forms:

- The Employer terminates the employment contract, with or without notice;
- The Employee is employed under a limited-term contract (e.g. a contract to cover maternity leave, or for a particular project only), and the contract is not renewed after the limiting term;
- The Employee resigns in response to a fundamental breach of contract (this is called "Constructive Dismissal"). The breach of contract may relate to an express term (e.g. a failure to pay wages), or an implied term (e.g. failure to take care of an employee's health and safety).
- The employer changes the Employee's job in a fundamental way without the employee's consent (e.g. demotion, reduction in pay, change in key duties), and the Employee claims that this amounts to a dismissal, but accepts re-employment on new terms and conditions.

If an employee is dismissed, four critical questions follow:

1 **Has the employee received their statutory payments?**
Holiday Pay. In every case, a worker (not just employees) is entitled to compensation for holiday that they have accrued but not taken. If they have been off sick during the previous year's holiday and unable to take their holiday, there is a legal right to carry this forward. The charity should check what

the contract says about entitlement to compensation for untaken contractual holiday entitlement.

Redundancy Pay. If the reason for dismissal is redundancy, and the employee has 2 or more years' continuous service, they are entitled to a redundancy payment. There is a straightforward formula for calculating the statutory redundancy payment, based on a person's age, length of service, and weekly pay. A week's pay is capped for these purposes. The easiest way to calculate the redundancy payment is using the online government tool: https://www.gov.uk/calculate-your-redundancy-pay.

2 **Was the employment contract ended in accordance with the terms of the employment contract?**
If not, the employee may claim "Wrongful dismissal", which is another term for breach of contract. Normally the main claim is that an employer has failed to give notice or pay in lieu of notice, in which case the employee seeks damages (notice pay).

3 **Was the dismissal unfair?**
Ordinarily, an employee is protected against unfair dismissal if they have 2 or more years of employment service. As a general principle, an employer who follows a fair procedure will end up making a fair decision which will be hard to challenge. Good legal advice is key.

There are five potentially fair reasons for dismissing an employee (which do not include retirement). They are:

· **Capability or qualifications.** Capability normally relates to an employee's health or ability. Repeated short-term absences, as well as long-term sickness absence can fairly result in a capability dismissal. Key to a fair dismissal is a reasonable and sufficient medical investigation, and a fair procedure which ensures that the employee is properly consulted. Qualification dismissals refers to an employee's aptitude or ability. Employees should be given a reasonable opportunity to improve; rarely will a single act of poor performance justify an employee's dismissal.

· **Conduct.** Misconduct by an employee is a potentially fair reason for dismissing an employee. Misconduct outside of the workplace in some circumstances, will be a sufficient reason for dismissing someone, particularly where the nature of the misconduct affects their suitability to do their job, or could bring the employer into disrepute.

Rarely will a first incident of misconduct justify dismissal. Matters which would not normally justify dismissal, but which an employee refuses to address (such as persistent lateness) can justify dismissal provided the employer follows a progressive/incremental disciplinary procedure. An Employment Tribunal will look at:

- Whether the employer followed a fair procedure (many employers fail to read and follow their own disciplinary procedure).
- Whether they complied with the ACAS Code of Practice on Disciplinary and Grievance Procedures (this is a straightforward Code which your Disciplinary Procedure must be compatible with – a failure to adhere to the ACAS Code of Practice is not only evidence of unfairness, but can also lead to an increase in any compensation by up to 25%).
- The organisation size and resources available to the employer.
- Consistency with the employer's handling of similar misconduct by another employee.

- **Redundancy.** The closure of a charity, a workplace, and the reduced need by the charity for employees to do work of a particular kind can all lead to a redundancy situation. Fair redundancy dismissals are primarily about following a fair procedure. The Employment Tribunal (if involved), will assess:
  - Did the charity give as much warning as possible of the redundancy?
  - Did the charity consult in a meaningful way with employees and their representative about the redundancy situation and about the selection criteria that it proposed using?
  - Did the charity select employees fairly for redundancy using objective criteria?
  - Did the charity consider any representations by affected employees and their representatives about the selection results?
  - Did the charity offer employees selected for redundancy alternative employment rather than dismissing them?

- **Some other substantial reason.** There are many other circumstances where an employer is permitted to dismiss its employees fairly, provided it has a substantial reason for doing so, for example, where an employer is trying to restructure its operations (and therefore change terms and

15

conditions). The reasonableness of the employer's actions is judged in its context.

- **Legal prohibition.** Where it would be against the law to continue employing someone, an employer can fairly dismiss them. For example, if someone doesn't have permission to work in the UK, or if they are hired to be a driver and have been banned from driving. An employer should follow a fair procedure.

Some reasons for dismissal are automatically unfair. Automatically unfair reasons for dismissing someone include:
- Pregnancy and maternity.
- Family leave (parental, paternity, adoption, shared parental, and time off for dependants leave).
- Acting as an employee or trade union representative.
- Joining or not joining a trade union.
- Being a part-time or fixed-term employee.
- Discrimination.
- Trying to enforce legal rights (e.g. to paid holiday).
- Taking part in industrial action.
- Whistle-blowing.
- Transfer of the employer's business to a new owner.

In most of the above cases, an employee does not need two years' employment service to bring a claim for automatically unfair dismissal. If they can show that they were dismissed for one of the above reasons, then the employer will not be able to show that it was fair because of the procedure they followed – the dismissal is automatically unfair.

4 **Was the dismissal discriminatory?**
When considering a dismissal it is essential to think about discrimination law. Someone who does not have 2 years' employment service can claim compensation if the dismissal was discriminatory. Please see section 16.

Terminating the Employment of a Minister of Religion

Managing the employment of a Minister of Religion can be particularly challenging for those involved. The challenges include:

- dealing with strong personal loyalties;
- assessing the strength of allegation and counter-allegation;
- complying with constitutional requirements (such as the approval of a church membership);
- ensuring unity while maintaining wider church or charitable Objects.

This situation can cause much anguish and even division and, unsurprisingly, often results in prevarication by the leadership rather than effective and constructive management. Involving a suitably qualified advisor or mediator will help to positively and sensitively address the issues involved.

For churches and faith-based charities, it is important to remember that any settlement will involve using money donated to the charity for its charitable purposes. Settlement should therefore be in line with legal advice, and should be approved in accordance with the charity's rules.

There are four main ways to approach settlement:

- **Settlement conversations.** Settlement conversations are about bringing an employment relationship to an end in a mutually agreeable way. When proposing a settlement conversation an employer should be clear that it relates to an existing dispute but does not presuppose the outcome of that dispute. Not all employment disputes lend themselves to resolution in this way. Complaints about automatically unfair dismissal, and unlawful discrimination, for instance, are not covered.
- **Using ACAS.** ACAS provides a statutory conciliation service. In most cases, an employee will not be able to bring an employment tribunal claim unless they have completed early conciliation. If the employer has tried unsuccessfully to resolve a dispute directly, or if direct conversation might not be suitable, a trained Conciliation Officer will go between the parties to promote settlement.

  Early Conciliation is a free but time limited service. Once settlement is agreed (verbally or in writing) through ACAS it is legally binding, and ACAS will record the settlement in a written form to be signed by both parties. They also provide a voluntary and confidential mediation service to help restore and maintain the employment relationship.
- **Informal mediation.** In addition to ACAS, it is possible to pay for mediators trained and experienced in resolving workplace conflict.

15

RESOLVING EMPLOYMENT DISPUTES

Employment relationships are a significant investment for employer and employee alike. When disputes arise, it has a very personal dynamic. All too quickly the dispute can gather steam, and the parties can find themselves polarised, and their different points of view can be set. Once this happens, it is difficult to find a reasonable and reasoned middle ground which both sides can accept. In this section, there are five key considerations which can help resolve an employment dispute before it escalates into expensive litigation.

- **Get good legal advice.** Many charities try to save money by not taking legal advice. In the end such economising usually proves costly. A specialist and experienced employment lawyer will explain the law, and guide the charity around the common pitfalls. If a dispute is misconceived, a reasoned legal opinion will help to expose the weakness of the case, and to close down the dispute as quickly and effectively as possible. Most employment disputes caught early enough can be effectively managed. Once legal proceedings start they are more difficult and expensive to resolve.

- **Be willing to listen.** Employees who feel that they have not been listened to, want someone to listen to them. If the employer won't, a judge might! It is better to hear what they have to say directly, and not in a Tribunal Judgement. Disciplinary, grievance, bullying & harassment procedures all allow for parties to listen and

This can be more economical, quicker, and less stressful than defending Tribunal litigation. Alternatively, for churches and faith-based charities, informal mediation by someone who is respected and trusted by both sides, and who has sufficient knowledge of the situation and of employment law, can help the parties to agree a framework for resolving the conflict.

- **Judicial mediation.** Each Employment Tribunal has a judge trained in mediation, and they are usually very effective in focusing the parties' minds upon an acceptable resolution.

Once a settlement is agreed in principle it needs to be legally binding, to prevent the employee taking the money, and taking the charity to an Employment Tribunal in any event. The terms of settlement therefore need to be recorded in the form of a Settlement Agreement.

Settlement Agreements (previously known as "Compromise Agreements") to understand each other. Unless the employer understands what an employee wants to say, they will not understand how an employment dispute can be effectively resolved.

- **Think around the dispute.** Understanding why someone is in dispute, enables the reason to be addressed directly. Settlement allows for an almost infinite number of ways to resolve a dispute, not just by money. For example, in a situation where a church is seeking to terminate the employment of its minister, items such as a reference, outplacement support, training provision, gift of the work laptop, etc are all possible elements of a settlement package. Non-financial elements of a settlement package can take the sting out of a dispute.

- **Don't delay.** Delay in dispute resolution generally equates to unnecessary expense. If the charity delays until an individual has started proceedings, the employee will be more concrete in their position, and the dispute is likely to involve the additional expense of lawyers, and tribunal/court fees. Press for an early resolution.

- **Balance confidence and humility.** Humility can involve sensible admissions, a willingness to say sorry, and consideration of an appropriate remedy for any wrong. Conversely, confidence in a carefully reasoned position will help the employer to draw the right boundaries in negotiations, so that they do not concede ground unnecessarily.

15

are legally binding agreements which can waive an employee's rights to bring legal claims in return (normally) for financial compensation or other benefit. They are increasingly lengthy and complicated agreements, reflecting the outcome of many different legal cases. Settlement Agreements must be in writing, and these should be drawn up by an experienced lawyer to specifically relate to particular complaints or proceedings. In addition, the Agreement will not be binding on the employee unless they have received advice from a relevant independent advisor (a qualified lawyer, or a certified officer, official, employee or member of an independent trade union, or a certified and authorised advice centre worker), who is properly insured, and identified in the Agreement.

Giving References

When providing a reference for someone who has worked for the charity, it is important to remember that the new employer will be relying upon the experience of and representations by the person giving the reference to confirm the applicant's suitability for the role. Job offers in most cases are subject to references: if the reference is bad, the job offer is likely to be withdrawn; if good, the job offer is likely to be confirmed. Either way, the new employer and the job applicant are likely to know that what has been said has been decisive.

Generally, providing someone with a reference causes no difficulties. However, a person giving a reference has a duty to take reasonable care to provide a reference that is "true, fair and accurate". Both the new employer and the individual concerned may be able to bring a legal claim if the reference provided is unfair, misleading, or inaccurate in some way.

For this reason, many employers as a matter of policy will only provide a limited factual reference, confirming that the individual worked for them between specified dates in a stated role. It is important to ensure that if this is the charity's policy, that it is applied consistently and without exceptions, particularly to avoid discrimination claims.

If the charity is going to provide detailed references (in some cases there may be no choice, for example, if it has agreed to provide a reference in a settlement agreement, or if your charity is in a regulated sector), then it is important to check what is said to make sure it is factual (not subjectively personal), balanced, and that it doesn't overlook key facts (for example, if the individual concerned was dismissed for misconduct, or persistently late for work). Failure to disclose these could make the person or organisation giving the reference liable to the new employer.

Discrimination Law

16

Mark Bainbridge,
Wellers Law Group

21

Introduction

Discrimination law is about promoting equal opportunity, and preventing unfair and less favourable treatment.

Not all discrimination is negative. Positive discrimination, for example, is permitted in law to address some of the real disadvantages which disabled people face.

Discrimination, or discernment, is key to making the right choices about employees, workers, and service providers. If an employer promotes someone because they have the best qualifications for a job, that is a good and proper reason for the promotion. Equality law is really about identifying which different personal characteristics should be protected in law. These are called "protected characteristics".

Not all unfair discrimination is unlawful. People discriminate and are discriminated against in many ways. Sometimes this is unfair. For example, a manager may prefer someone because they are neighbours, not because they are better at their job. This reason for treating someone more favourably seems unfair, but it is not necessarily unlawful.

It's good to recognise these points. If someone believes that they have been treated unfairly, they may believe that it is unlawful discrimination, and bring a legal claim which is expensive to defend. A good Equal Opportunities policy that is properly implemented can help to avoid such misunderstandings. For trustees, directors, and managers of a charity, it is important to build an organisation where equal opportunities is seen to be a reality. This chapter is designed to help you do that.

The Equality Act 2010 (The Act)

Prior to October 2010 there were nine major Acts of Parliament and almost a hundred sets of regulations about discrimination law. There were some common terms, but the same term could have different meanings. This was all very confusing. To simplify things, the Equality Act was passed in 2010, as a "simple, modern and accessible framework of discrimination law which protects individuals from unfair treatment and promotes a fair and more equal society" .

- **TO WHOM DOES THE ACT APPLY?**
Charities who are concerned with:

· the provision of goods or services to the public,
· the provision, disposal, and management of premises,
· employment,
· education,

are all affected by the Act.

The Act protects those who apply for or use the services, premises, and property belonging to or managed by a charity. It also protects job applicants, employees and workers (including contract and agency workers), and even former employees of charities. School pupils and students are covered from the moment they apply for admission to the school.

For charities that pay people to work for them, recruitment, promotion and training, work practices and policies, contractual terms and benefits, and dismissal, are all covered by the Equality Act.

● **PROTECTED CHARACTERISTICS**
There are nine characteristics protected by the Equality Act:

· **Age**
"Age" can be a particular age or a range of ages. A person's chronological age, their relative age ("younger", "older"), and their age group (such as "old age", "middle age", and "youth") are all covered.

· **Disability**
"Disability" is not the same as "sickness" or "illness". Someone can be sick or ill, and not covered by the Act. Under the Equality Act, a person has a disability if they have a physical or mental impairment which has a long-term and substantial adverse effect on their ability to carry out normal day to day activities.

"Impairment" is anything which worsens the condition of mind or body;

"Long term" means that the impairment has lasted, or is likely to last for at least 12 months or is likely to last for the rest of the life of the person concerned;

"Substantial" adverse effect is one that is more than minor or trivial. If a person has more than one medical condition, the combined effect of their different conditions is taken into account. For many conditions, medical treatment helps people to do more. When deciding if a condition amounts to a disability, an assessment is made of how, in the absence of medical treatment, the condition would affect normal day to day activities (this does not apply in the case of a visual impairment that can be corrected by glasses or contact lenses). The emphasis is on what a person cannot do, rather than on what they can do.

Certain medical conditions – cancer, HIV infection, and multiple sclerosis – are regarded as disabilities, irrespective of their effect on day to day activities.

A severe disfigurement is treated as having a substantial adverse effect on day to day activities provided it is long-term.

In the case of a progressive condition, such as arthritis, the law requires an assessment of the likely future effect of the condition on a person's ability to carry out normal day to day activities.

Past disabilities are covered. An impairment whose substantial adverse effect has lasted for less than 12 months is treated as continuing if its effect is likely to recur.

Some conditions are excluded from the Act's protection. They are: addiction to alcohol, nicotine or any other substance; a tendency to set fires; a tendency to steal; a tendency to physical or sexual abuse of other persons; exhibitionism; voyeurism; and seasonal allergic rhinitis.

All of these different terms have been developed and defined in case law. This can be a complex assessment. Typically, an employer will refer the question to an Occupational Health Doctor specialised in making this assessment. What is important is for charities to understand when someone may have a disabling condition, so that they think through accessibility issues, make reasonable adjustments, and avoid discrimination.

· **Gender Reassignment**
This characteristic covers transsexuals – those who have undergone, are undergoing, or propose to undergo the process (or part of the process) of reassigning their sex, moving away from their birth sex to the preferred gender, by changing their physiological or other aspects of their sex. A medical process is not necessary; An individual born a woman but living as a man is covered.

· **Marriage and Civil Partnership**
Any formal legally recognised union whether same-sex, or between a man and a woman is protected. Those who are single, divorced, or co-habiting are not covered.·

· **Pregnancy and Maternity**

· **Race**

Race is a broad definition and applies to race, colour, nationality, ethnic or national origin.

· **Religion or belief**

This includes the lack of religion and belief. Belief is more than an opinion. Only genuinely held beliefs as to a weighty and substantial aspect of human life and behaviour that are worthy of respect in a democratic society are protected. Political beliefs and belief in scientific theories are not covered. A belief which is incompatible with human dignity or which is in conflict with the fundamental rights of others may not be covered.

· **Gender**

Men and women are protected by the Act.

· **Sexual Orientation**

Gay men, lesbian women, heterosexuals and bisexuals are covered.

● **PROHIBITED CONDUCT**

The Equality Act prohibits certain types of conduct:

· **Direct Discrimination**

Direct discrimination simply means the less favourable treatment of someone because of a protected characteristic. This may be unintentional. A well meaning charity may unintentionally discriminate against someone because of a protected characteristic, and find itself liable in law.

Less favourable treatment means suffering a detriment, or being put at a disadvantage because of a protected characteristic. Not employing someone because they are disabled is direct disability discrimination. Direct discrimination cannot be justified, except in relation to age.

The phrase "because of" is wide; a person does not need to have the protected characteristic to be covered. Associative and perceptive discrimination are therefore covered.

"Associative Discrimination"

Where someone is discriminated against because of their association with someone who has a protected characteristic, they are protected by the Act. This means that if someone is discriminated against because they care for an elderly disabled relative then they may be able to bring a claim for direct age or disability discrimination.

"Perceptive Discrimination"

If someone is treated less favourably because they are perceived to have a protected characteristic, they may bring a claim for direct discrimination. A man who is overlooked for promotion because he is perceived to be gay, even if his employer knows he is not, would be covered.

Neither associative nor perceptive discrimination apply to the protected characteristic of marriage and civil partnership, or to pregnancy and maternity.

· **Indirect Discrimination**

Here the law recognises that something which is applied equally (such as a requirement to work a particular shift pattern) may have the indirect effect of disadvantaging persons who share a protected characteristic (particular shift patterns may make it more difficult for a single mother to work). Other examples include: imposing a work rota which involves a worker having to work on a religious day; advertising a church ministry vacancy but requiring candidates to have a theological degree gained in England or Wales.

Indirect discrimination is different from direct discrimination, in that it can be justified if it is a proportionate means of achieving a legitimate aim.

· **Harassment**

Harassment is about unwanted conduct related to a protected characteristic that has the purpose or effect of violating someone's dignity, or creating an intimidating, hostile, degrading, humiliating, or offensive environment. It includes sexual harassment (unwanted conduct of a sexual nature). Like direct discrimination, someone can suffer harassment even if the conduct was not directed at them, and even if they do not have the protected characteristic. It is not a defence to say, "I didn't mean to offend you." Charities can be liable not only for the actions of their staff and volunteers, but also for third parties when harassment has occurred on at least two previous occasions and the charity is aware that it has taken place, but have not taken reasonable steps to prevent it from happening again.

Harassment cannot be justified, and can lead to expensive legal claims.

· **Discrimination Arising from Disability**

This means that it is unlawful to treat a person differently because of something connected with their disability. A person with severe dyslexia who is demoted because they keep making spelling mistakes would be protected. Similarly, someone with kidney failure who is dismissed for poor attendance, because they regularly take time off for kidney dialysis, could bring a complaint of discrimination arising from disability. This type of discrimination is only unlawful if the employer knows (or could reasonably be expected to know) that the person has a disability. In limited circumstances, discrimination arising from disability can be justified.

· **Pre-employment Health-related Checks**

As a general principle, an employer should avoid asking health-related questions before they offer someone a job. Until that point the only health-related questions that you can be asked are:

· to help decide whether to make reasonable adjustments for the person in the selection process;
· to decide whether a person can carry out a function that is essential to the job;
· to monitor diversity;
· to take positive action to assist disabled people;
· to confirm that the applicant has a disability where it is a genuine requirement for the job.

· **Unequal Pay**

"Pay" covers all elements of contractual pay and benefits. A man or woman can complain if a term of their employment contract relating to pay or other benefits is less favourable than the equivalent term for someone of the opposite sex who is doing the same (or broadly similar) work, or different work which is rated as equivalent under the same job evaluation scheme, or which is of equal value.

To strengthen the legal right to equal pay, the Equality Act also makes it unlawful to prevent or restrict employees from talking about their pay to work out if any differences are because of a protected characteristic. Pay secrecy clauses in employment contracts are therefore unenforceable.

· **Victimisation**

The purpose of victimisation clauses are to protect an employee who has made or supported a complaint, or raised a grievance under the Equality Act, or is suspected of doing so. It is about ensuring that people can use their equality rights without suffering a detriment as a result.

· **Failure to Make Reasonable Adjustments**

This concerns employment of people with disabilities. It recognises that people with disabilities do not have equal opportunities because they face substantial disadvantages in employment, using premises, acquiring services, and when accessing education.

Broadly speaking, this is a positive right which requires charities to take reasonable steps to avoid putting a disabled person at a substantial disadvantage in comparison with persons who are not disabled.

• **CONSEQUENCES**

There are potentially very serious and costly consequences for charities that breach discrimination law. Charities are liable for the acts of their staff and volunteers. They are also potentially liable for the acts of third parties that they deal with.

Courts and Tribunals have the power to award compensation to someone whose discrimination rights have been breached. Whereas there is a limit on compensation for unfair dismissal, there is no such limit on awards of compensation for discrimination claims. The Courts and Tribunals are able to make awards not only for the financial losses suffered, but also for injury to feelings, psychological and psychiatric injury.

In addition to any compensation a charity may have to pay, discrimination claims can be very expensive to defend, and there can be significant reputational damage as a result. Reputational damage can be particularly significant if any discrimination relates to the charity's work; A charity that provides services to the elderly but is found to have discriminated against an employee on the grounds of age can expect a significant fall out in its support.

When Worldviews Collide

In recent years there have been a number of high profile cases where two specific protected characteristics:

· religion and belief,
· sexual orientation,

have wrestled with each other. Important principles for both sides have been at stake. Should, for example, Christian hotel owners be permitted as a matter of religious belief to refuse a double room to a same sex couple? Should the Christian owners of a bakery be able to refuse to make a cake with a pro-gay marriage slogan? Cases such as these have attracted a huge amount of media attention. How should the law balance the rights of a gay couple to access services without discrimination with the deeply held religious convictions of the business owners?

What about faith-based charities? Can they restrict their services to those who share that faith or ethos? Can they refuse to provide services to persons or groups who do not agree or at least sympathise with their religion or belief?

Christian churches and faith charities are concerned to understand how they can be faithful to their religious convictions without breaking discrimination law. The Equality Act recognises this tension for faith-based charities, and provides important exceptions for them which are not available to commercial organisations:. Some of these are:

- **OCCUPATIONAL EXCEPTION**

· **A General Exception**

It will not be an act of discrimination for an employer to require certain workers to have a particular protected characteristic if it is an occupational requirement given the nature of the job or the context of their work, and provided the occupational requirement is a proportionate means of achieving a legitimate aim.

For example, the post of the Chief Executive of Age UK. Given this charity's work and the public profile of this role, it is possible to see how the charity might apply an occupational exception for the Chief Executive to be of a certain age group.

· **Specific Occupational Exceptions**

There are two specific exceptions for faith based charities, which allow a limited type of selection in relation to job applicants and employees:

· The first is a specific exception which permits an employer who is concerned whether a job applicant either complies with the doctrines of a particular religion or is not in conflict with the strongly held religious convictions of a significant number of the religion's followers, to apply an occupational requirement:

  · to be of a particular gender;
  · not to be a transsexual;
  · not to be married or a civil partner;

- not to be married to or the civil partner of someone who has a living spouse or civil partner;
- about divorce or the end of a civil partnership;
- about sexual orientation.

· The second specific exception is for faith-based charities which have an ethos based on religion or belief, which allows them to apply an occupational requirement for job holders to have the same religion or belief, provided it is a proportionate means of achieving a legitimate aim, and provided they have reasonable grounds for not being satisfied that a person meets that occupational requirement.

Faith-based charities should not assume that these specific exceptions apply to all staff. For example, if a Church is recruiting a cleaner, it may not be able to show that advertising the vacancy with the requirement that the post holder is a Christian is permitted. Legal advice should be sought before stating or applying a genuine occupational requirement.

- **FAITH-BASED SCHOOLS AND EDUCATIONAL INSTITUTIONS**
  Certain faith-based schools are exempt from parts of the Equality Act including non-discrimination in admissions, and the way in which they provide education and access to benefits, facilities and services. Such schools are not exempt from the duty to make reasonable adjustments, nor are they exempt from prosecution for harassing or victimising pupils.
  The Equality Act allows certain faith-based schools to observe their religion and belief in acts of worship and in teaching the curriculum.

- **MEMBERSHIP ORGANISATIONS**
  There are many associations which restrict membership, benefits, facilities, and services to persons who share a protected characteristic. This is permitted by the Equality Act. This is an important exception, but one which could have negative implications for charities who need to show public benefit.

- **PROVIDING SERVICES TO A PARTICULAR GENDER**
  Some religious services are gender specific and even gender sensitive. Where this is important to comply with religious teaching, or to avoid conflict with the strongly-held religious convictions of a significant number of the religion's followers, the Equality Act allows a Minister of Religion to restrict the provision of those services in certain circumstances by:

- limiting them to persons of one gender;
- providing separate services for persons of each gender.

- **RESTRICTING SERVICES TO THOSE WHO SHARE A PROTECTED CHARACTERISTIC**

  It is not unlawful discrimination to provide services aimed at persons who share a protected characteristic, or to insist on providing the service in a standard way. A charity can also refuse to provide the service to those who do not share the protected characteristic if it is thought to be impractical to do so. Legal advice should be sought before refusing to provide a service to someone because they do not share the protected characteristic.

- **SAME-SEX MARRIAGES**

  Protecting and promoting religious freedom was an important part of the Marriage (Same Sex Couples) Act. As a result, religious organisations can refuse and not be compelled to conduct same-sex marriage services. The Act therefore provides four safeguards. The first three safeguards are relevant to independent churches:

- The legislation states that no religious organisation or minister can be compelled by any means to marry same-sex couples or permit same-sex marriages on their premises.
- The Equality Act 2010 has been amended so that no discrimination claims can be successfully brought against religious organisations or ministers for refusing to marry a same-sex couple.
- There is an "opt-in" system for those who want to carry out same-sex marriages, so that they can only take place where both the church's governing body and the trustees of the particular church building have opted in.
- The fourth safeguard is for the Church of England, whose clergy have a specific legal duty to marry parishioners. For this reason, the Act is clear that this duty does not extend to same-sex marriages.

In schools, while teachers are expected to teach the factual and legal position that marriage in England and Wales can be between opposite sex couples and same-sex couples, this does not prevent them from expressing their own beliefs (provided it is done appropriately, professionally and in a balanced way), and they are not expected to promote or endorse views which go against their beliefs. This also applies in faith schools, where teachers are allowed to act according to the school's ethos and faith position when teaching the curriculum.

It is important to distinguish between the exception given to religious organisations and ministers in relation to same-sex marriage services, compared with other services that they provide. For example, a church may be asked by a LGBT group if they can use their hall for a Wedding Reception. Refusal is discriminatory, and will be unlawful unless it is a permitted exception.

- **GENERAL EXCEPTIONS FOR ORGANISATIONS RELATING TO RELIGION OR BELIEF**

  The Equality Act provides a general exception for non-commercial organisations relating to religion or belief. Its scope is wide. It covers charities whose purpose is to practice, advance, and teach a religion or belief. It also applies to enable persons of a particular religion or belief to receive any benefit, or to engage in any activity within the framework of that religion or belief, as well as to organisations that foster interfaith relations.

  In these circumstances, a charity can apply a number of restrictions, about:

· membership of the organisation;
· participation in its activities;
· provision of its goods, facilities, and services;
· the use or disposal of its premises.

This applies to those parts of the Equality Act dealing with services, premises and associations (including membership organisations), where the issue is religion or belief, or sexual orientation.

The exception applies in limited circumstances. Where the restriction imposed relates to religion or belief, it is only permitted if it is imposed because of the purpose of the organisation, or to avoid causing offence on the grounds of the religion or belief to persons of that religion or belief. Where the restriction relates to sexual orientation, it is only permitted if it is imposed because it is necessary to comply with the doctrine of the organisation, or to avoid conflict with strongly held convictions of a significant number of the religion or belief's followers.

Ministers of religion (including non-salaried ministers accredited, approved, or recognised for the purposes of the organisation whom they represent) have a similar freedom to restrict participation in the activities they perform, and the goods, facilities and service they provide in the performance of their religious functions, if it relates to religion or belief, or sexual orientation.

To summarise, these exceptions apply to churches, religious institutions, and faith charities and are not available to commercial organisations.

Other Legislation

Although the Equality Act 2010 is the most substantial piece of discrimination law that you need to be familiar with, separate legislation provides similar protection for:

· part-time workers;
· fixed-term employees;
· trade Union members and activists.

Equality-proofing the Charity

It is important not to pay mere lip service to discrimination law. It is important to:

· Think about discrimination law
Many charities do not think about discrimination law until someone complains or brings a legal claim about the way that they have been treated. A person can bring a discrimination claim about a single event, and that can be costly. It is important to take steps to avoid discrimination occurring, rather than reacting to a complaint or claim that it has already occurred.
It is important to have an Equal Opportunities policy and to look at when it was last reviewed and implemented.

· Have appropriate policy documents
Many charities do not have a basic Equal Opportunities policy. Others do not have a suitable Equal Opportunities policy.
It is possible to obtain a template Equal Opportunities policy but it needs to be adapted to your charity.
An Equal Opportunities policy that covers employment, but says nothing about those who, for example, use a charity's services, is inadequate.
The policy needs to provide guidance which covers all aspects of its operations. In the case of a church, an Equal Opportunities policy that

covers employment only, is of no assistance to staff or volunteers who for example manage the hire of the building to outside groups. These kind of issues need to be thought through.

· **Be Consistent**

Policy documents have to make sense, by themselves, and when read alongside other policy or organisational documents. For example, in the case of a faith-based charity, its trust deed should record its statement of faith and define the scope of its services. Its statement of faith should then be reflected in each of its policies, including its Equal Opportunities policy, on its website, adverts, booking forms.

The importance of this is clear. If, for example, a member of the public applies for a job at the charity, or applies to use its premises, they shouldn't be surprised by its ethos.

· **Implement Policy**

Policy documents should not be seen as a comfort blanket to fall back on if it all goes wrong. Implementation involves requiring staff and volunteers to read the document (a log should be made of this), providing appropriate training, monitoring its use, and reviewing the document on a scheduled basis.

· **Review Policy in Practice**

If the Equal Opportunities policy says that the charity should do something, it is important to do it. If a charity has a policy but is unable to show that it has followed it, this inconsistency may support a conclusion of less favourable treatment.

Conclusion

Discrimination law has changed beyond recognition in the last 20 years. Charities need to check that they have kept up with the changes. Those who have an up-to-date and properly implemented Equal Opportunities policy will minimise the risk of a successful discrimination claim, and ensure that those who work for and benefit from the charity will feel valued and safe, as well as understand how the charity will carry out its objects in a proper and lawful manner.

Pensions, Insurance and Investments

Andrew Meade,
EQ Investors

While the primary concern of a charity is its charitable Objects, it is important that care is taken to plan for the future. The topics in this section are important because they address the following concerns:

· protecting the charity's ability to operate;
· investing prudently for the future to fund the longer term work;
· ensuring that the charity has the best workers by incentivising well.

Addressing these financial planning issues can ensure that the charity is able to face future challenges robustly. The third point is important as the trustees will have a responsibility to ensure that "auto-enrolment pension" legislation is adhered to.

Charities should take independent financial advice. This should be from a Chartered Financial Planner who has experience dealing with charities.

Protecting the Charity – Insurance

It is important to ensure that the charity uses its resources well and takes suitable steps to protect them. This applies both to property and people. Charities differ in the activities that they undertake and therefore each will have different needs. Ultimately the trustees are responsible for making this decision; some types of insurance are more important than others. The events that insurance covers tend to be relatively rare, but have significant impact when they do occur. It would be foolish to ignore them.

● **BUILDINGS AND CONTENTS INSURANCE**
Charities that own buildings need to ensure that they are properly covered for the full reinstatement value. This obligation includes contents and third party risks and perhaps business interruption. If the charity occupies leasehold property then there may still be an obligation upon the charity to take out cover; it is important that the charity ascertains its responsibilities.

Failure by the charity to properly insure its buildings could, in the event of a loss, render the trustees liable personally.

● **INSURING AGAINST ACTIONS**
If the charity is involved in the community, or provides some of its services outside of its building then it may be necessary to take out specialist insurance. This might include public liability insurance and legal protection for negligence or third party risks.

Trustees may decide to take out indemnity insurance. Where the charity operates in high risk countries it may be necessary to consider insurance against kidnap, ransom and extortion (see section 21).

It is wise to consult a professional insurance broker to insure that the charity holds the relevant insurances. The Charity Commission has produced a useful guide called "Charities and Insurance" which can be obtained from their website.

Protecting the People – Insurance

17

For many charities their people are their primary way of achieving their charitable purpose. There may be particular individuals whose death or diagnosis with a critical illness might have a devastating impact and could be costly to replace. Consideration should be given to the cost of "filling the gap" if a member of staff is diagnosed with a long-term illness that prevents them from working. Few charities will have the financial resources to cover these costs without having a detrimental impact on the work of the charity. Fortunately it is possible to insure against these risks.

In this section we have focused on protecting the charity from these risks but these types of cover can be provided as an "employee benefit". The majority of organisations provide a Death In Service scheme to all staff based on a multiple of their salary; this can be obtained at relatively little cost but provides significant financial stability to the charity's workers.

- **KEY PERSON COVER**
  Key person cover is designed to provide a financial contribution in the event that a person key to the charity's success can no longer work. This person might be the visionary, a major fund raiser, a technical expert or indeed the leader. This financial input would enable the charity to recruit a replacement, avoid having to cease a particular activity, or otherwise suffer financial loss. There are three types of cover; some or all may be appropriate. The cost depends on the amount of cover and the age/health/lifestyle of the person to be covered.

- **Life cover**
  This pays a lump sum (called the sum assured) in the event that the insured person dies during the term of the policy. This money is paid to the charity and can be used to ensure that the charity has sufficient financial resources to continue.

- **Critical illness cover**

  This is similar to life cover and in many cases will include life cover. The policy will pay out a lump sum in the event that the insured person is diagnosed with a Critical Illness. This condition must meet the definitions set out in the policy documents; if the condition is not listed then no payment will be made. The more comprehensive the policy, the greater the cost. The charity should understand the nature of the cover they are taking out. The priority is to ensure that the cover meets the needs of the charity; not just that the cheapest cover is put in place.

- **Income protection**

  If a member of staff is unable to work due to a long-term illness the charity is likely to still have a contractual (and moral) obligation to pay their salary. At the same time the charity will need to assess the situation and either reallocate resources or recruit a replacement on a temporary or permanent basis. This would have a significant drain on resources. Income protection provides a monthly payment to the charity that can be paid (via payroll) to the person insured. This frees up resources to cover the cost of covering the work they do. These payments start after an initial deferred period (typically 6 months but should take into account the charity's resources). There is typically no tax on the cost of the cover, but the usual taxes will be payable via payroll on the sums paid out to the staff member

  This cover is valuable but can be expensive where a short deferral period is required and/or the person insured undertakes a role that is not office-based. The cover can be used to protect an individual, or the charity may wish to take out cover for a wider group of staff.

Investing for the Future

It is important that the trustees consider the impact of the charity's investments on its work and reputation. For example, an alcohol awareness charity should not invest in the licensed beverages industry. This takes priority over financial returns.

- **INVESTMENT OF CHARITABLE FUNDS**

  Where a charity has more funds than are needed for the immediate needs then these funds need to be invested wisely.

  The Charities Act 1993, The Trustee Act 2000 and the Financial Services

Market Act 2000 set out the principles concerning investment by charities. Due to the nature of investments, this can be a complex area and this section contains a general overview of the subject. For more detailed information, the websites of the Charity Commission and the Ethical and Investment Research Services are helpful.

- **TRUSTEES' DUTIES**

Trustees can only invest a charity's money within the constraints of the charity's governing document and of the powers of investment otherwise available to them. The trustees can be liable for losses which result from any disregard of this principle.

Trustees have a general duty of care which is set out in the Trustee Act 2000. This duty is to exercise such care and skill as is reasonable in the circumstances paying particular with regard to:

- any special knowledge or experience that the trustee has or holds himself out as having, and
- situations where a trustee acts in the course of business or a profession.

The specific duties of charity trustees with regard to investments can be summarised as follows:

- To have regard to the suitability to the charity of any investments made.
- To have regard to the need for diversification of investments for the charity.
- From time to time to review the investments of the charity having regard to the suitability and diversification ("from time to time" depends on the nature and size of the charity's investment portfolio).
- Before exercising any power of investment, trustees must obtain and consider proper advice (if the amount of the funds to be invested are small and investment advice would not be cost effective then in such circumstances it need not be obtained).
- When reviewing the investment of charity's monies, the trustees must obtain and consider proper advice in regard to the suitability and diversification of the investment.

Consideration will also need to be had to the:

- the proportion of funds which will be allocated to different classes of investment (asset allocation) and the overall level of risk;

235

- the merits of individual investments within each asset class (stock selection), in terms not only of their economic prospect but also in terms of their individual contribution to the overall management of risk.

Where a charity has an ethical or socially responsible investment policy, the trustees will want to recognise the need for consistency with that policy.

With regard to "proper advice" the trustees should be quite sure that the person providing it is qualified to give this advice to his or her ability shown in practical experience and qualification. It is possible for the adviser to be one of the charity's trustees (provided one or more of the trustees can satisfy the others that they have the necessary financial ability and experience). The trustee giving the advice may, like any other adviser, incur a liability to the charity if losses result from advice that has been given negligently. It may be that the trustee so advising does not possess the necessary professional indemnity insurance cover that an external professional adviser would have. This is a valid consideration to bear in mind when trustees make a decision as to whether to use one of their number or an outside professional adviser.

The Trustee Act does not make any distinction between a regulated adviser who can provide advice based on the whole range of investment products and an adviser who can provide advice only in relation to a particular company or a particular company's products. It can hardly be in the charity's best interests for it to restrict investment to a narrow group of funds recommended by one company just because the adviser is employed by that company. Rather, it would seem to be best practice for charities to use an independent adviser who can give advice based on the whole range of investments available in the market place.

- **INVESTMENT RISK**

As investment requires the active consideration of risk, and it is important to outline what is meant by risk in this circumstance. Essentially there are two aspects. One is counterparty risk and the other investment risk.

Counterparty risk is the risk that one of the companies with which the charity carries out its investment business (bank, stockbroker, investment manager, Independent Financial Advisor) will default on its contractual obligations. Perhaps this risk is quite low in a climate where financial services are closely regulated and where a compensation scheme is in place. However, regulation does not cover the whole of the investment marketplace and trustees should be careful as to which companies they use and what counterparty risk they are being exposed to. It is considered important for charity trustees to choose regulated companies and individuals as opposed to non-regulated ones.

Investment risk is inherent in any investment and is based on the failure or the under-performance for a particular investment. However, this risk can obviously be mitigated by having a suitably diverse portfolio.

A bank account has a low investment risk (and a low return). At the other end of the spectrum, investments such as Futures and Options could give a great return one day and a loss the next.

Investment risk is managed by having a diverse portfolio and by looking at the different asset classes. One of the most important aspects of managing risk is ensuring the correct asset allocation in a portfolio. The main asset classes are listed below in increasing order of risk.

- Bank Deposits
- Government Gilts
- Corporate Bonds
- Global Bond Funds
- Absolute Return funds
- UK Commercial Property
- Balanced funds with UK Equities and UK Bonds
- Balanced funds with Global Equities
- and Global Bonds
- UK Equity
- Global Equity Funds
- US Equity
- European Equity
- Thematic Equity Funds
- Far East Equity
- Emerging Markets Equity
- Futures and Options

Government Gilts and Corporate Bonds are often referred to as fixed interest but there is a distinction between the two from a risk point of view. Gilts are government backed and tend to attract a lower volatility and lower risk ratings, whereas Corporate Bonds are issued by companies which can be big international ones or alternatively "smaller" companies. There can be quite a spread of risk between these types. The investment risk of Gilts and Corporate Bonds can be reduced by holding them until maturity.

Not only is diversity important with asset allocation but also within stock allocation. This means that once the asset allocation has been decided on, then the underlying investment within that allocation should be spread. For example, if UK equity makes up part of the portfolio then not all of the UK equity should be in one particular share or with one particular fund manager.

- **ETHICAL INVESTMENTS**

Increasingly, ethical and socially responsible investments are a very important part of a charity's investment strategy. Ethical investment is a wide phrase used to convey many different approaches to investment.

Usually the investor will apply their own ethical principles as to how they choose (or how they get their manager to choose) their investments. This can be done in two ways:

- negative criteria
- positive criteria

The negative criteria will give a list of activities that the investor does not feel that it is appropriate to invest in. Many Christian charities would feel that gambling, armaments or pornography are not appropriate areas for their monies to be invested in and would therefore clearly state their funds should not be in companies involved with those activities. Sometimes the negative criteria list can be quite long and therefore the opportunity to diversify a portfolio is diminished.

The positive criteria look at identifying companies or industries that are actively involved in creating solutions to social and environmental issues. For example, investors wishing to invest in an environmentally friendly way might look to companies involved in renewable energy and showing good governance and equal opportunities to their workforce. The governing document of a charity might impose ethical restrictions on the trustees' power of investment. Even if the governing document is silent on this point, increasingly trustees of Christian organisations are deciding to adopt an ethical investment policy. In doing so, however, the trustees must remember that their power of investment should be used to obtain the maximum return that is consistent with commercial prudence, in order to further the purposes of the trust. In the case of Harris (Bishop of Oxford) -v- Church Commissioners (1993) (commonly known as the Bishop of Oxford case) the Judge stated, "Most charities need money and the more of it there is available the more the trustees can seek to accomplish".

If the ethical criteria is so tight that it results in very little growth or income, then this will have an impact on the charity.

In recent years, the marketplace with regard to ethical investment products has grown considerably. There are a few discretionary managers who have great experience in the whole area of ethical and sustainable investment and there are also fund managers offering socially responsible and ethical funds. Many of those funds have performed particularly well historically and the reason for this could be because the sectors that they are investing in are areas where there is a lot of potential growth.

The trustees may consider the question as to how far they can allow their investment strategy to be governed by considerations other than the level of investment return? The Bishop of Oxford case highlights three possible scenarios:

· there may be instances (albeit rare) where investment in a particular type of business would conflict with the aims of a charity. (e.g. a temperance charity investing in the shares of a brewery)
· the trustees may need to consider carefully the likely effect of holding particular investments which could alienate supporters or beneficiaries and therefore hamper its work.
· the Governing Document of the charity may require trustees to take into account non-financial criteria.

In the first two scenarios above the trustees would need to balance the difficulties they would encounter or the likely financial loss the charity would sustain if it were to hold those particular investments against the risk of financial detriment to the charity if those investments were excluded from the portfolio. The greater the risk of financial detriment the more certain the trustees should be of the difficulty/loss to the charity before they incur that risk.

The Judge in the Bishop of Oxford case summarised the position as follows:

> "Trustees must act prudently. They must not use property held by them for investment purposes as a means of making moral statements at the expense of the charity of which they are trustees. Those who wish may do so with their own property, but that is not a proper function of trustees with trust assets held as investment." The judge went on to say "in most cases the best interests of the charity require that the trustees' choice of investments should be made solely on the basis of well established investment criteria having taken expert advice where appropriate and having due regard to such matters as the need to diversify, the need to balance income against capital growth, and the need to balance risk against return."

ERIS (Ethical Investment Research Services) have produced some comprehensive independent guides to ethical investments in general and for charities in particularly. These can be found on their web site www.eiris.org

- **INVESTMENT POLICY**

  It may seem hard to make this judgement but the trustees should decide their investment policy based on their own charity's needs and circumstances rather than trying to conform to "public opinion". The Charity Commission considers that trustees should:

  - consider the aims and Objects of the charity;
  - keep in mind the fundamental principle of maximising the term;
  - if an ethical policy is adopted, it should be set out in writing and should be clear both on positive aims and any exclusions;
  - if companies or sectors are excluded, the reason for exclusion should be clearly thought through. The more restrictive a policy (in terms of exclusion) the greater the risk there may be to returns;
  - the trustees need to evaluate the effect which any proposed policy may have on potential investment returns and this will usually require expert advice;
  - if the proposed policy increases the risk of lower returns, this must be balanced against the risk of alienating supporters and damaging reputation;
  - the trustees are unlikely to be criticised for adopting a particular policy if they have considered the correct issues, taken appropriate advice and reached a rational result.

- **FORMING AN INVESTMENT POLICY**

  Before obtaining advice on specific investments, the Charity Commission suggests that the trustees decide an investment strategy for their charity. It should be recorded clearly in writing and agreed by all the trustees. The policy should then be kept under regular review.

  For charities that use an investment manager, the Trustee Act requires trustees to have an investment policy. This enables them to hold the investment manager accountable to that policy. The trustees would include reference to this policy in their Annual Report as contained within the audited accounts.

  An investment policy should address the following considerations:

  - the creation of sufficient financial return to enable the charity (together with its non-investment resources) to carry out its purposes effectively and without interruption;

· the time period wherein the charity sets out to provide the service or length of time that the capital can be invested;

· the maintenance and, if possible, the enhancement of the value of the invested funds while they are retained;

· the management of risk;

· the charity's stand on ethical investments.

● TAXATION AND CHARITY INVESTMENTS

Charities in the UK are exempt from tax on most income and gains from investments, estates, land and property so long as that income/gain is used for charitable purposes.

A charity can arrange to have income received from some of these sources paid to it before UK tax is deducted. They include:

· bank interest

· income from land and furnished property

· royalties

The above statement said "exempt from tax on most income and gains from investments". This means that there are some investments that are not tax efficient in regard to a charity. This is why it is important that a charity has the right type of investments so that the tax is not taken away from them at source, or if it is then it can be reclaimed back.

The trustees need to be careful before selecting a form of investment in which there is either no tax relief in respect of the investment returns, or for which no such relief is necessary because the investment returns are generally non-taxable. Charity trustees are not prohibited from making such investments, but the inability to use the charity's tax advantage may mean that the investment is intrinsically disadvantageous as compared with one where the returns are relieved from tax in the case of a charity. This would question the suitability of the investments for the charity.

This is an area where a professional adviser can add real value enabling a charity to make the most of their investments and receive the greatest benefit back from HMRC. It is often a financial adviser working in conjunction with an investment manager and accountant where the most advantages are made and the charity's funds are best managed.

Social Investments

A Social Investment is the use of funds or property of a charity in a way which both advances the Objects and achieves a financial return for the charity. As such the power to make a social investment is distinct from the power to make a general investment as set out above.

The power given to a charity to make a social investment does not extend to the use of permanent endowment for such an investment.

Before making a social investment the trustees must:

· consider whether any advice on the proposed social investment should be obtained and if so obtain and consider it;
· be satisfied that it is in the interests of the charity to make the social investment having regard to the benefit that they expect for the charity.

Once made, the social investment should be reviewed by the trustees regularly and if applicable, with the aid of independent advice.

Pensions

In any organisation it is important that a charity looks after the welfare of its workers. An important part of this is helping them prepare for the future and for many this means retirement. The most common way of doing this is to use a pension scheme. The Charities Commission has provided useful guidance on their website.

● **WHAT IS A PENSION SCHEME?**
This is a tax-advantaged policy that is typically used to build up a fund to provide income in retirement. Personal pension contributions may receive tax relief and relevant employer pension contributions are normally an "allowable business expense".

Money is invested and grows free from most taxes. At retirement the member can choose to receive up to 25% of the fund as a tax free lump sum. The rest of the fund can be used to provide a taxable income through a variety of means including annuity purchase (guaranteed income for life) or income drawdown (taking money directly from the plan). Financial advice should be sought at retirement and trustees should encourage this.

The money in the pension can provide a tax-efficient death benefit. It is very important that the member completes an Expression of Wish form to ensure that their benefits are paid out in line with their wishes, as this can save possible Inheritance Tax.

The value of these benefits depends on (a) how much has been paid in, (b) how well the funds have performed, and (c) the nature and amount of charges. The pension cannot be accessed until age 55 under legislation current at the time this book was produced.

The details of how a pension works and the various limits that apply are outside of the scope of this book. Advice should be sought from a financial adviser.

WHAT ARE THE REQUIREMENTS?

The law states that employers must provide an Auto-Enrolment Pension Scheme. The requirement is being phased in and existing charities will be informed of their "staging date" which is when they must start to comply. There are financial penalties for failing in this responsibility.

The employer must formally choose a pension scheme (that meets the legislative requirements), ensure that employees are assessed, automatically enrol them into the scheme, and ensure that contributions meet (or exceed) the government minimums. The requirement to assess eligible workers is continuous (on a monthly basis). Employers must also choose the default investment fund for the scheme. There are also certain reporting and record keeping requirements including registration with the Pensions Regulator.

These are by no means the full extent of a charity's responsibilities and it is essential that financial advice is sought.

The maximum penalty for failing to comply with the legislation is £2,500 a day. Between July and September 2015 alone the regulator issued 469 compliance notices, 85 unpaid contributions notices, 107 fixed penalty notices and 2 escalating penalty notices. This is not an area that a trustee can afford to ignore.

Eligible workers are defined as:

- aged between 22 and State Pension Age;
- earning at least £10,000 per year;
- ordinarily working in the UK.

CONTRIBUTION AMOUNTS

The contribution amounts for employers will increase in 2018 and 2019 so charities will need to take this into account in their longer term budgets.

There are minimum employer contribution amounts but it is permitted to contribute more. The definition of qualifying earnings is based on the 2015/16 tax year.

	7% of all earnings		8% of pensionable salary provided 85% of total payroll is pensionable		9% of pensionable salary (Basic salary)		8% of qualifying earnings (£5,824 - £42,385)	
	Total must be	Employer must contribute	Total must be	Employer must contribute	Total must be	Employer must contribute	Total must be	Employer must contribute
Staging date to April 2018	2%	1%	2%	1%	3%	2%	2%	1%
April 2018 to April 2019	5%	2%	5%	2%	6%	3%	5%	2%
April 2019 onwards	7%	3%	8%	3%	9%	4%	8%	3%

It is important to note that "non-eligible" workers must be offered membership, and if they decide to join the employer must contribute as per the table above. There is a third category of "entitled" workers who can join but employers are not required to contribute.

- **SUITABLE SCHEME**
  The government has set out minimum standards that an Auto-Enrolment Scheme must meet. In some cases an employee's existing pension can be used, but most organisations will choose to establish a group arrangement. This will typically be with an insurer or pension provider rather than taking on the expense, ongoing financial and administrative liability, and regulatory burden imposed by "company pension schemes".

  The minimum standards include:

- Employer must agree to pay the employee's contribution by way of deduction from their salary.
- There must not be a penalty for members who wish to cease contributions or transfer to another provider.
- The maximum ongoing charge is 0.75% per year.

Some of the charity's staff, particularly more senior people, may already have their own pension schemes and it may be possible or desirable to direct their contributions accordingly. However this does not absolve the charity of its auto-enrolment responsibilities.

- **OPTING OUT**

Workers have the option to opt out of the pension scheme before they are automatically enrolled and at any point thereafter. It is important to note that the charity is not permitted to encourage them to do so in any way.

- **TAX RELIEF AND CONTRIBUTION METHODS**

Personal pension contributions are made net of tax. The pension provider then adds tax relief from the government (an extra £20 for every £80). Tax relief is available on contributions up to 100% of a person's earned income. Higher and additional rate tax payers may be able to claim further relief but this is subject to change and financial advice should be sought.

Employers may offer the option of facilitating contributions through Salary Sacrifice. The employee exchanges part of their gross salary for an increased employer pension contribution. As a result they pay less National Insurance and Income Tax; this is paid into their pension. Employers will make a saving on their National Insurance obligation and many choose to add some or all of this to the pension.

The table below briefly compares the two for a worker earning £20,000 who makes a £200 month gross (£160 month net) pension contribution. By sacrificing £2,823.53 they have the same income after contributions, but have an extra £813.18 in their pension over the year (assuming the charity reinvests their National Insurance Saving). These calculations are based on the 2015/16 tax year.

	Non-Salary Sacrifice	Salary Sacrifice
Gross Salary p.a.	£20,000.00	£17,176.47
Sacrifice amount		£2,823.53
Personal Contribution per annum (net)	**£1,920.00**	**£0.00**
Pension Tax Relief (Basic Rate) at pension	£480.00	£0.00
Total Income Tax	£1,880.00	£1,315.29
Class 1 NI	£1,432.80	£1,093.98
Total Tax & NI (after Pension Tax Relief)	£3,312.80	£2,409.27

▶▶

	Non-Salary Sacrifice	Salary Sacrifice
Gross Earnings less tax & NI	£16,687.20	£14,767.20
Net Disposable income	**£14,767.20**	**£14,767.20**
Employer NI	£1,640.54	£1,250.90
Employer Pension Contribution	£0.00	£2,823.53
Reinvestment of ER NI Saving	£0.00	£389.65
Total Pension Contribution	**£2,400.00**	**£3,213.18**

It is important to take legal advice before implementing a salary sacrifice scheme because there are certain HMRC reporting requirements and this constitutes a change to a contract of employment.

Other Opportunities for Tax-Efficient Pay for Charity Staff

It is possible to provide benefits to staff that are "non-cash" such as expenses and covering travel costs. Making use of these is good stewardship of the charity resources, but it is important that they are used legitimately. Employing the spouse of a minister for example may be a tax efficient way of remunerating the family provided they also undertake work. Care should be taken to ensure that the trustees comply with the spirit of the law.

An area often overlooked by charities is the obligation to pay the National Minimum Wage. (See section 15).

HMRC provides guidance on tax-efficient ways of paying staff. The following booklets may be of interest and can be found on the hmrc.gov.uk website:

CWG2 *Employers Further Guidance to PAYE and NICS*
480 *Expenses and Benefits*
490 *Employee Travel*

However, it is vital to seek professional advice from a tax adviser.

SECTION 18

Vulnerable Persons

David Pearson,
CCPAS

Introduction

Hardly a day goes by without the abuse of children or other vulnerable people making the news. The church and other faith groups have periodically been highlighted as places where abuse has taken place and for failure to adequately protect children and take appropriate action when concerns have been raised. As this book is being prepared, preparations are underway for the Independent Inquiry into Child Sexual Abuse to be chaired by the Hon. Lowell Goddard DNZM. The Inquiry will investigate whether public bodies and other non-state institutions, including churches, have taken seriously their duty of care to protect children from sexual abuse in England and Wales, and will demand accountability for past institutional failings.

Government, Charity Commission and insurance expectations require charities working with children and vulnerable groups to safeguard them from harm. People served by churches and groups may be vulnerable to abuse because of their age, health or physical or mental capacities.

Children and adults are abused by those in positions of "trust" – for example, church leaders, children's workers, music teachers, counsellors etc. Places of worship differ from many organisations in that they open their doors to all. It follows therefore that people who pose risks to children and other vulnerable groups may be attending or may even unknowingly (to the church) be involved in activities within the church, organisation or group. However, most abuse, statistically, occurs within the family. Churches are more likely than not to be working with children or adults experiencing abuse in a home setting and workers therefore need to be trained and equipped to observe signs of possible abuse and know how to appropriately respond to concerns.

Abuse is essentially about the misuse of the power and control that one person has over another. This is based not on whether an individual intended the harm but rather on whether harm was caused, and on the impact of any harm (or risk of harm) on the victim. A failure to take reasonable steps to prevent harm being caused to a person for whom you have a responsibility, or acting in a way that results in harm to a person who legitimately relies on you, constitutes abuse.

It is essential, therefore, that charities have formal policies in place to safeguard children and vulnerable adults. The trustees are responsible for ensuring that such policies are adopted in accordance with statutory expectations and other (e.g. insurance) requirements and that such policies are regularly reviewed. This is important so that the highest standards can be maintained in preventing and responding to abuse for both those in receipt of the services provided by the charity and those with whom the charity comes into contact.

Safeguarding and a Duty of Care

Safeguarding is a term which describes the responsibility of charities and other agencies working with children/young people, vulnerable adults and their families. It involves them in taking reasonable measures to minimise the risk of harm and acting appropriately when concerns of possible abuse arise.

Charity trustees, their workers and representatives, have a duty of care towards children and other vulnerable people with whom they have contact. Effective safeguarding policies and good practice guidelines within an organisation are not only essential in safeguarding and promoting the welfare of children and others, but necessary in addressing the charity's responsibilities towards staff and volunteers, parents and carers, statutory and other agencies, as well as the general public.

As far as the law is concerned a "child" is someone under the age of 18 years and our safeguarding responsibilities apply to all under that age. So far as adults are concerned, any one of us can become vulnerable at certain times in our life. It's not necessarily a permanent state. So we need to consider not only those whose ability to protect him/herself from violence, abuse or neglect is significantly impaired through a physical or mental disability or illness, old age etc but others in specific circumstances served by churches and groups. Such activities include pastoral care/counselling for relationship issues or debt advice services, street pastors, food banks and so on. We need to adopt the same safeguarding standards in how we run these services in regard to the recruitment of workers and in accountability, support and supervision of workers, safer practice etc. Where such services are not charities in their own right but run on a shared responsibility basis by more than one church (or group), decisions will need to be taken so that responsibility for these matters is clearly defined.

Legislation and Statutory Guidance

- **CHILDREN**

Current government guidance on safeguarding in England is set out in the statutory guidance *Working Together to Safeguard Children: a guide to inter-agency working to safeguard and promote the welfare of children* (2015), together with companion guidance *What to do if you're worried a child is being abused* (2015). Statutory guidance is issued by law; you must follow it unless there's a good reason not to.

Churches and other faith-based organisations are required to have arrangements in place that reflect the importance of safeguarding and promoting the welfare of children including:

- clear lines of accountability for services to children;
- a senior board (trustee) level lead to take leadership responsibility for the organisation's safeguarding arrangements;
- developing a culture of listening to children;
- clear whistleblowing procedures and the reporting of concerns;
- following safer recruitment practices for individuals whom the organisation will permit to work regularly with children, including policies on when to obtain a disclosure and barring service check;
- appropriate supervision and support for staff, including undertaking safeguarding training;
- clear policies in line with those from the Local Safeguarding Children Board (LSCB) for dealing with allegations against people who work with children.

Working Together 2015 defines four general categories of the abuse of children:

- physical abuse;
- emotional abuse;
- sexual abuse and exploitation;
- neglect.

These categories include issues of safety, domestic violence, forced marriage, female genital mutilation, children who live away from home or go missing, child sexual exploitation, race and racism, child slavery, extremism and abuse linked to faith or belief (e.g. physical and/or emotional harm linked to exorcism and witchcraft accusations)

The Children's Workforce Development Council (CWDC), published safer recruitment guidance for anyone appointing staff or volunteers to work with children and young people in England. Although the CWDC (a former government "quango") no longer exists, their guidance on recruitment and selection, vetting and checking candidates for work with children, safer practice and managing allegations against staff, still applies.

Although the issues and expectations in regard to safeguarding children are broadly similar throughout all four nations in the UK there are some procedural and legal differences in Wales, Scotland and Northern Ireland. Further information can be obtained from any local authority (in England, Wales and Scotland), Social Services and Health Board (Northern Ireland) or from the Churches' Child Protection Advisory Service (CCPAS). See Appendix 6.

As part of the Charity Commission (England and Wales) registration process, organisations working with vulnerable beneficiaries (children and adults) will be asked for information about policies and procedures as well as processes for appointing trustees.

• VULNERABLE ADULTS

The Care Act 2014 for the first time established a clear statutory framework for safeguarding adults in England. The Act, which came into effect in April 2015, defines adult safeguarding as the process of protecting adults with care and support needs from abuse or neglect. This applies to an adult who:

· has need for care and support (whether or not the local authority is meeting any of those needs);
· is experiencing, or at risk of, abuse or neglect;
· as a result of those care and support needs is unable to protect themselves from either the risk, or the experience of abuse or neglect.

The statutory guidance enshrines the six principles of safeguarding:

· **Empowerment** – presumption of person-led decisions and informed consent.
· **Prevention** – it is better to take action before harm occurs.
· **Proportionality** – proportionate and least intrusive response appropriate to the risk presented.
· **Protection** – support and representation for those in greatest need.
· **Partnerships** – local solutions through services working with their communities.
· **Accountability** – accountability and transparency in delivering safeguarding.

The categories of abuse that have been defined follow, though this is not a conclusive list as each local authority will identify additional categories of concern in their area:

· physical;
· domestic violence;
· sexual;
· psychological/emotional;
· financial or material;
· modern slavery;
· discriminatory;
· organisational;
· neglect and acts of omission;
· self-neglect.

Much of what has been stated already in regard to children e.g. the need to follow safer recruitment and good practice applies equally to work with adults who could be in need of care and support, but there is an important difference. With a child the expectation is that if there is a safeguarding concern an adult is expected to act (e.g. by contacting the authorities), the young person's consent is not required. With adults the position is different and their consent is a factor. Under the Mental Capacity Act 2005 for a vulnerable adult to give consent they should be able to understand and retain relevant information that is being given to them, believe it to be true and weighing it in balance, be able to make a choice. All action should be based on the presumption of mental capacity and on the consequent right of an adult to make their own choices in relation to their own safety. In practice, the advice is that all concerns should be referred to Adult Social Care in the local authority who will be able to determine a person's mental health state and capacity.

Some of the Essentials

This may all sound rather daunting but the main denominations will have their own policies which local churches would be expected to adhere to. The same may be true of other umbrella organisations. For others it isn't a question of having to reinvent the wheel! Model policies and safer practice guidelines for work with both children and vulnerable adults are available from CCPAS who can provide access through their membership service to an online manual with policies and forms that you can adapt. CCPAS also have a 24hr help line, available to members and non-members alike, which will be able to provide professional advice on policy issues or in regard to individual cases. They also have a range of publications you can freely download from their website covering in more detail many of the issues addressed in this chapter.

There is no failsafe system that can rule out the appointment of someone who is intent on abusing people, but in adopting recommended procedures and practice, trustees will minimise the risks of this happening. In addition, failure to follow such procedures might prove crucial to the outcome of a negligence claim against a church or organisation where there has been an incident of abuse. Church specialist insurance companies have also advised that failure to follow appropriate policies may invalidate any insurance cover.

We have already said that most abuse takes place in the home. More often than not, therefore, workers having to deal with these issues will be responding to concerns and suspicions which relate to circumstances outside the place of worship or organisation. Workers have no less a responsibility towards children in these circumstances, as illustrated in the case of Victoria Climbie, who died as a result of injuries inflicted by her carers. In the Statutory Inquiry into her death, three churches were severely criticised for not taking appropriate action in bringing her situation to the attention of the authorities.

The most important areas which need to be considered are:

- **The Policies**
  Safeguarding policies for both children and vulnerable adults need to contain the following:

  · how to respond if there are concerns/suspicions of abuse, including allegations/concerns in regard to employees (paid or voluntary);
  · a named contact (and deputy) in the charity to co-ordinate concerns and to take action. Separate child/adult/protection/safeguarding co-ordinators could be appointed in respect of children and vulnerable adults, or the same individual could fulfil both roles;
  · safer recruitment procedures for both paid and volunteer workers;
  · guidelines for running the charity's activities for children and vulnerable adults;

- actions and procedures necessary where someone who is a known risk is involved with a group (e.g. a sex offender who is a member of the church congregation);

In addition it is necessary to have good practice guidelines addressing specific issues in each group or activity for which the church or organisation is responsible. Some examples are given later in the chapter.

- **Responding to Concerns or Allegations**

Where safeguarding concerns arise, workers should immediately record in writing what they have seen or heard that has worried them and/or what they have been told by someone else.

In the case of suspected abuse or deliberate injury, if there are concerns for a child's safety or if the child is afraid to return home, the local authority Children's Social Care or the Police Child Protection Unit should be contacted. In circumstances where there are concerns regarding a vulnerable adult, Adult Social Care or the police should be informed.

CCPAS have issued the following guidelines for any worker or individual responding to a child or vulnerable adult who may have been abused:

- do not question (just receive the information);
- do not make promises you may not be able to keep, e.g. not telling anyone else;
- accept what you hear without passing judgement;
- tell the child/young person/vulnerable adult what you are going to do;
- make careful notes (the circumstances, what the child/vulnerable adult said, what you said etc) as soon as possible, preferably within an hour. Include dates and times of incident, record and keep the notes safely. Do not attempt to investigate;
- contact the person responsible for child/vulnerable person protection concerns in your church or organisation or, in their absence, take action yourself without delay;
- the child/vulnerable person protection co-ordinator/safeguarding officer should contact the appropriate Social Care Department in the local authority, the Police, or CCPAS for further advice;
- it may also be a requirement of your denomination, group and/or insurance company that they are contacted.

The government guidance to organisations "What to do if you are worried a child is being abused" underscores some key principles in work with children and families. Everyone in the organisation should:

· be familiar with and follow the organisation's procedures and protocols for promoting and safeguarding the welfare of children and know whom to contact in the organisation to express concerns about a child's welfare,

· remember that an allegation of child abuse or neglect may lead to a criminal investigation so don't do anything that may jeopardise a police investigation, such as asking a child leading questions or attempting to investigate the allegations of abuse;

· refer any concerns about child abuse or neglect to Children's Social Care or the Police. If you are responsible for making referrals, know whom to contact;

· seek to discuss your concerns with the child, as appropriate to their age and understanding, and with their parents, and seek agreement to making a referral to Children's Social Care unless you consider such a discussion would place the child at risk of significant harm;

· when you make a referral, agree with the recipient of the referral what the child or parents will be told, by whom, and when;

· if you make a referral by telephone, confirm it in writing within 48 hours. Children's Social Care should acknowledge your written referral within one working day of receiving it.

If you make a referral as an organisation (not as a private individual which would be different) you might be asked to participate in further assessment of the child, either through an early help assessment, through a child in need assessment (section 17 of the Children Act 1989) or a child protection enquiry (section 47 of the Children Act 1989), which will be led by a social worker.

If the social worker suspects that a child is suffering, or is likely to suffer, significant harm (i.e. their health and/or development has been or would be impaired compared with that which could reasonably be expected of a similar child), the local authority will hold a strategy discussion to determine the child's welfare and plan rapid future action. A strategy discussion can take place following a referral or at any other time, including during the assessment process. You should be prepared to contribute.

● **Appointing Leaders and Workers**
In order to meet the statutory guidance already mentioned, it is important that the organisation has written job descriptions for all leaders and those

working with children and young people or vulnerable adults. This should apply to all, whether minister or crèche worker, paid member of staff or a volunteer. All workers should be chosen with care; no one has a right to work with children and young people, or vulnerable adults. With a shortage of workers the temptation to appoint all who volunteer must be avoided. The following recruitment process should be followed:

· all would-be applicants should be advised of the recruitment process and that if successful it will be necessary to undergo disclosure and barring service check (DBS) if legally possible;

· a detailed application form should be completed, which would include a declaration as to whether the applicant has been the subject of criminal or civil court cases, and whether they have caused harm to any child or put them at risk. This includes "spent" convictions under the Rehabilitation of Offenders Act 1974. Applicants should be asked to declare all convictions and cautions, however old, and given the opportunity of voluntarily disclosing any relevant information. This will avoid having to go through a full appointment process if clearly someone is not going to be suitable for the position. It is also a test of their honesty, as information subsequently revealed by a DBS check could be checked against information that has been supplied, and again may prove useful in determining suitability;

· at least two references should be taken up. The charity should reserve the right to make any character checks they deem necessary;

· the applicant should be interviewed, and if it is decided to make an appointment, a DBS check at enhanced level (and against the barred list if a regulated activity*) should be then undertaken;

· those with responsibility for recruiting workers (paid or voluntary) should be satisfied that the applicant is suitable for the job;

· the position should be offered subject to satisfactorily completing a probationary period.

All workers should be made aware of the need to challenge behaviour when there are concerns, and advised of the organisation's child/adult protection policies.

---

* the statutory definition of regulated activity is based on a number of factors relating to child/adult contact and personal care which should be set out in the job description. It is beyond the scope of this chapter. Advice should be taken from your DBS umbrella body (e.g. CCPAS or your denomination).

- **Abuse of Trust**

  Churches and places of worship are unique in working with vulnerable beneficiaries, and in providing pastoral care within a context where people are in positions of power and authority e.g. church minister and member of the congregation.

  Under the Sexual Offences Act 2003, Sections 16-19 where a person aged 18 or over is in a specified position of trust with a child under 18, it is an offence for that person to engage in sexual activity with or in the presence of that child, or to cause or incite that child to engage in or watch sexual activity. This applies to people in certain positions of responsibility (e.g. school teachers) but though charities are not included, the same principles are applied to them in Abuse of Trust guidelines, "Caring for the Young and the Vulnerable – Guidance for preventing Abuse of Trust (Home Office 1999)". This guidance can be accessed via the CCPAS website (see Appendix 6).

  Concerns regarding a possible "Abuse of Trust" in a church environment typically arise in what might appear in other respects to be a normal boyfriend/girlfriend romantic relationship, but where one of the individuals is a young worker in a position of trust in regard to the other who is under 18. Such a relationship should not be permitted to continue and concerns of this nature should be reported to local authority designated officer(s) – see next section.

- **Reporting Concerns About a Worker or Charity Activity**

  In addition to reporting concerns of possible abuse to one of the statutory agencies (Children's/Adult Social Care or the Police), an organisation has additional reporting responsibilities if there is a question of a worker's conduct:

- the Designated Officer or team of officers (previously LADO) is a local authority role responsible for managing and overseeing concerns, allegations or offences relating to staff and volunteers with children in any organisation across a local authority area. In the case of a worker with adults then contact Adult Social Care;
- the Protection of Freedoms Act 2012 established the DBS (Disclosure and Barring Service) which processes criminal records checks and manages the Barred Children's and Barred Adults' Lists of unsuitable people who should not work in regulated activities with these groups. The DBS decides who is unsuitable to work or volunteer with vulnerable

18

groups and it is illegal for a barred person to apply for such work (paid or voluntary), or for a charity to employ a barred person in such work. It is also a legal requirement for the organisation to refer someone in a regulated activity to the DBS if:

- they have dismissed them because they harmed a child or adult;
- they have dismissed them because they might have harmed a child or adult otherwise;
- the person resigned first.

- Charity Commission (worker/trustee or connected with charity activity). Charity trustees need to report actual or suspected serious incidents to the Commission and should do so as soon as they are aware of them. A serious incident covers a number of areas relating to the charity's money or assets and also in regard to safeguarding:

  - Suspicions, allegations or incidents of abuse or mistreatment of vulnerable beneficiaries (in other words children or adults).
  - Any actual or suspected criminal activity within or involving your charity or if your charity has been subject to an investigation by another regulator.
  - Not having a policy to safeguard your charity's vulnerable beneficiaries.
  - Not having "vetting" procedures in place to check your prospective trustees, volunteers and staff are eligible to act.

- **Guidelines for Day-to-day Running of Activities**
  There are some general principles which should be followed. These include:

- treating everyone with respect;
- respecting personal privacy;
- being available, but also being ready to refer a situation or problem to someone more experienced to deal with it;
- being sensitive to needs, likes and dislikes;
- avoiding questionable activity, e.g. rough/sexually provocative games and inappropriate language;
- following accepted guidelines relating to physical contact;
- challenging unacceptable behaviour;
- reporting all allegations/suspicions of abuse.

Other Matters

Practice guidelines should be prepared in relation to each activity, which needs to include:

· procedures for recruitment, training and supporting of workers;
· guidelines specific to each group activity (see below);
· a statement that the interests of the child/vulnerable adult are paramount at all times;
· an ability to depart from general guidelines (in particular circumstances and in the interests of the individual concerned), this will only be done with the knowledge of the worker's supervisor or in an emergency reported in writing after the event.

18

The issues which need to be considered, depending on the activities, include the following:

· Essential practice guidelines
· Definitions of abuse
· Recognising possible signs of abuse
· How to respond to a child/adult when there are concerns
· Action following disclosure
· Handling of DBS disclosure information and associated guidance
· Discipline policy (for children)
· Leader-to-child ratios
· Guidelines on physical contact
· Safety of premises
· First aid and medication
· Taking children off the premises
· Practice guidelines as applicable

· Home visits
· Children attending the group without a parent's knowledge
· Babysitting arrangements
· Peer group activities
· Working with disruptive children
· Appointing workers from abroad
· Transporting children
· Children with special needs
· Swimming trips
· Use of the internet and safety issues
· Videos and photography
· Drop-in centres
· Working overseas

Within the context of this chapter, it is impossible to cover all these aspects, but detailed information is available from specialist organisations such as CCPAS.

· **Safe Supervision of Known Offenders**
Another essential area in safeguarding children, young people and vulnerable

adults is how the leadership responds if someone attending church has committed sex or other offences that could constitute a risk of harm to others. They must never be allowed to work with children or vulnerable adults or be left alone with them at any time. Indeed, if an individual has been banned from working with children, the church could be committing a criminal offence if they allow this to happen, in any capacity.

Sexual offending can be extremely addictive. For this reason, however repentant an offender may appear to be, there are no cast-iron guarantees that they will not re-offend. Even if the offender has undergone treatment or received prayer ministry, it should not be assumed they are safe. The follow-on from repentance is to "go and sin no more", so apart from the safeguarding considerations it would be irresponsible to place someone in a position of vulnerability where they might be tempted to re-offend. Sex offending needs to be approached in the same way as any other addictive behaviour.

When an offender starts to attend a place of worship, or leaders first become aware of a situation, it will be important, in consultation with agencies such as police and/or probation, to carry out some sort of risk assessment. In some situations it would not be appropriate to even try to work with an offender – for example in circumstances where the building is small and overflowing with children. There may be other churches without children attending who are better placed to help.

In circumstances where it is judged possible to safely supervise an offender, behavioural boundaries need to be put into place. These should help the offender feel secure and less at risk of false accusations. More importantly, these boundaries will serve to protect children and vulnerable adults attending activities. Such boundaries need to be personal to the individual involved and regularly reviewed. The following would need to be considered:

An offender should not be permitted to get close to children (either physically or emotionally or by use of the internet or mobile phone).

An offender should never be allowed to work with children and young people.

He or she should not sit in the vicinity of children at church or attend house/cell group meetings where there are children.

They should not hold positions of leadership or responsibility where seen by children within the church, even in a role such as handing out hymn/ song books. This is because a child is likely to regard them as someone they can trust. The additional stress that leadership brings could also increase the temptation to re-offend.

N.B. these principles are equally applicable for vulnerable adults.

Such a contract (or covenant of care) would need to be reviewed on a regular basis and would be on-going. Risk is not related to the period someone might spend on a sex offenders register and therefore would need to continue even though statutory involvement might come to an end.

Where there are reasonable grounds for concern, the church will still need to respond even if an allegation is denied (or someone is not convicted) and in particular by applying appropriate boundaries. Failure to do so could place children at risk. It is also in the interests of someone who feels they have been falsely accused to work within given boundaries in order to minimise the risk of further allegations.

The help and pastoral support available in the church needs to run alongside the monitoring of an individual by police and probation. Multi-Agency Public Protection Arrangements (MAPPA) exist in all areas of England and Wales. MAPPA places a duty on the police, the probation service and the prison authorities to assess and manage risks posed by offenders with whom they are working. Similar arrangements apply elsewhere in the UK.

Safeguarding Issues

- **ABUSIVE PRACTICES AMONGST NEW AND EMERGING COMMUNITIES**

There is now a great wealth of cultural and ethnic diversity within the UK. It has emerged that, alongside the positive experiences of living within a multi-cultural society, certain practices are occurring (some of which may have been acceptable or tolerated in other countries) that are illegal and/or abusive in the UK. It must be emphasised that these practices are carried out by a very small number of individuals and are not exclusive to minority ethnic groups. They nevertheless need to be challenged wherever they are found. Advice and support for safeguarding coordinators and others dealing with unfamiliar practices that they suspect may be abusive is offered by the CCPAS helpline.

Places of worship throughout the UK are becoming increasingly diverse. Many of our major cities and even rural communities are becoming home for peoples from across Europe and the rest of the world. A proportion of these immigrants who are practising Christians will attend churches from the main denominations which may also cater for their nationality, ethnicity, or language. There are however significant numbers of smaller denominations and independent churches which cater specifically for the particular cultural needs of their congregations. New and emerging communities bring new challenges in terms of implementing child safeguarding policies and procedures in the UK.

The following areas are of specific concern from a safeguarding point of view.

Human Trafficking

The trafficking of human beings is happening world-wide and should be understood in this context. It is not the domain of one particular nationality or ethnicity. Having said this, there is evidence that, within the UK, children are being trafficked, predominantly from West or Central Africa, Eastern Europe, and South East Asia.

There are no accurate national statistics as to the prevalence of child trafficking purely because of the concealed nature of this criminal offence. However, UNICEF estimates that 1.2 million children are trafficked each year. Other organisations believe the figure to be far higher but, whatever the statistics, it is shocking that this should be happening at all, that children as well as adults are being traded across the world as commodities. The Modern Slavery Bill currently being debated in parliament is a response to the national outrage about human trafficking. The government has set up a National Referral Mechanism in order to identify and support victims of trafficking in the UK.

See http://www.ecpat.org.uk/content/national-referral-mechanism

The reasons for trafficking are complex and cannot be disassociated from migration generally. Trafficking is not always for criminal exploitation; it can purely be for a child to receive what is perceived to be a better life or education and the trafficking of children may sometimes be linked to arrangements that are covered by "private fostering" regulations (see below).

Human trafficking is an abuse of fundamental human rights and it should therefore be reported to the Police or Children's Social Services.

Private Fostering

Not an abusive practice in its intended and legal form, the law on private fostering is covered by a number of pieces of legislation including the Children Acts 1989 and 2004 together with the Children (Private Arrangements for

Fostering) Regulations 2005.

Children who are being cared for by adults who are not their birth relatives are very vulnerable, particularly when they are living far from home. Most private foster carers do a great job but there are other private fostering arrangements in which children have been seriously abused and neglected.

There are many reasons why parents from overseas place their children into private fostering arrangements, but often the parents believe that their children will have better opportunities for education if they live in the UK.

Children's social care should be notified of all private fostering arrangements at least 6 weeks prior to commencement in order that they can ensure that the foster carers are suitable and the placement is safe. Private fostering arrangements are subject to national minimum standards which are outlined in the document "Minimum Standards for Private Fostering" which can be obtained from:

https://www.gov.uk/government/publications/national-minimum-standards-for-privatefostering

The regulations surrounding private fostering arrangements are very important because, should a person become aware of an unauthorised private fostering arrangement and fail to inform the appropriate local authority, they could be committing a criminal offence.

Female Genital Mutilation (FGM)

The practice of female genital mutilation (FGM) is centuries old and it is sometimes referred to as female circumcision. Worldwide it affects more than 120 million women, and an estimated 2 million girls are circumcised each year.

FGM is common to certain traditions and cultural beliefs, and where it is still practised incidents are more commonly found amongst faith communities. It is particularly difficult for the statutory authorities to investigate this offence because of the age of the victims/survivors and the family setting.

The procedures are mostly done outside of the UK in unsanitary conditions by people without formal medical training which can lead to serious infection and death. The peak age for female victims is between 10 and 12 years although it can happen to all ages through to adulthood.

The Female Genital Mutilation Act 2003 is the primary legislation that deals with this criminal offence. It is not only illegal in the UK but it is also illegal to travel outside the UK to have it performed. If such an incident comes to the notice of anyone responsible for a child below 18 years of age, there is an obligation in the interest of the child, for individuals to report the matter to the police or Children's Social Services.

In February 2014 ministers from across the government signed a declaration to stop the practice of FGM. New steps were introduced to record information about FGM practices carried out in NHS hospitals and funding was made available to community projects involved in raising awareness about FGM.

https://www.gov.uk/government/news/new-government-measures-to-end-fgm

Child Abuse Linked to Faith or Belief

Over recent years there have been several high profile criminal cases involving child cruelty associated with beliefs about witchcraft and spirit possession. These include cases of children receiving severe beatings, torture and even murder. Victoria Climbié was one such case and the horrific murder of Kristy Bamu around Christmas 2010 was another. The blend of faith and traditional practices has led to a number of children being at risk in the UK.

The issues should also be seen in a wider global context, however, and in recent years such offences are generally but not exclusively confined to African and Asian Diaspora communities.

Belief in witchcraft, spirit possession and other forms of the supernatural can lead to children being blamed for bad luck, and subsequently abused. Fear of the supernatural is also known to be used to make children comply with being trafficked for domestic slavery or sexual exploitation.

A growing awareness of the harm done to children by these beliefs and practices led to a national action plan to which CCPAS made a significant contribution. This plan was published in 2012. See:

https://www.gov.uk/government/publications/national-action-plan-to-tackle-child-abuselinked-to-faith-or-belief

This action plan was created for anyone who works with children, to raise awareness of child abuse linked to faith or belief. It will also be of interest to religious groups and communities in general.

The plan identifies problems and solutions, and includes case studies of work already being done to stop or prevent this type of abuse.

Forced Marriage

There are clear differences between a forced marriage and an arranged marriage. An arranged marriage has families of both spouses involved and the choice to accept the arrangement remains with the individuals. A forced marriage is one where at least one party doesn't consent and some element of coercion is involved.

Forced marriage is primarily an issue of violence against women. Most cases involve young women and girls aged between 13 and 30 years, although there is evidence to suggest some victims are male.

Parents who force their children to marry often justify their behaviour as protecting their children, building stronger families and preserving cultural or religious traditions.

Child Sponsorship (UK Organisations Working Overseas)

Many organisations run child sponsorship programmes some of which have been operating successfully for many years. The benefit for the sponsor is that they can see very practically how they are helping to make a difference in the life of the child or children they support. Very often the sponsored child will send letters and photographs, and friendships develop.

While the organisation will aim to maximise the benefit of these programmes, the underlying priority must always be to safeguard the children involved particularly as the children can be a target for people wanting to abuse children.

In order to ensure harmful relationships aren't allowed to develop the following safeguards should be put in place by the organisation. They must be prepared to decline sponsorship for any reason including safeguarding concerns:

- consult with external bodies, including the police if there are serious doubts about an individual sponsor - for example, if they are in prison;
- correspondence between the sponsor and the person sponsored should be sent via the organisation to ensure it does not contain the sponsor's contact details; check for inappropriate written or visual material that raise safeguarding concerns, or political/religious comment that may cause offence or be illegal;
- sponsors should agree not to share any information about the person they have sponsored over the internet;
- enabling sponsors to remain in contact after the sponsorship has ended should be facilitated by the organisation and only if the sponsored person and/or their parents/carers agree.

Organisations should use all the standards contained in this section as a basis for safeguarding the children involved in any sponsorship programme and have a formal procedure for all direct contact with the sponsored child.

Children and Young People Placed with Host Families

Some organisations run projects and activities that involve children and young people staying with host families. Some may be well known to the organisation, but others and members of their household might not. It is therefore important to adopt a policy and safe working practice where this happens.

Prior to the child or young person's visit, the host family must have been interviewed for suitability and a home visit made. The organisation should obtain:

- names and ages of all members of the household;
- home address and contact details (phone numbers and email);
- a Disclosure check on all occupants in the household who are 18 years of age or over;
- details of any current criminal investigation, or any criminal charge or conviction;
- offence by a member of the household;
- details of sleeping arrangements, meal times etc.

It is important that all concerned are protected from the possibility of false allegations made against members of the host family. Every host family should therefore be given:

- a copy of the organisation's safeguarding policy;
- name of the child or young person together with any other relevant information (e.g. medical details);
- name, address and telephone numbers of the parents/carers;
- an itinerary/programme of activities.

Every parent/carer should be provided with:

- details of the host family;
- a statement that all host families have been assessed by the church prior to the visit;
- a statement that the place of worship/activity has a safeguarding policy;
- the phone number of a contact person if there are any concerns;
- a programme of activities.

Organisations Working in Schools

Organisations are sometimes involved with schools, including providing services such as After School Pastors, School clubs, contributing to RE and Personal Health and Social Education (PHSE) teaching, Listening and/or Counselling services.

It is important that the organisation has an agreement with the school as to what they are providing. The agreement should cover:

· a commitment that the organisation has undertaken safer recruitment in line with "Recruiting Safely" or "Safer Recruitment in Education" and "Working Together" including criminal records disclosures at the appropriate level for any workers;

· ensuring that arrangements for maintaining appropriate confidentiality are in place, which is especially important where an organisation provides a counselling service;

· arrangements for reporting safeguarding concerns, accidents or incidents requiring medical attention whether in school hours or outside e.g. regular clubs or special trips, with the additional requirement that should a concern be expressed about a worker, the safeguarding co-ordinator for the organisation will be informed;

· clear practice guidelines provided by the school for the workers from the organisation.

Proprietors of Independent Schools

Proprietors of independent schools have similar responsibilities to those of governing bodies of maintained schools but cannot rely on local authorities to provide advice and support in the same way as they do for maintained schools. Many local authorities do provide advice and support but they will charge fees for the work undertaken. Independent schools that do not purchase services from a local authority can approach the Local Safeguarding Children's Board (LSCB) for advice. Safeguarding training may also be available from LSCBs but there is likely to be a charge per head for those attending. In any event, proprietors need to ensure that appropriate safeguarding procedures are in place and that staff and volunteers are aware of them and know what to do in the event of any safeguarding concerns arising.

CCPAS may be able to assist with safeguarding arrangements in schools, including audit, review and training for DSPs. See Link: Specialist Services for Places of Learning.

Day Care and Early Years Services

If an organisation runs (or is thinking of running) a playgroup, crèche, day nursery, holiday play scheme or out of school club, the organisation needs to ensure that they meet any statutory requirements for day care providers. These can include national minimum standards which are designed to ensure consistency in the quality of care across the country. These standards specify the qualification requirements of providers, and they standardise requirements across all types of provision including any overnight care offered by childminders.

Those seeking to work in day care or early years provision may be prohibited from doing so if they live with another person who is disqualified from working with children or on the DBS barred list.

Counselling Services

Organisations offering counselling services to children, young people and vulnerable adults should:

- act at all times in the best interests of the client;
- operate a confidentiality policy for all staff and volunteers. The confidentiality policy needs to acknowledge that any safeguarding concerns need to be reported to the relevant authorities;
- refer any child or young person where there are serious concerns about their mental state or physical safety. The organisation providing the counselling should refer the person to Children's Social Services or Adult Social Services, the Police Public Protection Team or a GP;
- ensure that counsellors are trained to a professional standard and follow the safeguarding procedures laid down by the organisation.

Pregnancy Advice Centres

It is vital that any organisation offering pregnancy advice adopts clear policy and practice for all workers when those approaching the organisation for help and advice are under the age of consent (16 years), those under 18 years of age and vulnerable adults.

Pregnancy Advice Centres need to have policies and procedures that:

- recognise the importance of the welfare of children, young people and vulnerable adults and their right to protection from all forms of abuse;
- recognise a duty of care to children, young people and vulnerable adults by its staff;

- will take all allegations of abusive behaviour and/or practice in all forms seriously and will respond to such allegations quickly;
- considers that the emotional wellbeing of all clients is of paramount importance;
- will treat all children, young people and vulnerable adults with dignity and respect in attitude, language and actions, listening and responding appropriately;
- give consideration as to whether a male and/or female worker should be involved or more than one worker;
- respect the privacy of children, young people and vulnerable adults, avoiding any questionable activity such as making sexually proactive comments;
- staff will not arrange to meet with a child, young person or vulnerable adult whose first point of contact is either the helpline or online service, but will refer them to the nearest pregnancy advice centre if face-to-face support is required;
- where a child, young person or vulnerable adult lives in an area not served by a pregnancy advice centre, online support can be offered, but parental consent should be encouraged wherever possible in the case of anyone below 18 years of age;
- incorporate a confidentiality policy;
- will not employ, in any capacity, staff under the age of 16 years;
- are committed to safe recruitment, supervision and training for all staff working on the Helpline or online.

18

SECTION 19

Immigration

Rosalind Nunoo,
Wellers Law Group

Introduction

In England and Wales, immigration is controlled and regulated by the UK Visas & Immigration UKVI (formerly known as the UK Border Agency).

A charity wishing to employ non-EU citizens is required to have a Sponsorship License.

Before applying for a Sponsorship License, it is vital to check that the charity is eligible. There is a requirement to have appropriate systems in place in order to be able to monitor the sponsored employees. The charity will also be required to have a clean record with the UKVI and associated organisations such as HMRC.

The type of license required will depend on the position to be sponsored.

There are five categories (tiers) of license but only two relate to the charity sector:

- Tier 2 (skilled workers with long-term prospects);
- Tier 5 (skilled temporary workers).

Tier 2 is split into:

- General;
- Minister of Religion;
- Intra-company transfer;
- Sportsmen and women.

Tier 5 is split into:

- Creative & sporting;
- Charity worker;
- Religious worker;
- International agreement;
- Government Authorised Exchange.

A charity may apply for a License to cover both Tier 2 and Tier 5 and is responsible for ensuring that the sponsored workers are suitable and qualified for the position for which they have applied.

Before making the application it is important to appoint an individual(s) within the charity who will be responsible for managing the sponsorship process (the Key Person).

The roles that are required to be filled are those of:

- An Authorising Officer;
- A Key Contact;
- A Level 1 User.

The charity can appoint different people to take each position or one person can fill all of these roles.

Once the application is submitted, the UKVI will conduct suitability checks on the Key Person and the application may be refused if the Key Person(s) has a criminal record or has been fined by the UKVI in the past 12 months.

Before the UKVI will grant the sponsorship license, they will need to establish the following:

- The charity is genuine, and lawfully operating in the UK;
- The Key Person is honest and reliable;
- The Key Person is capable of carrying out the duties imposed on sponsors;
- The charity can offer genuine employment that will meet the requirements of the UKVI.

Applying for a License

The actual submission and payment of fees must be done by appointed personnel of the charity. The application will be rejected if the charity allows a representative to make the submission.

Following the submission of the application online, the charity is required to validate it by sending to the UKVI the submission sheet and all supporting documents by post within 5 days. Failing this the application is likely to be deemed invalid and rejected. A charity is permitted to use a representative to complete and check the application.

A Sponsorship License holder has a number of reporting and record-keeping duties to the UKVI and must take these responsibilities seriously.

- It is the responsibility of the sponsor to check that the sponsored workers have the necessary skills and qualifications or professional accreditations to perform their duties. It is also good practice to keep copies of their credentials in the event of a visit from UKVI before or after the License has been granted.
- It is also the charity's responsibility to assign certificates of sponsorship

when the job is suitable for sponsorship and there is a genuine vacancy to be filled.

Record Keeping The charity must keep records of an employee's passport, UK immigration status document, biometric card and up-to-date contact details.

For an employee who is sponsored for less than one year, the documents must be kept for the duration the migrant is working for the charity.

Reporting Duties

UKVI expects to be informed if a sponsored worker:

· does not turn up for work on the first day;
· resigns;
· is absent from work without permission or a reasonable explanation.

There is also a duty to inform UKVI:

· if there are significant changes in the migrant circumstances, for instance if they can no longer carry on with their duties;
· if there is information and proof that the sponsored worker is breaching the conditions of their leave by working elsewhere;
· if there are significant changes to the charity e.g. change in address, dismissal of a sponsored employee, change in allocated roles.

Monitoring

UKVI will require the charity to have a suitable HR system in place that will allow monitoring of the employee's immigration status on a regular basis. This will include setting up reminders for the expiration of each employee's leave to remain.

It is wise to keep a record of employee contact details and their next of kin in case of emergency and to report to UKVI if there is a problem.

It is helpful to manage and communicate with UKVI via the Sponsorship Management System (SMS) to:

· manage the License;
· create and assign certificates;
· make and renew applications;

- report worker activities;
- manage batches of licenses.

Charities and Illegal Working

UKVI in recent times have described illegal working in the UK as one element of a wider, hidden and illicit economy. A charity is obliged to comply with the regulations imposed on employers in the UK regarding employing workers from non-EU countries.

UKVI is using communication and enforcement activities in order to deter employers from using illegal migrant labour to run its operations. All charities must therefore be watchful when it comes to relying on volunteers as well as paid employees from overseas.

Charities and Volunteers

Generally, there should be no problem with an organisation accepting an individual from outside the United Kingdom as a volunteer, but the individual must ensure that the current Immigration Rules allow them to work with the charity, even in an unpaid capacity.

All UK and EU citizens are free to volunteer with a charity with the exception of those on certain types of benefits. It is therefore advisable for potential volunteers to seek guidance from the Department for Works and Pensions before they volunteer for a charity.

People who come to the UK with visas that allow them to take up employment may also be able to work as volunteers so long as there is a clear definition that they are volunteers and would not give more hours for the charity than their sponsored employment.

For all other visa holders, the charity must be vigilant in accepting volunteers to work for them as otherwise the charity may be liable for a fine. For example, an individual on a tourist visa may undertake incidental volunteering provided it lasts no more than 30 days in total and it is for a charity that is registered with either the Charity Commission for England & Wales or Charity Commission for Northern Ireland or the Office of the Scottish Charity register.

Resolving Disputes

It is almost inevitable that disputes will arise from time to time in a charitable organisation – that is not to say that a charitable organisation is any better or worse than any other organisation. It is perhaps a reflection on human nature that where two or more people work together in close proximity for a period of time, stresses and strains can develop into full blown disputes.

The Charity Commission does not look to get involved in resolving disputes within charities. It considers it to be the trustees' responsibility to run the charity and will only get involved in internal disputes in exceptional circumstances. The trustees must, therefore, take the lead in ensuring disputes are dealt with properly.

For a charity, the critical issue is not the existence of the dispute itself, but rather how the charity will manage or respond to that dispute. There are insufficient pages in this book to set out all the circumstances that could give rise to a dispute, although there are three main areas that seem to generate more than their fair share of difficulties:

· personalities;
· programmes;
· pressure.

When disputes arise, it is likely that the parties themselves, as well as the charity, will look for appropriate intervention to enable the dispute to be resolved. People working in any organisation look for a forum in which to raise concerns, expect to be listened to positively, and require a response.

The cost of a dispute to a charity can be considerable. The aggregate of the cost of people's time, the damage to the goodwill and image of the organisation, the effect on its financial support and fundraising potential, as well as the negative effect on its programmes and the remainder of the staff, all need to be considered.

In addition, if the dispute goes to either litigation or mediation, the charity needs to consider the effect of:

· the delay;
· damage to relationship and morale;
· stress;
· the limiting of the work of the organisation;
· possibly legal fees.

Larger charities may well have a dispute resolution procedure in place.

Denominational churches can often appeal to regional or national bodies to assist in times of dispute.

Fundamentally, however, when a dispute arises it is important:

- to identify and recognise the existence of the dispute;
- to agree a forum whereby the nature of this dispute can be understood and the parties can be encouraged to try and work towards a resolution. A third-party facilitator can be significant at this juncture;
- to recognise that if the parties will not commit to try to work the issue through, then steps may have to be taken to isolate the parties concerned from the day-to-day running of the organisation, while the issue continues to be addressed;
- to ensure that steps are taken to minimise the fallout on the remainder of the charity and its work.

Spotting the Dangers

Taking the three areas of possible dispute mentioned above we should look at them in a little more detail.

20

Personality
- character – dominant leader/bully/independent spirit;
- ambition – plotter/manipulator/controller;
- frustration – inadequate leadership/blocked goals.

Programmes
- too much activity/insufficient rest;
- too much exposure to a crisis situation;
- inadequacy of programmes towards perceived need;
- lack of finance.

Pressure
- resistance to change;
- hostile environment;
- political or board "interference";
- lack of adequate staff;
- temptation;
- no-one to talk to/no accountability.

Options for Dispute Resolution

If the dispute cannot be resolved "in house" then the options include:

- **THE TRUSTEES**

Given their role as governors of the charity and the fact that they are likely to be separated from the day-to-day activities; the trustees (or maybe two or three of them) may be well placed to be a catalyst for reconciliation and understanding between disputing parties. One of the advantages of becoming involved is that they will understand the unique culture and operation of the charity plus they do have the ultimate sanction as governors. If, however, the trustees are considered to be part of the problem (e.g. because of their inter-ference) then their involvement in dispute resolution is likely to inflame the situation.

- **MEDIATION**

Mediation is fast becoming the preferred methodology for resolving disputes, particularly when the subject matter of the dispute is between personalities, or concerns issues such as doctrine.

The main characteristic of mediation is that it is the parties themselves, with the help of a professional mediator, who will work out a mutually accept-able solution. In this respect, it differs from litigation or arbitration where the solution is imposed on them.

In mediation each party outlines their position before the mediator, and thereafter each party meets in confidential sessions with the mediator. The mediator then "shuttles" between the parties, analysing and isolating the main areas of disagreement and exploring ways in which difficulties can be over-come. The parties can be legally represented during the process and, if the mediation reaches an agreement, then the settlement itself is written down and signed by the parties and the mediator.

The success rate in mediation is quite high and, given that it is the parties themselves who ultimately come to an agreement, they therefore "own" the settlement and the settlement tends to become binding in the vast majority of cases.

Other advantages of mediation include its cost effectiveness, the fact that it is private (court hearings are very often reported publicly), and that almost 80% of mediations are settled within one day.

The mediator can either be a trained professional or one endorsed by a regulatory organisation such as the Centre for Dispute Resolution (CEDR).

Churches and Christian organisations who would like a Christian mediator can contact organisations such as Resolve Christian Mediation and Arbitration Service UK.

● LITIGATION

In certain circumstances, it may be right for a charity to go to court, either to protect an asset or establish a right. However the courts will not adjudicate on "the truth, merits or sincerity of differences in religious doctrine, or belief, or on the correctness or accuracy of religious practice, custom or tradition". The courts are also cautious in adjudicating on the "fitness or otherwise of a particular individual to carry out the spiritual duties of a religious office". That does not mean that faith groups enjoy a spiritual independence, or are exempt from the law of the land; rather it explains that the courts are reluctant to decide such matters, unless presumably, the belief or practice leads to actions that put the organisation in clear breach of the law of the land.

It has long been recognised that a line has to be drawn between what can and cannot properly be decided by a secular court in disputes relating to religious doctrine and practice, including internal governance.

Generally speaking charities do not require consent from the Charity Commission before commencing an action in court. However some types of dispute, e.g. "charity proceedings", require the Charity Commission's prior authorisation. Charity proceedings are those brought with respect to charities, or the administration of a trust for charitable purposes. In practice, this tends to mean internal disputes between trustees or members of a charity as opposed to those between charities and third parties.

It is suggested, however, that even if Charity Commission authorisation is not required, it is a wise step to seek it, in order to protect the trustees from the risk of personal liability for the costs of a legal action.

A trustee should be entitled to be indemnified by the charity for costs incurred in connection with bringing or defending legal proceedings in connection with it. Any trustee who, without the consent of the court, starts or defends an action unsuccessfully, does so at their own risk, even if acting on legal advice. Therefore it is wise to seek the prior approval of the court or the Charity Commission to the proposed course of action.

Trustees of an unincorporated charity will often find themselves personally named in court proceedings relating to the charity in which they serve.

As an unincorporated charity is not a separate legal entity from its trustees, the lack of limited liability, (which would be the case of a charitable company or CIO) could result in their facing personal liability to pay damages or costs to the other party, particularly if there are insufficient funds in the charity to make the payment in question.

Litigation is expensive and the outcome uncertain. Therefore unless all other options have been exhausted, and/or the charity has been professionally advised that they have a strong case, litigation should be avoided if at all possible.

- **THE CHARITY COMMISSION**
  The Charity Commission shows a marked reluctance to engage with a charity in dispute. They certainly will not intervene in disputed issues outside their remit, which is basically to focus on whether or not the trustees of the charity are acting within their powers and complying with their legal duties. Their involvement (if indeed they get involved), is to ensure properly appointed trustees are in place, or providing authority for trustee elections to take place.

  Apart from the above, the Charity Commission works within its own "Risk Framework", under which it identifies any issues that may concern it as Regulator, which it considers may necessitate an Investigation and/or Enforcement.

  The Charity Commission's position on disputes can be summarised thus:

  · Primarily the trustees of the charity are responsible to seek resolution when a dispute arises.
  · If the charity is a membership charity then those members (akin to shareholders in a trading company) usually have the power to hold the charity trustees to account and may replace them.
  · They are not a referee between parties in dispute.
  · Their focus in any dispute is to ensure the proper administration of the charity by its trustees.
  · In some cases they may make an order appointing trustees or setting out a process for elections to appoint new trustees.
  · They will disengage from involvement where there is continued disruption or lack of cooperation on the basis that it is not an effective use of their resources. This seems to be the case even if it results in the charity ceasing to operate or splitting. Ultimately they take the view that

any resulting loss of charity resources is the responsibility of the trustees and those engaged in the dispute.

If the Charity Commission does intervene in a dispute, the options it can include are:

- appointing additional trustees to break a deadlock between the existing trustees;
- suspending a trustee or an officer of the charity for a period of up to twelve months, pending consideration as to whether or not that person should be removed;
- vesting property of the company in the Official Custodian of Charities;
- preventing a person who holds property on behalf of a charity from disposing of that property without the consent of the Charity Commission;
- appointing an interim manager in respect of the property and affairs of the charity.

The above powers may be exercised by the Charity Commission, providing it is satisfied that there has been misconduct or mismanagement in the affairs of the charity, or that it is necessary to act in such a way as to protect the property of the charity.

In addition the Charity Commission has powers to impose a permanent resolution by:

- removing any trustee or employee of the charity who the Charity Commission believes by their conduct has contributed to or facilitated misconduct or mismanagement; and
- to make a Scheme for the administration of the charity.

However, before one of these permanent solutions can be imposed, the Charity Commission must first institute a formal inquiry into the charity and be satisfied that the proposed course of action is necessary to protect the property of the charity, and that notice to this effect had been given to each of the charity's trustees.

The Charity Commission is of the opinion that disputes concerning the management and administration of the charity are initially a matter for the charity trustees themselves to resolve. It will not overrule a charity's decision that has been validly taken within the powers that the trustees have. It is for

20

those trustees to decide policy for the charity and this may include:

- resolving differences over spiritual or doctrinal matters within faith-based charities;
- deciding how community facilities (schools, community centres) are used;
- deciding applications to admit or remove from membership, and whether proper procedures have been complied with;
- deciding how to consult support groups about decisions and policies of the charity they use or support;
- the terms and conditions of occupancy of any land owned or administered by the charity;
- issues relating to employment or claims for unfair dismissal;
- disputes between charities and people or organisations who have entered into contracts with the charity – including landlord and tenant disputes;
- issues connected with a planning application or enforcement of planning law.

It is considered that as Regulator, the Charity Commission should become actively involved in a dispute where there is evidence that the assets or funds of the charity are at risk, the charity's income is not being used for its stated purpose, or trustees, and/or the charity is in breach of a court order, or prior direction of the Charity Commission.

The reluctance by the Charity Commission to offer greater support to charities facing a dispute is, in my opinion, disappointing. Proactive involvement by the Regulator could well prevent a number of disputes escalating, and save charities considerable sums of money, that would otherwise be spent on court proceedings. Perhaps their stance is a reflection of their reduced government funding in recent years? If so, then it is the charity sector that is suffering. I am aware of charities that have spent six figure sums in going to court to seek resolution in areas of dispute that would have been settled by direction from the Charity Commission in years gone by.

It is a personal reflection but it is suggested that most, if not all, the 165,000 registered charities in the UK would be willing to pay an annual fee (perhaps on a sliding scale to take account of size) and have a properly funded fully involved Regulator of the charity sector. Given that the Charity Commission's budget has been effectively frozen until 2020, the position is unlikely to improve in the short term.

SECTION 21

21

Charities Working Overseas

Charities working either wholly or partly overseas often find that the mixture of culture, environment and local laws presents a challenge over and above the charitable Objects that the organisation seeks to undertake in that country.

There is a challenge, too, for the charity's UK-based trustees who need to ensure that the assets of the charity are expended exclusively in the furtherance of the Objects of the charity in the overseas country(s) in which it is working. Not only does this require good systems of governance and management, but the trustees must also be prepared for the "What if?" scenario.

The principles contained in this section are applicable only to organisations that are governed by the laws of England and Wales.

At the outset, it is essential that the trustees of the charity select the correct legal framework for their work in the overseas country. A consultation with a law firm in that country, and perhaps other NGO's working there, will establish the best way for the charity's work to be structured. A key question to ask is: what are the risks to the charity for its intended activity in that particular country? This is sometimes referred to as the "onion skin principle" i.e. how to avoid the tears should the organisation's layers get peeled by the authorities!

Clearly the trustees will want to be certain that its charitable activities are actually lawful in that particular country.

Local Subsidiaries

It is wise to ascertain at the outset whether the charity is required to be registered in the particular country in which it intends to work. Even if not, there may be benefits for the charity in voluntarily registering in that country.

Registering in a foreign country (a local registration) usually involves: a certified copy of the charity's governing document; its Certificate of Incorporation (in the case of the charitable company); a Power of Attorney appointing a local resident as the contact point in that country; being legalised by the UK foreign office (forms downloadable form the FCO website), before being submitted for "legalising" by the particular country's embassy in London. The documents so legalised are then produced for registration in the particular country. It may also be necessary to ensure that the legalised documents are translated into the local language by an accredited translation firm.

The requirement for a Power of Attorney is to ensure that at least one person who is ordinarily resident in the particular country can transact business there, on behalf of the charity. Care should be taken in the appointment of that person, as they will have considerable freedom to enter into contracts and obligations on behalf of the charity (under laws that may be distinct from UK ones). Sometimes this person can be a senior member of the UK charity, but some countries require a national to operate in that role.

Benefits of local registration can include:

- the possibility of closer cooperation with other NGOs, governments and other locally based entities;
- the ability to hire staff locally;
- simplified procedure for obtaining visas or work permits for expatriate staff;
- in some cases certain tax benefits in the particular country.

The possible drawbacks to local registration include:

- the necessity to comply with all local laws;
- the need to have a local audit of finances;
- the possibility of influence or control from the government of that country.

Issues relating to the audit arrangements for local subsidiaries can complicate the UK charity's audit as the local figures must be audited in the subsidiary's country and presented to the UK Auditor in an acceptable way. The UK-based charity trustees are ultimately responsible to ensure that the locally registered subsidiary fully reflects the charitable purposes for which the UK charity has been set up.

Many UK charities working overseas testify to the fact that time spent in building good local contacts, particularly with the various ministries of the government who supervise charitable activity in that country, is time well spent. It is wise, too, to ensure that the British or EU Embassies in the country are aware of the existence and activities of the UK charity, as they may offer guidance, advice and support in appropriate cases.

Fundamentally, it is essential that the UK charity trustees have control over how its monies will be used, and influence over the selection of beneficiaries or projects that will be supported. It is not sufficient that the UK charity is merely a conduit to pass funds through to the entity in another country, in circumstances where it has no say in how those funds are to be used.

Charity trustees based in the UK may nevertheless feel detached and therefore uncomfortable when a sizeable proportion of the charity's resources are sent overseas to support its charitable activities in other countries, even if those trustees have a considerable say in how those funds are to be used. Trustees who are concerned to ensure the proper discharge of their governance responsibilities may choose to adopt one or more of the following steps:

- If the charity has a Chief Executive, or leader, who travels overseas regularly to supervise the charity's work in various countries, the board may consider inviting them to become a member of the board. (Provided that the charity's governing document allows that person to be salaried and a board member). As that person travels overseas they will be representing the other members of the UK board and making decisions as a board member, as well as, as a paid member of staff. In other words, they will be the trustees' ears and eyes from a governance perspective as well as an executive one.
- The trustees may consider it advisable for one or more of them to travel overseas, from time to time, to personally view and appraise the nature and effectiveness of the work in those countries. Their reasonable travelling expenses may well be a legitimate expense of the charity, provided that the expense is in proportion to the total income and expenditure of the charity, and that it is properly agreed that one or more of the trustees should actually travel (of course, if they are paying their own expenses then they are free to travel whenever they wish!).
- Charities working overseas often prefer to employ local people rather than to second staff from the UK. This can be beneficial to the charity in enabling the charity to more readily understand local laws and customs, and it also provides additional benefits to the community in which they work. It is important, therefore, that charities fully understand the local employment laws. Money spent on good quality local legal advice will often prove to be a wise investment in such matters. If the UK charity has not effected a local registration in the particular country, then the staff hired are effectively hired by the UK charity, although it is by no means certain that, in the event of a grievance, that person would choose to pursue their claim in the UK courts.

Joint Ventures with Local Entities

Some charities working overseas enter into a joint venture with a local entity. There are pros and cons in this arrangement:

· **Benefits** – these include local know-how, easier access and instant credibility.
· **Downsides** – issues of control, risk and possible conflict concerning different management and governance styles.

UK charities considering a joint venture in these circumstances need to choose their partners carefully and establish their exit route from the outset.

Compliance with Local Laws

For charities working overseas, there is no substitute for gaining a good understanding of the local laws and customs that could affect the charity's work. In addition to the law of the land, in some countries tribal or religious laws or cultural obligations may be just as significant. To breach any of these can have serious implications on the reputation and standing of the charity in that country. Good intentions count for little, if the local cultural, tribal or religious laws are broken.

(On a visit to a Central Asian country on behalf of a client charity, I recall being regaled by an official of that country with a true story of how a foreign worker had been in ignorance of the cultural sensitivities concerning a matter and as a result had felt threatened by the reaction of the nationals and had summoned his country's Embassy for help. The Embassy had dispatched a helicopter who had winched the person concerned out of the charity's compound and taken him to place of safety at the Embassy – much to the amusement of the local people!)

Some charities working overseas have entered into agreements with national governments in order to pursue a common purpose. Invariably such agreements are written under the laws of that particular country. Some of those that I have seen enable the government, in the case of the failure of the particular project, to call on the assets of the parent charity in the UK!

Charities working overseas may be offered the opportunity of working together with a national government in an arrangement akin to a joint venture. Often the documentation involved can expose the charity to financial liability in the event that the project is not successful. While the charity may feel that such a joint venture gives it an excellent opportunity to develop its work in that country, the trustees need to weigh carefully the risk against the potential benefit. In such circumstances, it may be preferable for the charity to consider setting up a wholly-owned subsidiary (probably a company limited guarantee but without charitable status), with which to enter into the joint venture. Providing that the Objects for that subsidiary company are in line with the charity's own Objects and the company precludes the distribution of any profits to its members, then the charity can properly advance monies to that subsidiary for it to undertake the joint venture project. In the event of financial or other failure, the funding from the UK charity would cease and it is only the assets of the subsidiary company that are at risk, rather than the assets of the parent charity itself.

Charities intending to work overseas might be best served to either carry out their vision through partnership with a locally based entity or to set up a locally registered entity with its own local trustees who will oversee the governance. In that way they may be more likely to achieve integration of their vision with those they are seeking to help as well as minimise many of the difficulties involved in managing risk and responsibility in a country far away.

In some cases, a charity may seek to delegate operational decisions to a field council or perhaps to a body that is an amalgamation of several charities working in a particular region. The trustees of the charity need to be comfortable with the limit of authority that is given to the field council, as ultimately they remain responsible for what is carried on in the name of the charity and under their remit.

Calculating and Managing Risk

As has been stated elsewhere in this book, a charity faces many risks in undertaking its work. For those charities working overseas, there are some additional issues which may need to be dealt with:

- kidnap or abduction;
- war or political instability;
- earthquake or other natural disaster;
- disease;
- terrorism;
- serious accident or injury;
- murder or accidental death;
- missing persons;
- imprisonment or expulsion;
- entrapment;
- corruption
- safeguarding issues;
- fraud/bribery.

Charities and their trustees need to be aware of the potential risks and ensure that the staff member, volunteer or worker who is to be sent overseas is fully aware of the situation to which they are being exposed. In instances where the charity is working in countries where there is a higher than average risk the charity should take the following steps:

- Consult with appropriate organisations such as the Foreign and Commonwealth Office in London (www.fco.gov.uk), the Hospital for Tropical Diseases (www.thehtd.org) and possibly the embassy of the particular country, to get the most up to date and complete picture in order that the charity's workers can fully briefed before travelling.
- Ensure the charity has in place adequate procedures dealing with emergency evacuation (with an appropriate method of communication between the worker and the charity). NB: This procedure should be communicated to the staff worker's next of kin in the UK as well.
- Possibly require the staff worker to sign a declaration before they travel promising to abide by the charity's emergency evacuation policy and acknowledging that in default of compliance the charity has no further responsibility.
- A policy that clearly sets out the charity's procedures in the event of kidnap or abduction (including whether or not ransoms would be paid).
- The setting up of a crisis management team in the UK or in the particular country, which is empowered to make decisions and implement pre-agreed policy in response to the particular challenge that has arisen.
- The setting aside of an emergency fund that can be utilised quickly, to enable the crisis management team to respond purposefully to the challenge.

In the particular country in which the crisis has arisen, the charity and its staff will need to be sensitive to the authorities and how they may wish to respond to the incident, as the authorities may be minded to exclude the charity from direct involvement and try and resolve the issue themselves.

Crises do arise, and it is how the charity and its trustees respond to those crises that is important. Time spent in agreeing appropriate policies and procedures in advance will be time well spent.

In cases where the charity is sending workers overseas who perhaps have been seconded to the UK charity from other countries, then the UK charity must bear in mind that staff members, friends and families from the seconding country may well have a different interpretation as to how the charity should respond in an emergency. In the midst of a crisis situation, the charity will not wish to receive a claim from friends and family of the staff member who live in another country, and who feel that the charity should be sued for exposing that person to unreasonable risk or having a less than efficient system of managing those risks overseas.

The charity Global Connections (www.globalconnections.co.uk) has some guidelines in crisis management for charities working in high-risk areas overseas. They are available to be downloaded from their website.

Kidnap, Ransom, Extortion, Safeguarding and Health and Safety Issues

Charities working in certain high-risk areas may wish to consider the possibility of purchasing specialist indemnity insurance to cover the risks of kidnap, ransom and extortion. This can provide an indemnity against any ransom or extortion monies that may be demanded, together with related expenses. Such policies are available from Lloyds of London.

Charities sending workers in to "high-risk" areas:

- need to register with the appropriate embassy;
- should take advice from other major agencies working in those countries such as the United Nations;
- should ensure they receive basic security training.

By their very nature, many charities working overseas focus their work with the most disadvantaged and needy members of society, in circumstances which could be open to abuse. The trustees are responsible for ensuring that the beneficiaries of the charity's work are not harmed through their contact with the charity. For example a charity working overseas with children should ensure that its UK Safeguarding policy is fully binding on its staff and volunteers overseas.

It is considered best practice that where charities are working with children or vulnerable persons overseas, the charity should ensure that all its workers and volunteers have the appropriate DBS Disclosure certificates before they travel overseas to work for the charity. For any staff or volunteers who are recruited locally in that country, it may be possible to take up references locally so that the charity is at least seen to be doing what it can to maintain minimum standards. The website of CCPAS has practical information on this important subject (www.ccpas.co.uk). See also section 18.

The health and safety of the charity's workers overseas is a paramount consideration. Prolonged exposure to relief work amongst people who have been affected by natural disasters, famine, disease, war and poverty can have a lasting impact on a person's health and mental well-being. The wise charity considers ways in which the needs of the staff members can be met and these can include:

- access to appropriate medical support and advice;
- provision of counselling;
- specialist training including personal security;
- appropriate support, encouragement and guidance from senior people working for the charity in the country or in the region;
- the provision of regular periods of rest and relaxation away from the main area of activity;
- a confidential medium of communication to senior leadership either in the region or in the UK;
- reassurance that the charity's work will not be abandoned.

Before allowing workers to travel overseas, many charities require the worker to complete a Power of Attorney appointing a near relative to handle their affairs in the UK, and to leave a valid Will, together with instructions for any funeral arrangements.

Visas and Work Permits

Charities intending to send workers overseas for any period of time should take specialist advice on the issue of visas and work permits.

Understanding local requirements and cultural sensitivities will be key to the success of the charity's intended work in those countries. It is essential that in any application for a visa or work permit the exact nature of the charity's proposed activities are set out. While it may be tempting to describe the intended applicant's work as "business" as a cover for other activities, nevertheless, that should be resisted if it is not genuine.

Working with Other NGOs

Increasingly many charities now work closely with other charities or NGOs overseas, in order to pool resources and reduce unnecessary management overheads. The benefits of charities working together can outweigh the disadvantages. Before deciding to work with another organisation on a particular project, the charity must ensure that its Objects and those of the other party(or parties) are compatible. If the arrangement is likely to last for a period, say, in excess of one month, then it is advisable that a formal agreement is signed by the parties setting out exactly what each party brings to the arrangement and what is the desired goal. Funding arrangements, accountability, decision-making, audit requirements etc. are all valid issues that need to be considered.

Charities responding to natural disasters often decide to pool their resources for the common good. In practical terms, there may be a charity that has an established base or reliable contacts in the geographical area in question, and it makes sense for that charity to be the main coordinator of the response to the disaster. Other charities bring money, personnel and other resources.

The international community's response to large-scale disasters such as the 2004 Tsunami has shown that there can actually be significant duplication of resources and efforts when charities come together. Trustees need to be convinced that working with other charities or NGOs is the most efficient way of utilising resources to respond to the need in question.

Sending Money Overseas

HMRC now take a keen interest in charities that send monies overseas and have established some guidelines to which all charities must adhere. Failure to comply with these guidelines could result in the payments being deemed non-charitable and HMRC taxing them,

Fundamentally, a charitable payment made to a body (charity, company, organisation, agent, partner, beneficiary or individual) outside the UK, will only be regarded as charitable expenditure provided that the charity can clearly demonstrate to HMRC that it has taken steps (that HMRC consider are reasonable in the circumstances), to ensure that the payment is applied for charitable purposes.

This will require the sending charity to carry out appropriate research in relation to the intended overseas recipient followed by ongoing monitoring and evaluation. The charity will need to be able to describe the steps they take, explain how those steps were reasonable and produce evidence that they actually took them. It will not be sufficient for the charity simply to establish that the overseas recipient was a charity under the local law of that country; nor will it be enough to keep records of how the money was spent. While it is important, the trustees must do more.

HMRC will consider:

- the charity's knowledge of the overseas recipient/previous relations with it;
- the previous history of the overseas recipient;
- the amounts to be given;
- the charity's observance of its own financial management and decision-making procedures and whether or not these were adequate.

In practical terms a charity proposing to send money overseas should expect to be able to provide information and supporting documentation concerning:

- the person or persons to whom the payment was given;
- the specific charitable purpose for which the payment was given, the reason for it and how the decision to provide the payment was arrived at;
- the assurances that have been obtained from the overseas body that the payment will be applied for the purpose for which it was given and what financial controls are in place, including sufficiently detailed financial records;
- the steps the trustees took to ensure the payment will actually be applied for charitable purposes (for example, ongoing monitoring, reporting and oversight);
- the follow-up action taken by the trustees to confirm that the payments were applied properly.

HMRC need to be satisfied that the steps taken by the charity are reasonable in the circumstances.

In the case of a small one-off payment an exchange of correspondence between the charity and the overseas body will normally suffice. However, the correspondence should be on headed paper and give details of the payment, purpose for which it was given, and provide confirmation that the sum has been, or will be, applied for the purposes given.

Clearly these requirements impose additional and serious obligations on charities sending money overseas. In part it reflects increasing supervision on the international transfer of monies, given that charities represent an attractive conduit for money launderers, and those wishing to move monies internationally for illegal purposes. However, it also reflects an increasing interest in charitable activity overseas, and a desire to ensure that monies given to a UK charity for a specific purpose are actually expended on that purpose when they are outside the jurisdiction of the English courts. The onus is therefore on the UK charity to prove compliance with these regulations, and charities would be well advised to prepare a protocol in line with these requirements that can be clearly understood and complied with, by all staff, whenever monies are sent overseas.

Care should be taken when sending money overseas to use reputable banking arrangements, and, wherever possible, avoid money transfer agents who are not subject to the same supervision and accountability as the major

Some suggested guidelines to help charities comply are these:

- Obtain as much evidence of the existence, activity, status and bona fides of the overseas recipient as is possible. This can take the form of press cuttings, evidence of a body's local registration, publicity material and links to known individuals within the UK charity who may have visited the overseas body. Beware of the fact that, in some countries, material may be fraudulently produced with a view to attracting overseas funds; therefore a charity should not just rely upon material produced by the intended overseas recipient. Third party verification would be essential.
- The use of a written grant procedure between the UK charity and the overseas recipient could be helpful. This would particularly apply when more than one payment is to be made and would allow the UK charity to make subsequent payments only when the recipient had achieved certain pre-agreed benchmarks or timelines, or disclosed particular items such as audited accounts or third-party verification. This could include the retaining of a third-party who would visit the recipient and report back to the UK charity, particularly useful when the UK charity is supporting a building project.
- Personal visits by members of the UK charity to the recipient who can then report back with photographic documentation, in order to give the UK charity independent verification of the application of its monies.
- Payment of anything other than a small amount to an individual should be discouraged.

international banks. Charities would need to ensure that such companies are legitimate, that full records are kept and that there is some means of redress should the funds not reach their intended destination. It follows that sending money to a recipient overseas in cash (perhaps hand-carried from the UK) should not be done.

Some charities may work in countries where "non-traditional banking methods" are common. This would include Hawala banking (used in Muslim communities) and Chitty banking (used in Hindu communities). It may be that a charity has to use a non-traditional banking method to move monies although these could pose more risk than the traditional methods.

These risks can be mitigated by putting specific controls in place:

- ensuring that all transfers are fully documented with the records being kept in the UK;
- ensuring that the documents include the details of the beneficiary, the commission paid, the gross and net value of the transaction as well as the names of any intermediary and the particular country of transaction.

It might be wise to speak with other charities working in that country to learn from their experiences as to the best way to move money.

Accounting and Management Issues

Charities working overseas will invariably need to set up banking facilities in the country in which they are working. Primarily the bank account should be operated in exactly the same way as the main account is operated by the charity in the UK. In areas where access to banks is somewhat restricted, there is often the temptation for charities to hold money in cash; in addition to the possible threat to the security of the staff members concerned, this is not considered to be a satisfactory method of working, unless full receipts are obtained for all monies dispersed.

Monies spent overseas have to be accounted for either in the UK audit of the charity or, in the cases of charities that are registered locally, in the local audit. It is quite permissible for charities working overseas to keep reserves in a currency other than the local currency (e.g. Sterling or US dollars) and then convert it into the local currency on an "as needed" basis. This can provide protection against violent currency fluctuations or, possibly, the collapse of the local banking system. Charities are reminded of the need to respect the local laws. In some cases these require all money transfers to be done within the country itself and it may be illegal to bring large amounts of foreign currency in or take local money out, other than through the national banking system.

Overseas countries are now seeking to control the inflow of foreign exchange that is destined for charitable activity. Again this is connected to the anti-money laundering procedures being applied worldwide and the authorities need to be certain that such monies coming in are for charitable purposes. It is unwise to try to circumvent those controls as such activity would be illegal.

The U.S. Treasury Department's Office of Foreign Assets Control (OFAC) lists countries under sanction, as well as people or entities, involved in drug smuggling, terrorism and international crime. While this is not specifically binding on UK charities, sending monies to countries, organisations or individuals on that list may not sit comfortably with HMRC! HM Treasury has its own "Consolidated List of Financial Sanctions Targets" as well as "Business and Enterprise Guidance on Sanctions, Embargoes and Restrictions" available on the gov.uk website and charities would be well advised to view this.

Charities anticipating transferring considerable sums of money overseas may decide to forward-buy the foreign currency or enact other steps with the bank to take out a foreign currency Futures or Option.

As intimated above, charities working overseas need to keep accurate records of all financial transactions so that their accounts can be prepared:

- In situations where the charity has registered in a particular country then accounts will need to be prepared in that country and audited to the appropriate Generally Accepted Accounting Principle (GAAP), so they can be included in the audit of the parent charity in the UK. Difficulties arise where it is not possible to find an auditor locally who can undertake the work to GAAP.
- In the event that the charity is not registered locally, then all receipts and payments made in the country need to be recorded in the books of the UK charity and included in its income and expenses and therefore its audit. UK Auditors are not impressed when vouchers are not available and this can lead to the UK charity's audit being qualified and its audit fee significantly increased.

NB: Care needs to be exercised in the disclosure in a charity's accounts of the existence of a large grant, as this could prejudice the charity' s operation in a particular country or, indeed, expose its key staff to increased personal danger in countries where there is civil unrest. The Charity Commission has assisted in the past with a procedure that can be utilised in such cases to enable the grant to be excluded from the accounts.

Charities working overseas need to be aware that they could become a target for:

· money launderers who wish to use the charity to move monies to and from the country in question;
· those who would use the charity's "people focus" to smuggle people into countries illegally;
· those that would seek to use the money raised by charities in a particular country to fund terrorist organisations or drug deals;
· use of the charity's educational programmes as a base to recruit young people for military or terrorist activities or to spread propaganda;
· fraud.

Finally charities working overseas need to review their risk management strategies (see section 26) to ensure that it includes the overseas activity.

Safeguarding Issues

● **UK-BASED ORGANISATIONS WORKING OVERSEAS**
The UN Convention on the Rights of the Child (UNCRC) or regional equivalent is universally recognised as the foundation on which safeguarding policies and procedures all across the globe must be based.

All charities involved in overseas work with children, young people and vulnerable adults must have a safeguarding policy for all workers, paid and voluntary, as well as procedures for safe recruitment.

These policies need to be consistent with all the standards and should be developed with the assistance of local agencies, and underpinned both by the laws of the country in which the charity is operating and by international law. If the safeguarding laws, policies or procedures in the country are insufficient or absent then the United Nations (UN) Convention on the Rights of the Child (children and young people) and UN Universal Declaration of Humans Rights legislation (vulnerable adults) will always apply.

Within the organisation's safeguarding policy there must be an appropriate process for reporting and responding to concerns and allegations of abuse. Any reporting mechanism should be consistent with local procedures in the country where the organisation is operating and it is the responsibility of that organisation to provide guidance on this to its workers.

In addition to the standards of practice contained in this section, the organisation needs to ensure:

- A reporting mechanism is in place that uses a locally appointed individual and a named individual at the headquarters of the organisation in the UK who will deal with safeguarding concerns.
- There is commitment to work with the governing authorities in the country concerned but not at the expense of leaving a child, young person or vulnerable adult in a situation where they could suffer further abuse from an individual connected with that organisation.
- Child protection is kept separate from disciplinary procedures. The child protection procedures need to clearly state what action will be taken in the light of allegations or serious concerns against someone connected to the organisation, including provision for suspension and repatriation as a neutral act while investigations are being carried out.

It is understood that the costs associated with repatriation are likely to be significant. Decisions will need to be made locally based upon an assessment of risk regarding whether it is safe to withdraw a worker from contact with vulnerable people and provide close supervision for the duration of the time overseas, or whether repatriation needs to take place with immediate effect.

UK CITIZENS WORKING OVERSEAS

Where a charity is working with a project, church, school or NGO overseas they should ensure as part of any partnership arrangement that they have a safeguarding policy and appropriate procedures including safer recruitment.

It is now possible for organisations based overseas who wish to employ (in a paid or voluntary capacity) British citizens or individuals who have lived in the UK for six months or longer, to conduct a criminal record check. This would apply to those who would not qualify for a Disclosure through the Disclosure and Barring Service because the organisation is not a UK based entity. The overseas organisation can ask the individual wishing to work for them to obtain an International Child Protection Certificate (ICPC). This is particularly helpful to international schools.

Details of the ICPC can be obtained from www.acro.police.uk/icpc

- **DIFFERENCES IN LAW, CULTURE AND PRACTICE**
  Charities working overseas may well face additional difficulties in responding to safeguarding concerns, particularly if the safeguarding infrastructure in the relevant country is still relatively undeveloped:

- differences in legal frameworks e.g. the definition of sexual abuse in the UK may be classed as indecent assault or rape in the foreign country because the legal system treats children as adults;
- the belief that sexual abuse doesn't really happen;
- different cultural attitudes particularly where the age of consent and marriage are lower than in the UK;
- no equivalent to the UK statutory agencies to ensure an independent and thorough enquiry;
- lack of experienced and appropriately qualified personnel to investigate and provide skilled support/therapy;
- poor supervision of an isolated project making "cover-up" relatively easy;
- logistical problems faced by an agency in the UK in determining an appropriate response to something that has happened thousands of miles away;
- ensuring the safety of a child and other children, young people or vulnerable adults once a report is received;
- knowing what action to take when there has been an allegation of abuse against an employee, volunteer or other personnel, where other family members (i.e. partner and/or children) and other children, young people or vulnerable adults have been affected, such as those served by the agency or living in the local community.

- **RESPONDING TO CONCERNS**
  Even if the concern seems relatively minor it is important to bear in mind that it could be the "tip of the iceberg". There is an understandable temptation to play down the situation. To do so, however, may result in children continuing to be abused and any suggestion of cover-up could also have serious consequences for the charity involved. The needs and interests of both the victim(s) and innocent adults who could be implicated demand a proper

inquiry when concerns are raised or allegations are made.

The response needs to be measured and the charity would be well advised to seek external advice (e.g. from CCPAS) to ensure a response appropriate to circumstances and to ensure that the agency is not seen as covering up a situation. It will be important to adopt clear, written procedures.

In order to know how to respond appropriately it is important that the person with responsibility for child safety (safeguarding and child protection) is aware of:

- Local laws regarding abuse and safeguarding procedures for responding to abuse, including policy on reporting to local relevant authorities.
- There may be occasions where a report to the local authorities could put the alleged perpetrator at risk, children at risk, or other personnel at risk. Such considerations should be covered in the charity's policy on the basis of good local knowledge. This MUST NEVER be used as an excuse to not report abuse to the local authorities.
- Knowledge of safeguarding procedures and relevant law and legislation for the personnel involved in the alleged incident of abuse, including any extraterritorial proceedings and the possible recourse of extradition. e.g. sex tourism laws.
- Where no local statutory investigation is possible, the charity should have procedures for commissioning and producing an external independent investigation.
- Protocols for reporting in other countries from where the alleged perpetrator holds a passport.

- **GOOD WORKING PRACTICE**
  When UK charities are working overseas, the following good practice should be considered:
- All concerns/incidents should be reported to a named person locally and there should be clear guidance on the action that needs to be taken. This should include immediately notifying the named person at headquarters who has been appointed to deal with concerns of this nature. The procedures outlined in this section should be followed and deputising arrangements in place in case the person appointed to deal with allegations is unavailable or implicated.
- There needs to be a willingness to work with the local authorities of the country in which the project is operating. The policy should state clearly

what these expectations are. If the authorities carry out an investigation, then they will have their own procedures which will influence the action that is taken. Inaction by the authorities in the country where the charity is operating does not mean that the charity should not deal with the issue directly. If the standards that apply in the country fall below those in the UK, every attempt should be made with the authorities to ensure the child, young person or vulnerable adult is safeguarded.

21

- The future safety of children, young people and vulnerable adults must take priority where allegations are made. The charity should be satisfied that arrangements made for them and the alleged perpetrator will prevent further acts of abuse. If this cannot be guaranteed, consideration should be given to moving the adult to another location or immediate repatriation to the UK.

- The charity should monitor the process by which allegations are investigated by the local authorities. In no circumstances should an alleged victim (child or adult) be required to face their abuser. Some organisations have been complicit in allowing this to happen. It may not only compound the problem but also put extra pressure on the victim, which may lead them to withdraw the allegation.

- Children, young people or vulnerable adults should have access to people they feel are independent and unbiased, not someone who, for example, has a close family relationship or employment connections with the alleged perpetrator.

- The charity should consider the possibility that the alleged abuser may have abused other children, young people or vulnerable adults either overseas or in the UK. If there are allegations concerning a person's conduct in the UK then an investigation in this country might be necessary.

- Children and other family members affected by what has happened may well need pastoral care and support. The alleged perpetrator will also need support, but the principles outlined in Standards 7 and 9 should be followed to ensure there is no collusion and to prevent any inappropriate use of information.

- There may be safeguarding concerns about an individual once they have returned home (e.g. they have children of their own) requiring advice from Children's Social Services in the usual area of the children's residence. Children's Social Services will then be able to take appropriate action to ensure the children's safety, provide support and guarantee any appropriate investigations are made in this country.

- Where repatriation is considered, this should only occur with the agreement of the authorities in that country where an investigation is happening and following a risk assessment having been undertaken.

SECTION 22

Finance

Peter Drown,
Beavis Morgan LLP

Introduction

Every charity, of whatever size, is required to prepare a Trustees' Annual Report. There are some basic contents which are mandatory but otherwise the content will depend on the size and constitution of the charity. Most charities are required to submit these accounts to the Charity Commission but some are not required to do so.

Accounts are normally prepared for a twelve month period and each charity needs to decide what year end it is going to use (the accounting reference period). The accounting year end can, if required, be changed from time to time. There may be factors that affect the year end. If the charity were connected with another charity then it would help if the year end of both charities were the same. Charities involved in education may well wish to work to a year end that coincides with the academic year (1 September to 31 August). Charities involved with Local Government may prefer 31 March as a year end. As gift aid recoveries normally relate to a tax year, 6 April to 5 April, then this may be a reason for adopting a 5 April year end.

There are two things to be filed with the Charity Commission:

· An Annual Return.
· Annual accounts.

An unincorporated charity does not have to file accounts if the income is below £25,000 per annum. A Charity Commission Annual Return is not required if the annual income is less than £10,000. Incorporated charities have to file both whatever their income.

Unregistered charities do not need to submit their accounts to the Charity Commission. However, they are still required to prepare accounts in a format that complies with the Statement of Recommended Practice applicable to charities (the SORP) and these must be subjected to independent examination or audit as appropriate (see below).

Some churches may be required to submit account to their denominational body but there may very well be a separate format required; for instance, the Church of England requires accounts to be submitted to the Diocese in a format not too dissimilar from the SORP required by the Charity Commission.

Unincorporated charities with a total income below £250,000 may prepare accounts on what is called the cash basis (receipts and payments). This means that they only bring into their accounts such items as have actually been paid or received in the year. Any sums paid or received after the end of the year are ignored but incorporated into the following year's accounts. Once an income or expenditure of £250,000 is reached, the charity is required to prepare accounts on an accruals basis. This means that any sums due to be paid or received at the end of the year must be incorporated into that year's accounts. An example of this would be tax due under Gift Aid from HMRC. If the charity has a year end of, say, 31 March then the tax recoverable up to that date will obviously not be received until April or even later. Under cash accounting, it is permissible to leave this sum out of the accounts for the year ended 31 March. Under the accruals basis a debtor will be brought into the accounts of the amount of tax that will eventually be repaid. A debtor is an amount of money owed to the charity at the end of the year.

Charitable companies are not allowed by company law to adopt the cash basis.

The Accounts

The objective of the trustees' annual report and accounts is to provide information about a charity's financial performance and financial position that will be useful to a wide range of stakeholders in assessing the trustees' stewardship and management of charitable funds, and to assist the user of the accounts to make economic decisions in relation to the charity.

Although past, current and potential funders, donors and financial supporters of a charity are the primary audience for the financial information contained in a charity's report and accounts, interest in this information may also extend to other parties e.g. bankers and HMRC.

The report and accounts should help users of the information to understand what the charity is set up to do, its solvency, the resources available to it, how these resources have been used and what has been achieved as a result of its activities.

The actual format of the accounts is somewhat different from that of a normal trading business. The format applicable to accruals accounting charities is laid down in the SORP issued by the Charity Commission and the office of the Scottish Charity Regulator. There are two SORPs applicable to charities, and trustees must decide which accounting standard to follow. The two SORPs are Charities SORP (FRSSE) and Charities SORP (FRS 102). The FRSSE may only be used for smaller charities. Separate SORPs may exist for a particular class of charity e.g. registered social housing providers or further and higher education institutions. Such charities should adhere to these SORPs. From time to time the formats are amended and charities will need to consult their Accountant or the Charity Commission website to obtain the formats applicable to them at the time. The Charities SORP (FRSSE) cannot be used for accounting periods beginning after 1st January 2016. A consultation is ongoing on whether/how it should be replaced.

In very simple terms, the SORP formats attempt to classify funds under certain headings. There are three fund types recognised by the SORP.

- There are general unrestricted funds of the charity which can be used for any charitable purpose.
- There are unrestricted but designated funds. These are sums of money that have been set aside (designated), sometimes by the charity itself, for a specific purpose. The charity decides on the designation and then keeps the monies in a separate fund.
- Lastly there are restricted funds, i.e. sums raised or given for a specific purpose such as a building project. The donors normally restrict these themselves. If somebody donates money to a charity for a specific purpose then the use of those funds is restricted to that purpose. These funds must be shown separately in the accounts and these distinctions are absolutely essential in the accurate production of accounts (see below).

The accounts of a charity may extend over many pages and will include a Trustees' Annual Report, a Statement of Financial Activities (SOFA), a Balance Sheet and Notes to the Accounts. A parent charity is likely to be required to prepare consolidated accounts i.e. that include financial information on the parent and all subsidiaries.

The Trustees' Annual Report

The Trustees' Annual Report, contained in the Accounts, can be as long as the trustees wish. There are, however, some basic matters that must be included in every trustees' report. These are part of the charity's public benefit reporting and include:

- Objects and activities;
- achievement and performance;
- financial review, including reserves policy;

- structure, governance & management;
- reference and administrative details;
- exemptions from disclosure; and
- funds held as custodian trustee on behalf of others.

The items required under each one are as follows:

Objects and Performance

This sets out the Objects of the charity as set out in its governing document, and the main activities undertaken in relation to those Objects.

This is an opportunity for the trustees to show how the charity has achieved the objectives referred to above and how successful has been their performance in fulfilling the objectives. Charities seeking to raise funds from outside organisations will undoubtedly wish to expand on this and the previous section. Smaller charities will often only give minimal information in these 2 sections. However, grant-making trusts will look at these sections in detail. Many charities will therefore expand these sections with graphs, pie charts, etc.

Financial Review

This area summarises the financial position of the charity at the end of the financial period. The trustees will need, in particular, to consider the solvency of the charity, whether there are adequate reserves and its ability to continue trading as a going concern. If in doubt, take professional advice!

Structure, Governance and Management

This will refer to the nature of the governing document (e.g. trust deed, Articles of Association, Royal Charter, etc.) and how the charity is (or its trustees are) constituted (e.g. charitable company, unincorporated association, trustees incorporated as a body, CIO, Co-operative and Community Benefit Society).

Charities may withhold certain governance and management details where the criteria for exemption from disclosure are satisfied (see "Exemption from disclosure"). It may also give details of how trustees are recruited, appointed and trained. There can then follow details of the management structure of the charity and the decision-making process. Also under this heading comes the Risk Assessment.

The trustees of each charity are required to assess the risks to the charity and what action has been taken to minimise or prepare for those risks. For instance, a charity may operate out of certain premises either leasehold or freehold. One major risk would be the destruction of those premises by fire or other disaster. The trustees would obviously take out appropriate insurance but should also consider in advance what action would be taken in the event of a catastrophe to enable the charity to continue its activities were it to lose those premises (see also section 26).

Reference and Administrative Detail

This used to be called Legal and Administrative Details which probably sums up more accurately what it should contain. It must contain the following:

- the name of the charity which, in the case of a registered charity, means the name by which it is registered;
- any other name which the charity uses;
- the charity registration number(s) for the jurisdiction(s) in which it is registered as a charity and, if applicable, its company registration number;
- the address of the principal office of the charity and, in the case of a charitable company, the address of its registered office;
- the names of all those who were the charity's trustees on the date the report was approved or who served as trustees in the reporting period;
- bankers;
- auditors or independent reviewers;
- solicitors;
- investment managers/advisers.

Charities may withhold certain reference and administrative details where the criteria for exemption from disclosure are satisfied (see "Exemptions from disclosure").

Exemptions from Disclosure

On occasions, the disclosure of the names of trustees or of the charity's principal address or the disclosure of the name(s) of any chief executive officer or other senior staff member(s) could lead to that person (or others) being placed in personal danger (e.g. in the case of a women's refuge). In such circumstances, the applicable law and regulations may permit the withholding of these details. Where a report omits the name of a trustee, chief executive officer or senior staff member or the charity's principal address, it should give the reason for the omission.

Charities in England and Wales may omit the names of those persons and the charity's principal address from their report provided the Charity

Commission has given the charity trustees the authority to do this. In Scotland there is also a provision under charity law for such information to be excluded.

The directors of charitable companies registered in the UK should note that, with the exception of the name of the auditor, or senior statutory auditor in the case of an audit firm (section 506 Companies Act 2006), there is no corresponding dispensation in relation to the disclosure of names.

Funds held as custodian trustee on behalf of others

If a charity is, or its trustees are, acting as custodian trustees, the charity must refer to the SORP module "Accounting for funds received as agent or as custodian trustee."

Larger Charities' Accounts

A greater degree of public accountability and stewardship reporting is expected of larger charities. Larger charities in compiling their report must meet the requirements placed on all charities as set out above and also provide additional information.

Statement of Financial Activities (SOFA)

In a commercial business, this would be described as the Profit & Loss Account or, if on a cash basis, the Receipts & Payments Account. It is really a presentation of the Income & Expenses of the charity during its financial year. However, the Charity Commission is not so much interested in whether the charity has a surplus or deficit as to the use made of funds available. The general public will also be interested in this aspect e.g. overheads or running costs as a percentage of monies received as donations, grants etc. For this reason, the charity is required to list its expenditure under certain headings so that the Charity Commission and the general public can assess the charity's use of the funds available to them. An example of the current layout of the SOFA is available on the Charity Commission's website.

Balance Sheet

Whereas the SOFA is a statement of what has happened over a period of time, the Balance Sheet is a snapshot of the financial position of the charity at its accounting year end date. It shows all the items owned by the charity which are known Assets and all the amounts owed by the charity which are known as Liabilities. The Assets may be Fixed Assets or Current Assets.

Fixed Assets are items used in the charity that will be retained and used for a period exceeding 12 months e.g. properties, office furniture, computers etc. Current Assets, on the other hand, are likely to change their form over the next 12 months e.g. debtors (amounted owed to the charity) and cash in its various forms. Normally, investments are Current Assets but if treated as an endowment they may be shown as Fixed Assets.

Liabilities are divided into Current Liabilities, which again are likely to change their status within the next 12 months, and longer term Liabilities. These are normally divided into Creditors (amounts owed by the charity) due to be paid within one year, two to five years and longer than five years.

The difference between the Assets and Liabilities will represent the Reserves held by the charity at the year end and which will, as described previously, be split between general unrestricted funds, designated funds and restricted funds. None of these funds should be "overdrawn" at the year end as that will indicate solvency issues. As a general guide, the general unrestricted fund should contain between three to six months of general overheads i.e. normal running costs.

Notes to the Accounts

This can extend over many pages and will include the accounting policies used in the preparation of the accounts e.g. income recognition, going concern, depreciation rates charged, etc.

Many items in the SOFA and Balance Sheet are broken down into further detail in the Notes to the Accounts. These could actually be shown on the face of the Accounts but it would make the Accounts harder to read. The Notes will give detailed information, for instance, of fixed assets, debtors, creditors (within and over 1 year), capital commitments and transactions with related parties.

Audit and Independent Examination

Any charity with total income under £25,000 is not required to have any outside person or body review their accounts, although Parochial Church Council's (PCCs) have to have at least an independent examination. Neither are they required to submit their accounts to the Charity Commission whatever their size. Incorporated charities have to file accounts with the Charities Commission.

Except for NHS charities, any charity with income between £25,000 and

£250,000 is required to be subject to an Independent Examination. The Independent Examiner can be anybody competent to carry out the work and by definition, independent of the charity. Therefore, the Independent Examination cannot be carried out by one of the trustees or someone associated with the charity in any way.

A charity with total income between £250,000 and £1 million is still only subject to Independent Examination but the Independent Examiner must be an appropriately qualified Accountant.

Once income exceeds £1 million the charity is subject to an audit. An audit will also be needed if total assets (before deductions) exceed £3.26 million and the charity's gross income is more than £250,000. This work must be carried out by a Registered Auditor who must also be totally independent of the charity. This does not mean that the Auditor cannot carry out other advisory work for the charity as long as the relationship does not become so close that the independence of the Auditor is undermined. There is no legal requirement for a charity to change its Auditors every 3, 5 or 7 years. There is no reason why the same Auditor cannot carry on undertaking the Audit for a long period of time, provided the Auditor is satisfied that he remains independent.

When accounts are submitted to the Charity Commission they should be signed by the Independent Examiner or Auditor. It was formerly a requirement for a copy signed by the trustees to be submitted to the Charity Commission but this has recently been changed because of the incidence of people copying signatures of charity trustees. There must be a copy of the accounts signed by the trustees held on file but the copy submitted to the Charity Commission does not have to be a manually signed copy. The accounts need to be submitted to the Charity Commission, and Companies House if a charitable company, within nine months of the end of the charity's financial year.

Where an independent examination or audit is needed then the report of the examiner/auditor has to be attached – but some accounts (e.g. incorporated charities with less than £25k income) can be filed without such a report.

Taxation Issues

As a general rule charities are not liable to taxation. Amounts donated to a charity are not liable to tax in the charity's hands even though the charity may recover tax under Gift Aid and the donor may even have saved higher rate tax on their donation to the charity.

If charities receive bank interest then this should either be paid to them gross (before the deduction of tax) or they should apply to HMRC for a refund of any tax deducted by the bank or building society concerned.

If a charity receives a dividend which has had tax deducted then the charity cannot recover the tax credit reflecting the fact that the dividend came from income taxed within a company. These credits used to be recoverable but in 1997 that ceased to be the case and from April 2016 the concept of tax credits on dividends was withdrawn altogether. This may appear to suggest that equity investments paying dividends are not such a good investment for the charity, however this could be balanced by the prospect of growth in equity values.

If a charity makes a capital gain on the sale of an Asset this will not be subject to Capital Gains Tax.

Charities are not exempt from taxation, but they need to register with HMRC in order to take advantage of the reliefs that are available for charities established in the UK.

For example, a church may make a very large amount of its income from the commercial hiring out of the church building. This income would be taxable but expenses may be deducted from the income before the tax is assessed. These expenses would relate to some of the expenses of operating the premises.

Charities will either be structured as unincorporated ones which are within the income tax regime or incorporated ones to which the corporate tax regime applies.

Periodically, HMRC send charities tax returns. The charity must complete that return or suffer a penalty of £100 if the return is not submitted within 12 months of the year-end. When a tax return is received then advice should immediately be sought from the charity's Auditors or a *qualified* Accountant.

Donations

Charities should encourage individual donors who are income tax payers to give under the Gift Aid Scheme. The effect of this is that the charity can recover tax on amounts donated to it and the donor may even save higher rate tax on the amount of the grossed-up donation. For example, if the standard rate of income tax is 20%, the higher rate of income tax is 40% and a donor gives £80 to a charity. The charity can recover £20 from the HMRC because the £80 is deemed to be the net amount after the taxpayer has deducted 20%

tax. And if the taxpayer is a higher rate taxpayer then he or she would be entitled to relief from higher rate tax on the £100 gross amount (i.e. £80 gift and £20 tax) that is to be given. That is to say, the donor's own personal tax liability would reduce by £20 (the higher rate tax no longer being payable) so in real terms the £60 net he would have had in his pocket becomes £100 to the charity. Should they choose to, donors may be able to eliminate paying higher rate tax by using Gift Aid! A recent attempt to put an annual maximum on the amount of relief claimable on charitable giving was not brought into law.

22

Realisable Donations

Where charities receive gifts of items for sale in their shop – but not items for ad hoc fundraising events – provided the donor signs a gift aid declaration, what is realised (net of any expenses) may be treated as gift aided (see section 23).

Payroll Giving Scheme

Many employers and pension providers also offer a payroll giving scheme. This allows individuals to donate directly from their wages or pension before tax is deducted. The advantage of this method over cash gifts as described above is that the individual receives tax relief immediately. However the drawback is that donations are made through an agency charity who pass them on to the chosen charities. These agencies may charge an administration fee (around 4%) which is usually deducted from employee's donations before they pass funds to their chosen charities, unless the employer chooses to pay this fee.

Donation of Qualifying Investments

Those not having cash available for donations may wish to consider giving qualifying investments. Charities should make it clear to potential donors that they can accept alternatives to cash donations which may be tax efficient for individuals and companies. HMRC's list of qualifying investments includes shares listed on any recognised stock exchange including AIM, property and land, amongst others. Companies and individuals are able to deduct up to the full value of the gift from their income reducing their corporation tax or income tax liabilities accordingly in the year of gift.

Capital Gains Tax (CGT)

Gifts of shares and property not only benefit from income tax relief but also from exemption from CGT. Neither the donor nor charity need be liable to CGT on any increase in value of the asset during the donor's ownership when the gift is sold. Note that if the investment were to be sold on the open market and the proceeds donated to charity, the donor would be subject to CGT on any uplift in value. Making the donation of a qualifying asset itself is therefore more tax effective than selling the asset and gifting the cash proceeds.

The donor benefits by not paying CGT on disposal *and* receiving income tax relief on the market value of the investment, and the charity by receiving the full value of the investment. However, If an asset does not fall within HMRC's qualifying list, then *only* CGT relief is available.

Charitable Bequests

All gifts to charity by individuals are Inheritance Tax (IHT) free. However with effect from 6 April 2012, HMRC announced that IHT would be reduced from 40% to 36% for estates or parts thereof where at least 10% of the relevant value of the estate is left to charity. This has an interesting effect for those already planning to distribute 4% or more of their estate to charity. By increasing the estate's contribution to charity to 10%, they could not only leave a greater charity legacy but also increase the amount available to distribute to beneficiaries because of the lower IHT rate. It is therefore very worthwhile highlighting this to donors who can claim this reduced rate by inserting an appropriate clause into their Will.

Annual Budgets

Each charity should prepare an annual budget and cash flow projection to be approved by the trustees. While not specifically laid down in the Charities Act, it would be unwise for trustees to embark on a year's activities without having some idea of the financial implications of the decisions made at their trustees meetings. If the charity does not have the expertise to prepare annual budgets then advice should be sought from a qualified accountant.

There are two distinct documents that should not be confused. The budget is an estimate of the income and expenditure for the coming year across the three different funds of unrestricted, designated and restricted. The format and figures can be based on previous years' accounts. Once prepared, the trustees can monitor actual results with budget, at each trustees meeting. This will enable appropriate action to be taken in good time.

The other document is the Cash Flow Projection. This is arguably the most important financial document for any charity as it answers the question "Will we have enough cash for our plans?" Whereas the budget will usually cover the year on an accruals basis, the cash flow is usually a monthly estimate of cash in and out. This will make clear any months where an overdraft may need to be negotiated or loans raised. Again, when monitored against actual figures any problems can be identified at an early stage. Both the figures in the budget and the cash flow projections should agree with, and be reconciled to, each other.

Credit Control/Cash Flow

Charities have as much of a responsibility as trading companies to control their cash flow and maintain their solvency. If there is any form of trading by the charity then credit control will also come into the scenario. Each charity needs to ensure that there are sufficient funds available for their day-to-day expenses. As well as preparing year-end accounts, there should be a continuous monitoring of cash flow to ensure that adequate funds are available to meet expenses as they arise. For example, a church may be considering an extension to its building. The trustees will need to look at the resources available to the church, the total cost of the project to be undertaken and the availability of other funds that can be borrowed to pay the initial building costs. They will also need to consider the repayment of the resulting loan as regards both interest and capital. It would be negligent for the trustees to embark upon any project without first ensuring that adequate funds would be available.

Receiving and Accounting for Cash

Many charities have cash transactions. A good deal of their funds may actually be raised in cash from either collections or other means. The trustees of the charity have a responsibility to ensure that cash is correctly accounted for and that risks of fraud or error are minimised. For example, when church offerings are counted, this should be carried out by two people, neither of whom is the treasurer; the funds should then be banked after a signed statement has been prepared by those counting the collection as to the amount involved.

Similarly, charities undertaking any form of street collection should ensure that the risks of fraud and error are reduced as far as possible. At the end of the day, there has to be an element of trust in these situations but as most charities are using volunteers, it would be unusual for those volunteers not to handle the finances of the charity appropriately. The underlying moral is to ensure that all volunteers recruited to the charity are appropriately checked and references taken. Systems should also be in place to minimise any risk to the charity.

Payments

All payments over, say, £100 should be approved by two or more properly authorised individuals. Any commitments to expenditure (including for staff) over a pre agreed level should be authorised by the trustees and recorded as such in the minutes of the trustees meeting. All trustees are collectively responsible for the finances. Charities should set practicable limits depending on their size.

Borrowing Money

As long as the governing document of the charity permits, a charity may borrow funds. There are many sources of funds. Mortgages are dealt with in Section 11 of this book. There may be a need for borrowing on a day-to-day basis. It may be appropriate or inappropriate for trustees to personally give a guarantee against bank or other borrowing and/or allow a charge over their personal property to secure such a loan. It may be that from time to time a charity has an offer of a loan from either an employee or trustee. If this is the case, then the minutes of the trustees meeting must clearly state the terms on which the loan is made as regards interest, capital and repayment. Such a loan should obviously be on no more onerous terms than could be obtained from outside borrowing. Market rates should apply. Professional advice should be taken in such circumstances from the charity's lawyers or accountants.

Investments

From time to time charities may well find themselves holding excess funds which require to be invested. Indeed, many charities have large capital funds available to them that have been built up over the years. These should obviously be invested wisely and with a view to maximising returns and capital growth for the charity. The Charities Aid Foundation operates bank accounts on behalf of charities which will often give a better rate of interest than is normally obtainable from High Street banks. If considerable sums of money are going to be held for an indefinite period then professional advice should be sought from advisors who are experienced in handling, and advising on and managing, a portfolio of investments on behalf of charities. This will ensure that any decision-making on investments is carried out by an independent third party that will advise the trustees as appropriate (see section 17).

Needless to say, there are investments available, which may offer a very attractive return but which carry a higher risk of loss. It would not be in trustees' interests to take risks with the capital sums owned by the charity in the hope of receiving a slightly enhanced income. Thus, any substantial sums that need to be invested should only be invested with the advice of an independent and appropriately qualified financial advisor.

Record Keeping

All charities must keep the accounting records (e.g. cash books, invoices, receipts, Gift Aid records etc.) for at least 6 years. The accounting records and the accounts must be available to the public on request.

Gift Aid

A registered charity can claim Gift Aid on cash donations of £20 or less even if the donor has not made a Gift Aid declaration. It is possible to claim a total £1,250 in anyone tax year in respect of cash donations. However, a charity cannot claim more than ten times the total Gift Aid claim in any one tax year. For example, if a charity claims a total £1,000 in respect of cash donations that charity must also have claimed at least £100 in respect of ordinary Gift Aid *during* that year.

Fundraising

"Research has shown that when it comes to charitable giving the public are often ruled by their heart, not their head.

Researchers have looked into why people donate, why they don't do it as much as they would hope to and how to bridge the gap. The explanations for charitable giving fall into three broad categories:

· the purely altruistic – "I donate because I value the social good done by the charity";

· impurely altruistic – "I donate because I extract value from knowing I contribute to the social good done by the charity";

· not-at-all altruistic – "I donate because I want to show off to potential friends how rich I am".

As an illustration of the above, it was found that people are more responsive to charitable pleas that feature a single, identifiable beneficiary, than they are to statistical information about the scale of the problem being faced. It was also revealed that advertising which emphasises the proven effectiveness of the charity does not increase giving. In short when it comes to charitable giving we are apparently ruled by our hearts and not our heads."*

Charities can achieve very little without adequate funding. While charities exist to spend money rather than accumulate it, they have first to raise the income before it can be dispersed.

In today's increasingly competitive environment charities are exploring new and innovative ways to raise funds – the "Sponsored Walk" of the past has given way to the "Himalaya Trek" or "Sponsored Sky-dive" of today. Indeed, very few of us can pass through the high streets of our towns without being approached by individuals acting on behalf of a charity anxious to solicit our funds and support.

Ultimately it rests with the charity's trustees to decide on a particular methodology for raising funds. Churches and other faith-based organisations still rely heavily upon gifts from the congregation and other like-minded people or organisations that closely identify with the Objects of the charity. However, there is growing evidence that many charities are now beginning to explore other means of attracting income. I deal with some of these in this section, not in an attempt to highlight them as being more effective or desirable than other ways; rather they are mentioned due to the particular legal ramifications that affect them.

* Michael Sanders and Francesca Tamma, Behavioural Insights Team, 23 March 2015

The Charities (Protection and Social Investment) Act 2016 brings into being a fundraising regulator for the charity sector as a direct response to public criticism of charities for their fundraising practices. Charities will be expected to register voluntarily with the new body. Agreements between professional fundraisers, commercial parties and charities will be required to:

· set out any scheme regulating fundraising that the professional fundraiser or commercial party has voluntarily agreed to follow;
· contain details of the measures taken to protect members of the public from aggressive fundraising practises;
· set out how charities will monitor compliance with the above.

The key objective is to protect the public from unreasonably persistent approaches or the application of undue pressure on a person for the purpose of soliciting monies or other property for a charity.

Before a particular fundraising activity is undertaken, it is essential for the charity's trustees to review the methodology and ask themselves whether its adoption by the charity would lead to disapproval by the charity's main constituency and could damage the charity's reputation in the medium-to-long-term. While the possibility of substantial one-off gifts are attractive to a charity, ultimately most charities are underpinned by the small regular gifts of a number of donors, and the reduction in, or loss of, those donors would be immeasurably more damaging to the charity in the long-term.

Perhaps, before undertaking any major fundraising initiative, it would be wise for the charity to work out a strategy and to assess the likely cost of the fundraising exercise over and against the amount of money that can realistically be raised. Such a strategy should also set out the likely areas that the charity will explore to raise funds – for example, grant applications to companies or government, the hiring of a professional fund-raiser or direct mail campaign. The Trustees Annual Report will be expected to contain a statement explaining the approach taken by the charity for the purposes of fundraising for the year in question.

This section highlights five ways in which charities can attract income. As mentioned above, they are not the only ways and for a fuller discussion on the possible avenues open to charities wishing to raise funds, the reader is directed to organisations such as the Institute of Fund Raising, the National Council for Voluntary Organisations and the Charity Commission's guidance on fundraising.

Irrespective of the type of fundraising activity the charity decides to pursue, there are four specific issues that are relevant in each case:

- The purpose of the fundraising should clearly be stated. If the funds are for the general work of the charity then that should be made clear and care taken not to mislead potential donors by implying that the gift will be used for a specific purpose.
- If the fundraising is for a specific project then again that should be made clear to potential donors. Furthermore, the charity needs to say what will happen with any excess funds that have been raised. For example, if the aim is to raise £30,000 to enable the charity to buy a vehicle for its work in Africa, then what happens to the balance if the fundraising actually brings in £40,000? Conversely, if the fundraising only brings in £20,000 will the charity wish to return the money to the donors or to spend it on another project? Again this needs to be made very clear in all communications concerning the fundraising.
- If the fundraising is for a specific purpose, and more funds are raised than is required, and the appeal did not specify what would happen to any surplus funds, then the Charity Commission will need to be consulted as to whether a Scheme will be required to enable the money to be used for other charitable purposes. If insufficient monies have been raised, then the charity has a duty to return any monies given by donors that can be identified. If the donors can be found and do not want their money back, they can sign a disclaimer allowing the funds to be used for the general purposes of the charity. If the donors cannot be found, advertisement may need to be made, following which the Charity Commission would need to be consulted on the possibility of their making a Scheme, to enable the money to be used for other charitable purposes.
- All income received as a result of the fundraising needs to be paid directly to the charity and under control of the charity's trustees. In circumstances where the trustees appoint a fundraising consultant or organisation to lead the particular fundraising project, then the trustees need to be certain that they have ultimate control over the monies that are received from public donations, and ensure that it is paid into a bank account controlled by the trustees.

Five Possible Ways to Attract Income

- **GIFT AID**

  As a registered charity, it is possible to claim back 25p (at current rates) every time an individual donates £1 to the charity, provided the donor is a tax payer.

  The donor must have paid at least as much in Income Tax or Capital Gains Tax in that tax year that equals the amount that the charity wants to claim in Gift Aid.

  The donor makes a Gift Aid declaration and the charity claims the Gift Aid from HMRC on line. It is possible to claim Gift Aid on cash donations of £20 or less even if the charity does not hold a Gift Aid Declaration for the sum given. The total sum that can be claimed in this way is £1,250 per year provided that the sum claimed is not more than ten times the total Gift Aid Claim for that year. For example, if the charity claims £1,000 a year under Gift Aid in respect of cash donations, then the charity would need to have claimed at least £100 in respect of other non-cash Gift Aid payments.

  HMRC insist that in order to be valid, the Gift Aid declaration must explain the donor's position if the donor has paid insufficient tax to cover the tax reclaimed by the charity. If the explanation on the declaration is not worded in the required terms, the Gift Aid declaration is invalid and the charity may need to repay the tax to HMRC. Even if the declaration is valid but the donor has not paid sufficient tax in that tax year, then the charity can be required to repay the Gift Aid claimed on that particular gift (usually done by way of a reduction of a subsequent Gift Aid claim).

  See section 24 Trading.

- **FUNDRAISING FROM THE PUBLIC**

  The Charity Commission has issued detailed guidance on the matter of fundraising from the public and this applies irrespective of whether public fundraising is a small or major part of the charity's income, and whether it is carried out by the charity or a another person or organisation on the charity's behalf. Fundamentally, responsibility for fundraising remains with the trustees who should both be aware of and approve the fundraising strategies to be adopted by the charity. This will include:

- approving the charity's fundraising plan;
- approving the assets and resources to be used;

23

- agreeing how the fundraising will be explained to the charity's supporters and the public;
- supervising the fund-raisers.

There is a Code of Fundraising Practice issued by the Institute of Fundraising and charities are expected to comply with this.

If the charity intends working with a commercial partner in its fundraising strategy then the following steps are suggested:

- The charity should ensure that the commercial partner will be a suitable and appropriate body with which to work. In other words undertaking some due diligence will be important.
- The trustees will be concerned to ensure that the cost of the service will be proportionate to the likely benefit and is otherwise in the best interests of the charity.
- A properly drawn-up written agreement with the commercial partner is important. It will include the requirement that the charity will have proper control of the funds raised and that the charity will be protected against inappropriate risks to its reputation, finance, data and its name/image.
- The charity should have control over any fundraising communications.
- The arrangement must be free from any conflicts of interest that have not been identified and properly dealt with.

If the charity intends to use an online giving platform then useful guidance has been produced by both the Charity Finance Group and the Institute of Fundraising.

Charities will be concerned to avoid fundraising fraud, and suspicious donations, in connection with charitable appeals and collections. The Charity Commission has useful guidance on this subject too. See also section 25.

It will be the responsibility of the charity trustees to ensure full compliance with all laws that apply to the different types and aspects of fundraising, for example:

- **The collection of goods** – this may need a local authority licence or a licence from the Metropolitan Police (for collection in the City of London).
- **Advertising and marketing** – the Advertising Standards Authority regulate all advertisements to ensure they are not misleading, harmful

or offensive. OFCOM regulates the TV and Radio sectors, as well as telecoms and mobiles.

· **Data Protection** – the Information Commissioners' Office regulates data privacy and has issued advice and guidance for charities.

· **Fraud** – Action Fraud provides a contact point for information about fraud and internet crime, and if a charity becomes aware of a charity scam they should report it to Action Fraud as well as the Police, local authority trading standards organisations and the Charity Commission.

· **Tax** – the HMRC works to prevent tax avoidance and evasion.

The reader is advised to consult the websites of the Metropolitan Police or other local Police Force which will have details of the permits/licences required by anyone collecting for charitable purposes, whether on the streets or house-to-house. Failure to comply is an offence which may result in prosecution.

Charities can be fined if their street fundraisers breach the rules designed to protect members of the public. This regime is enforced across the UK by the Public Fundraising Regulatory Association.

Charities proposing to undertake a specific fundraising event, such as a dinner, a performance or an exhibition, may consider that there could be a risk of loss to the charity if the fundraising event was less than successful. It is suggested that if a particular fundraising event is projected to have a turnover that is likely to exceed 25% of the charity's annual income, then it may well be preferable for the activity to be undertaken by a trading subsidiary, rather than the charity itself. While a major concert or dinner may be an enticing way of raising substantial funds, it could be risky and the charity's general funds should not be used as "risk capital" to underpin such events. By undertaking them in a wholly-owned trading subsidiary it may also be possible to obtain outside sponsorship that underpins the event itself rather than risk the charity's own funds.

● **GRANTS**

The making of grants is a favoured way for businesses, large organisations and government agencies to fund charities, no doubt because it enables a degree of accountability and performance to be factored into the arrangement.

The grant-making process usually involves the charity writing a grant proposal and submitting it to the potential grant-making organisations. The grant proposal is akin to a business plan as it will set out:

- the particular issues which the charity intends to address;
- the appropriate explanatory background;
- the charity's proposal for meeting the perceived need or responding to the challenge;
- the timetable and milestones involved in the programme;
- the details of staff and other key facilitators who will be responsible for carrying out the programme;
- a detailed breakdown of the cost involved in the project (in larger projects this may involve cash flow forecasts), the proposed start and finish dates for the project and therefore the length of the term of the grant;
- the measurable outputs;
- the indicators or benchmarks that will indicate the end of the project;
- the indicators that will measure the success of the project.

Potential grant-making donors will expect the grant application to show that it will produce positive outcomes and that it represents good value for the sums that have been requested. The grant-making applications will be assisted if the charity can also demonstrate sustainability and competence in the particular field, perhaps with evidence of good outcomes and results from previous charitable activity.

If the donor decides to award the grant, then effectively it becomes a contract between the donor and the charity. The charity needs to consider carefully the contents of the grant (i.e. the promises and representations it has made). A breach of any of the terms, or a failure to achieve the agreed benchmarks or timetables, can require the charity to repay the grant (either in whole or in part), or allow the grantor to withhold subsequent payments (grants are seldom advanced in one lump sum; they are usually drip-fed over the period of the grant against the agreed timetables and milestones).

Often the grant will require the charity to prepare a report at its conclusion, disclosing the results of the activity. The grant-maker may require this information so that it can, in turn, advertise its generosity. However, from the charity's perspective there may be a significant conflict in their disclosing fully the results of the particular project. For example, if the charity is involved in work among the victims of abuse then the charity may well be bound by its duty of confidentiality not to disclose the sensitive information that it may well have received as a result of the activity for which the grant was made. Yet this may be the precise information that the grant-maker wishes to publish.

Some charities themselves exist to make grants to other charities (grant-making trusts). As mentioned above, grant-making is an effective way for an organisation to have a degree of influence on the charity that is proposing to expend the money through the award of the grant. Grant-making charities need to ensure the following:

- The purposes for which the granted monies are to be used are exclusively charitable.
- There is an appropriate reporting and accountability mechanism in the grant arrangement.
- In certain circumstances a representative of the grant-making charity should be permitted to observe the programme that it has funded and to visit the proposed beneficiaries.
- If at any time they have reason to believe that the funds are not being expended for the purpose for which they were originally granted, then it should take steps to cease funding pending clarification, and conceivably request the return of the funds that may have been paid under a misapprehension. It is not sufficient for the grant-making charity to shrug its shoulders on the basis that "it is all in a good cause".

- **LEGACIES**

Under current legislation if a UK tax payer makes a will in which they leave 10% or more of their net estate to charity they will benefit from a reduced rate of Inheritance Tax, which comes down from 40% to 36%. This estate relief also includes jointly owned assets which pass by survivorship to the other joint owner and assets held in trust that are taxable on the deceased's death.

However, it is important that the 10% test is met – a gift of 9% does not give rise to any relief.

By way of illustration:

- If the net value of the estate is £1,000,000 and a gift of 4% is made to charity (£40,000), this results in £384,000 payable in IHT and £576,000 passing to the family.
- If the net value of the estate is £1,000,000 and a gift of 10% to charity (£100,000) results in only £324,000 payable in IHT, yet the same £576,000 passes to the family.

The charity gets an extra £60,000 at the expense of HMRC!

The success of the nationally-promoted "Make A Will Week" by several charities shows the importance that charities are now giving to gifts that they may receive in people's wills.

There are two types of gift that can come from a will:

- **Legacy** – usually a specific amount or a specific object that is given in the will to the charity.
- **Share of residue** – this means a specific share of whatever is left in a person's estate after legacies, tax, debts and funeral expenses have been paid. Often an exact amount will not be known until the estate has been finally administered.

Once a person leaving a will has died, and that will is admitted to probate and the will itself becomes a public document. There are organisations who read the wills admitted to probate each day, and advise charities if they are mentioned in them. This enables the charity to liaise with either the executors, or the firm of solicitors representing the estate, to ensure that there is an ongoing dialogue during the administration period. This can be especially helpful in circumstances where, for example, the gift to the charity is a portfolio of shares. The charity may wish to sell those shares at an early stage, in order to be sure of the value they will receive. By liaison with the executors during the administration, that request can usually be accommodated. If the shares are "appropriated" to the charity during the administration period, this will avoid the risk of Capital Gains Tax being payable on their sale.

The following points are relevant to charities that are recipients of a legacy or a share of residue:

- It is important to check whether or not the legacy or share of residue is given for the "general purposes" of the charity or for a "specific purpose". If it is for a specific purpose then the charity can only use the gift for that purpose, and if that purpose is no longer attainable by the charity there may be some difficulty. It is suggested that, in such circumstances, the charity should immediately open discussions with the Charity Commission to see if a Scheme can be made to accommodate the change in purpose (see section 28).
- If the deceased person was domiciled in the UK and paying UK tax, then it is likely that the gift to the charity will not suffer an Inheritance Tax

deduction. The charity needs to take particular care in ensuring that it receives all of the monies that it is entitled to in those circumstances. For example, if the estate itself was of a size whereby Inheritance Tax would be payable, then that portion of the estate which is the gift to the charity must be deducted from the gross estate before the Inheritance Tax calculation is made, in order that the charity receives in full the amount of money, or the share of the residue, that has been given to it. The tax calculations in these circumstances are very complex and specialist advice should be always be sought to ensure the charity receives the correct funds.

- The charity is entitled to interest on a legacy from a date twelve months after the date of death through to the date upon which the charity finally receives payment. If interest is paid to the charity net then it should ask for a tax deduction certificate so that it can reclaim the income tax directly from HMRC. This provision also covers interest or dividends that may be payable on the assets themselves during administration, until such time as those assets are sold or realised and the money is paid to the charity. A share of the residue in an estate is paid together with interest earned during the period of administration.

The charity should always ask for a copy of the will. If the charity is receiving a share of the residue, it should also ask to see the finalised estate accounts and should scrutinise those before finally accepting the gift. Charities receiving a share of the residue are, in effect, the ultimate beneficiaries and should satisfy themselves that the charity has got everything that it is entitled to under the will. The charity's own lawyers may need to be involved at this stage in order to consider the final accounts and ensure that the charity's best interests have been served.

Care should also be taken if the executors ask the charity to indemnify them when the final distribution is made. Some zealous solicitors acting for executors ask charities to sign forms of indemnity that are much too wide.

In some cases a charity is given a residual gift in a will but that gift is subject to an intervening life interest. For example, the charity may be left a freehold or leasehold property subject to the occupancy of a surviving spouse for the remainder of their life. Normally the charity would bide its time until the life interest ceased, whereupon the charity would receive the property. It is however possible for the charity to consider buying out the life tenant and in effect accelerating its gift. For example, the life tenant may wish to downsize or indeed may need to go into residential care and need money for that purpose. The charity, after taking specialist legal and actuarial advice, could well agree a figure to buy out the value of the life tenancy. However it is a fairly complicated procedure and it is only applicable in certain circumstances, requiring great care, discretion, sensitivity and wisdom on the part of the charity.

- **TRADING**

Charities may wish to undertake trading activities as a way of raising money. This is called "non-primary purpose trading" and charity law does not permit a charity to carry out non-primary purpose trading themselves on a substantial basis in order to raise funds. It may therefore be possible to undertake non-primary purpose trading by setting up a wholly-owned trading subsidiary. There are special rules to assist charities that wish to carry out a very small amount of non-primary purpose trading in circumstances where all the profits from that trading are used by the charity in furtherance of its charitable Objects. Unless prohibited by its governing document, the charity can carry out small levels of non-primary purpose trading and be exempt from the tax on the profits, providing those profits are applied for the purposes of the charity.

For a further discussion on trading see section 24.

Trading

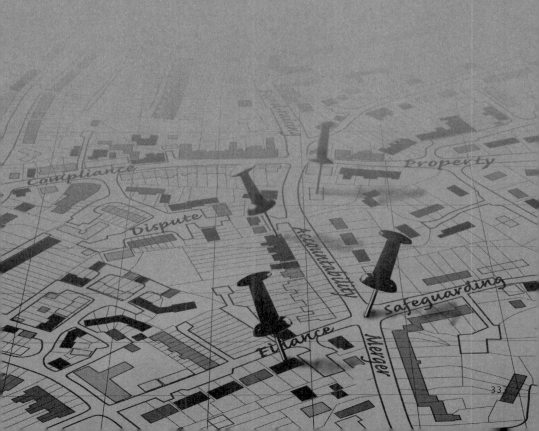

The question that is often asked is, "Can a charity trade?" The short answer is "Yes, but …!"

There are three kinds of trading that are permitted:

· **Primary purpose trading** – this is a trade that is undertaken in the course of carrying out the primary purpose (Objects) of the charity, for example, the provision of education by a charitable school in return for course fees, or a trade in which the work is mainly carried out by the beneficiaries of the charity, (e.g. where a school is set up for people who suffer from a disability and which sells goods or products made by the students).

· **Ancillary trading** – is where the charity carries out a trade that is ancillary to the primary purpose of the charity, for example, the sale of refreshments by a theatre charity to members of its audience.

· **Occasional trading** – where a charity holds the occasional jumble sale or fete at which items are sold.

In circumstances where a charity is trading specifically to generate funds for the charity (as opposed to primary purpose trading), care must be taken to ensure the charity does not become involved in commercial activity that would put the assets of the charity at risk. If it does, then a trading subsidiary should be utilised for this purpose.

Furthermore, the trustees should ensure that, in all decisions they make with regard to the trading subsidiary, the interests of the charity are paramount. This means that as far as the charity is concerned, the interest of the trading subsidiary, its directors, creditors and employees must be secondary to the interests of the charity. If the charity's assets are put at risk for the benefit of the trading subsidiary, its directors, creditors or employees, then the trustees of the charity may be personally liable for any loss or reduction in the value of the charity's assets.

It is important to bear in mind that the exact definition of "trading" for tax purposes is a matter for HMRC to decide, and the fact that the profits of the activity are to be used for a charitable purpose does not in itself prevent that activity from being classified by them as "trading".

"Trading" does not include the sale of goods that have been donated to a charity or the granting of a lease of land or a building by the charity.

If the charity is to be involved in trading that fits one or more of the above categories then there are three important considerations for the trustees to bear in mind:

· **The appropriate vehicle for the trading activity.** Fundamentally, the trustees must consider whether or not the governing document of the charity prohibits trading. If it does not, then the trustees may decide that the trading activity can be safely undertaken by the charity within the terms of its governing document. In other words, the charity itself will be doing the trading. The trustees should consider whether the trading activity will put the other assets of the charity at risk, or whether the trading activity will undermine the charitable nature of the organisation in any way.

If the trustees determine that the trading activity will be best carried out in an organisation that is distinct from the charity itself, then the trustees could either (a) consider contracting with an outside organisation for them to undertake the commercial trade in return for a share of the profits coming back to the charity or, (b) set up a wholly owned trading subsidiary which would exist as a distinct entity from the charity, although ultimately controlled by it. Further consideration of trading subsidiaries is set out below.

· **Tax.** In principle the income or profit that a charity receives from a trading activity is exempt from either corporation tax or income tax providing the trade is:
  · primary purpose trading;
  · ancillary trading; or
  · occasional trading.

However, the exemption only exists where the profits are applied solely for the purposes of charity. Apart from the above, trading profits are liable to tax.
  · Income Tax in the case of an unincorporated charity/CIO;
  · Corporation Tax in the case of a charitable company.

If a charity undertakes trading solely to raise funds then such trading is not supporting the primary purpose of the charity, and such activity is contrary to charity law. Furthermore any profits may well be taxed. (Small scale non-primary purpose trading in order that the profits will be used by the charity, is permitted, provided that the amount of income or profit made is within certain limits – the "small-scale exemption" – see the Charity Commission website for further details.)

Charities are subject to VAT on the sale of goods or services in exactly the same way and same registration levels as a commercial company, unless their trade is either zero-rated or other exemptions apply (see Appendix 1 paragraph 30).

· **Losses.** Any losses that result from non-primary or non-ancillary purpose trading may not be covered from the assets of the charity. Such losses may be regarded as non-charitable expenditure and indeed there could be a breach of trust (potentially exposing the directors/trustees to liability) if the loss were incurred irresponsibly.

Losses from primary purpose or ancillary purpose trading would normally be covered from the assets of the charity.

Trading Subsidiaries

Where the charity wishes to trade to raise monies in order to undertake its charitable purposes generally, or where the trading activity involves an unacceptable level of risk, the charity may decide to set up a wholly-owned subsidiary (a trading subsidiary) to undertake the trading activity. The profits of the trading subsidiary can then be passed back to the charity under the Gift Aid scheme, thereby reducing or eliminating the tax liability of the trading subsidiary each year.

The benefits of using a trading subsidiary include risk management and the ability to separate the commercial activity and charitable work from both an accounting and management perspective. The disadvantages, however, include the additional costs involved in two sets of administration and the possible loss of some charity benefit, such as exemption from Stamp Duty Land Tax on any property acquired by the subsidiary.

Before a trading subsidiary is set up the trustees of the charity need to consider (and take professional advice where applicable) to ensure:

· that, based upon their business plan/forecast, there is a realistic likelihood that the trading activity will be successful;
· that the governing document of the charity allows for it to make an investment in a trading subsidiary.

While the "investment" may initially involve the costs of setting up the trading subsidiary and subscribing for the share capital, nevertheless the charity may also have to fund initial working capital until the trading activity is such that the company can be self-reliant. In such cases the charity must ensure that its own investment powers allow it to make such an investment. Fundamentally, any monies advanced by the charity to the company must be justifiable as a proper investment of the charity's resources, and so the trustees will need to consider whether:

· this is a fair investment for the charity when compared with other forms of investment that could be selected;
· they are satisfied as to the financial viability of the trading subsidiary and its business prospects.

The trustees have a duty to review periodically such an investment to ensure it continues to be in the charity's best interests for the investment to remain in place. In the event that the charity decides to advance working capital which could be in the form of loans and/or guarantees to the trading subsidiary then the following should be borne in mind:

24

· The trustees must minimise any loss to the charity that would result from the trading subsidiary failing. For example, if new working capital is required to go into a company that is operating at a loss, then it is unlikely that the trustees could properly advance the working capital.
· Any monies advanced should normally be on the basis of a secured loan on market terms, and for an agreed length of time and properly determined as such (it is important that the charity's assets are not otherwise tied up in long-term investments in a trading subsidiary).
· It is unwise for a charity to advance monies unsecured or interest-free to a trading subsidiary. If they do, and the subsidiary company fails, the trustees may be personally liable for any loss to the charity's funds.

Great care must be taken if the charity's assets are to be exposed to any kind of guarantee for the liabilities of the trading subsidiary, for example, to guarantee any overdraft or bank loan made to the subsidiary. Professional legal and accounting advice should be taken, particularly as this could undermine the requirement to protect the charity's assets.

There are important tax considerations where monies are invested by a charity in a trading subsidiary, and further taxation advice needs to be taken in each circumstance.

Charities can normally make grants or loans to non-charities (including their wholly-owned trading subsidiaries), providing that the grants are made for purposes that further the charity's own Objects. For example, a church charity may set up a wholly-owned trading subsidiary to undertake a building programme to provide a new church building. Providing that the trading company exists for that purpose, and that appropriate safeguards are in place, the church charity could make a grant or a loan to the trading subsidiary in certain circumstances.

Although it is usual for the profits of the trading subsidiary to be passed back to the charity, either by way of a share dividend or Gift Aid payment, care should be exercised in circumstances where, if the whole of the profit is passed back to the charity, that would leave the trading subsidiary with no funds for working capital. If cash flow difficulties involve the charity needing to lend more monies to the trading subsidiary because the trading subsidiary has little or no substance (as it has Gift Aided its profits to the charity), then such an investment cannot be made under charity law. It may be important therefore for the trading subsidiary to retain some profits and accept the liability to pay corporation tax on them.

Other practical considerations include:

· If the trading subsidiary is to use all or part of the charity's land or property, then there should be a formal lease or licence to cover such use at a commercial rent (Charity Commission consent may be required for this, given that the trading subsidiary and the charity are "connected persons"). See section 11.

· If staff are to be used in common between the trading subsidiary and the charity, then their expense should be costed against the two entities in proportion to the time spent with each.

· It is probably inadvisable to have the same persons serving as trustees of the charity and directors of the trading subsidiary. In such circumstances, it is difficult for them to make decisions objectively from either standpoint. While it may be helpful to have some who are both trustees and directors, there should be preferably no more than 30% of the board for either organisation.

· The trustees of the charity should, on an annual basis, review the relationship between the trading subsidiary and the charity, to ensure that the continued investment is still in the charity's best interests and that the trading subsidiary is actually delivering real benefit to the charity.

- It is important to make the distinction to the general public that the charity and trading subsidiary are two separate entities, perhaps with different names.
- Care should be taken if any of the directors of the trading subsidiary are to be remunerated by that company. If these people are also trustees of the charity then it is unlikely they can be paid by the company, unless specific consent is obtained from the Charity Commission. A "related party" note will be need to be included in the accounts of the charity. See section 6.
- The charity's assets should not be used to settle the debts of the trading subsidiary.

Under no circumstances should a charity lend money to, or otherwise invest in, a trading company (notwithstanding that it is set up to raise money for the charity and actually Gift Aids its profits back to the charity), if the shareholders of that trading company form all or the majority of the trustees of the charity. The benefit for the trustees, by virtue of their shareholding in the trading company, would be interpreted as an indirect benefit that they are receiving from the charity itself. Indeed, in extreme circumstances this activity could result in the charity losing its charitable status.

Fundamentally, the charity should bear in mind that the activities of the trading subsidiary should not in any way be allowed to damage the reputation and standing of the charity itself. As mentioned earlier, the trustees should ensure that, in all decisions they make with regard to a trading subsidiary; the interests of the charity are paramount. It is for the trustees to set the appropriate guidelines within which the charity should relate to the wholly-owned subsidiary.

Charity Shops

These are represented on most high streets today, and it is not only the large national charities that are operating them. In many cases, local charities may set up a shop in their particular area.

Whether the charity sets up the shop in its own name or through a wholly-owned trading subsidiary, there are important issues to bear in mind:

- The trustees should consider carefully as to whether they have the skills and qualifications to take on a commercial venture.

- If the shop itself is to be taken on lease, then the lease will impose obligations on the charity as the tenant, and probably on the trustees of the charity, who could be asked to join in as guarantors. This means that if the shop does not prove to be successful in its trading operation, it may be impossible to close it down without an ongoing liability under the lease, until the lease can be sold on or expires; see section 11.
- A robust business plan will need to be prepared by the charity before the venture is undertaken. Many such shops rely upon goods being donated by members of the public and also on voluntary labour to staff the shop. If the shop is to trade successfully, the charity will need to be satisfied that they can rely both on the supply of goods and labour.
- Research will need to be undertaken on the catchment area around the shop, the competition from other charity shops, the availability of parking etc.

Given that the charity's reputation is borne by the shop, the charity would wish to ensure that a reasonable level of profitability is returned by the shop to the charity and that it is commercially viable. The charity should be able to demonstrate that a sizeable proportion of the gross takings of the shop are actually passed through to the charity itself. Notwithstanding that the goods and labour may be contributed at nil cost, the effort and risk involved in running a shop is scarcely worth it, if the actual contribution that the shop is making to the charity is only a small proportion of the charity's income each year.

The landlord of the shop (if it is rented) together with surrounding shop-keepers are unlikely to be well disposed to the charity if its shop bears all the appearance of a high street version of a jumble sale! The shop needs to be well run and its products imaginatively displayed, if it is both to attract customers and not to have a negative effect on the retail values of the surrounding shops.

Gift Aid and Goods Donated to a Charity

Gift Aid applies only to gifts of money and so if a person donates goods to a charity the charity cannot claim Gift Aid on those goods. That rule is however subject to an important exception.

A charity or its trading company can offer to act as an agent for the individual and sell the goods on their behalf, so that at the time of the sale the proceeds actually belong to the individual. The charity or its trading company can then invite the owner of the goods to donate the sale proceeds to the charity. If the owner does so, then Gift Aid can be claimed by the charity on the net sale proceeds.

Some important conditions apply to this exception:

- It must be clear to potential customers that the shop is selling the goods on behalf of the owner and not the charity.
- The owner of the goods has the right to keep all of the net proceeds but can choose instead to donate all or part of them if they wish.
- Before the net proceeds are donated to the charity, the owner of the goods must make a valid Gift Aid declaration.
- The amount which qualifies for Gift Aid is the net sale proceeds (after any sale commission and VAT are deducted).
- The scheme is only available to tax payers.
- The goods themselves must belong to the individual personally and not any other person.
- The charity must explain these arrangements to the individual donor and the donor should sign a written agreement with the charity (which can be an information sheet or a leaflet setting out the conditions).

24

What Can Go Wrong?

Charities are quite an attractive target for those who would seek to take advantage of the wholesome trusting image of an organisation set up for altruistic purposes but which attracts volunteer labour for much of its activity.

However there is much that can potentially go wrong and charity trustees and managers will find in this section details of some of the more common pitfalls. While this is not an exhaustive list it is nevertheless indicative of the major areas that pose risk.

Fraud and Money Laundering

Charities can be an easy target for criminals. The National Fraud Authority's 2013 data shows that 10% of charities reporting an income of more than £100,000 a year had fallen victim to fraud in the previous year. The National Fraud Authority report that the UK charity sector loses around £1.3 billion, or 2.4%, of annual charity income a year.

The risk is not only from those outside; a fraud can be perpetrated just as

In the light of this potential risk and in order that a charity is not the victim of fraud or another form of deception, its internal systems need to be robust to ensure it has established basic systems of control which will identify unusual gifts or activity. In particular:

- The charity should not accept an individual cash gift of more than £1,000 unless a senior member of the charity can identify and personally vouch for the donor.
- The charity should not disclose its bank details or pass blank letterheads to any outside party unknown to it who request that information for the purpose of making a gift. The real aim of a fraudster is often to get the bank details (to empty the account) or to get letterheads (in order to commit further frauds).
- A gift from an unknown source that is conditional upon a portion of those monies being paid on to a third party, should not be accepted.
- If a party wishes to make a gift to the charity that is out of all proportion to the charity's normal income levels, steps should be taken to verify the authenticity of the "donor" and the source of the funds, before the gift is accepted.
- If possible a member of the board of trustees (preferably with a legal or accounting background) should be the final arbiter of whether or not an "unusual" gift is accepted.

easily by those who are working within the charity. Neither is it a risk that only affects large charities.

Examples of fraud have included:

- outright theft of cash or assets from the charity;
- fraudulent investment advice;
- advanced fee fraud;
- falsification of records ;
- bribes and other "payments";
- misuse of charity credit card;
- claiming over-inflated/non-existent or inappropriate expenses;
- false invoices with fake supplier identities in respect of non-existent goods or services;
- unauthorised fundraising;
- credit card scams;
- fake grant applications.

In addition, charities are now the target of potential money launderers who would seek to use the good name and reputation of the charity to "wash" dirty money and legitimise it. Such monies can be the proceeds of crime, terrorism or drug dealing. I have come across the following examples:

- The charity should not put over-reliance on any one member of the charity in matters concerning finance. Any newly recruited staff, who will be handling money, should be subject to proper reference checks before they are hired.
- The trustees should receive adequate management information. Regular management accounts that are supported with copies of bank statements should be provided.
- If the charity has an investment portfolio then the internal monitoring of that portfolio (even if it is managed by outside professional managers) needs to be the responsibility of two senior people in the charity.

- Staff should be adequately trained and the systems within the charity should develop and grow in line with the growth of the charity itself.
- The charity should have appropriate controls on its IT system to prevent cyber-crime; furthermore laptops/mobile phones containing the charity's financial details should not be operated on public wi-fi systems (for example, in a coffee shop). Fraudsters have been known to be present to thereby gain access to sensitive accounting details.
- There should be appropriate safeguards relating to the hiring of agency or temporary staff.

25

- a Christian charity being offered a charity donation of $1.5 million from a donor via a firm of "lawyers" overseas, provided that the charity signed an agreement and remitted "costs" of £39,000 to the donor;
- a UK church being offered a large sum of money towards its redevelopment programme, from a source overseas, if it agreed to pass a sizeable proportion of that gift on to an unconnected named person, based in another country;
- a charity being advised by a firm of "solicitors" that it was the recipient of a legacy which would be paid to it in conjunction with a branch of a well-known church. Enquiries showed that the "solicitors" did not exist and that the church had had its database plagiarised and its name was being used to "legitimise" certain activity;
- the Foundation for New Era Philanthropy in the United States collapsed in 1995 owing some $135 million. It had raised some $500 million from 1,100 donors, promising them to double their initial investment within three months by matching each donation with contributions from secret donors, thereby doubling the amount of the gift that could then be given to the charitable work. The programme was exposed to be a sham and approximately 180 Christian groups, colleges and seminaries invested in New Era and lost considerable sums of money.

Remember the old adage: "If a gift looks too good to be true – it probably is!"

In addition, when the charity is working overseas, monies sent overseas and administered there will heighten the potential risk of fraud. Care needs to be exercised in the dispersal of funds overseas, to ensure that "partners" with whom the charity operates, are not themselves operating as a front for illegal activity. See also section 21.

Remember that the charity operates under the laws of England and Wales, and the trustees are ultimately answerable in this country. In some regions of the world the attitude to fraud and deception may be a little more relaxed than UK charities and their staff may be anticipating.

The Charity Commission details some of the methods whereby criminal groups would seek to use charities to further their objectives, these include:

- using charities to smuggle people into countries illegally;
- using residential schools as possible recruitment and training centres for terrorist activity;

- using charities that provide facilities for young people as areas in which they can organise and recruit volunteers;
- using charities as a base to spread propaganda

An offer of a donation (in cash or otherwise), whereby the charity can receive the interest on the capital, on condition that it returns the capital to the donor at the end of specified period, should be very carefully analysed before being accepted. (Sometimes the donation may be in foreign currency with the condition that the capital is returned in sterling).

Finally if charity trustees, or their senior management, have suspicions as to the true intentions of a potential donor (i.e. they think that they may be involved in criminal activity of any kind), then they must promptly report full details of this to the Police and to the Charity Commission.

Trustees are responsible for ensuring that they manage the risk of financial abuse; sound financial controls, good management and oversight are vital to ensure this.

The Charity Commission publishes some helpful guidance in the form of a check list covering internal financial controls for charities.

25

Lack of Governance

In section 5 governance was defined and the reason for it explained. It therefore follows that if the charity does not have good governance, then it is likely to suffer, be it from a lack of direction, policy, long-term strategy or shared vision. If the key staff and volunteers of the charity are to be empowered and motivated to carry out their assigned role in an environment where the charity suffers from lack of good governance, it is likely that the staff and volunteers will become a group of individuals each doing "their thing" with little or no organisation, team work or shared goal.

Many of the issues that cause damage and disunity in a charity can be traced back to lack of governance, and, although in faith-based organisations many staff and volunteers will claim they are working for a "higher reward", the charity is unlikely to be sustainable in the long term without the critical issues of governance being addressed.

Depending on whether you are a trustee or a worker in a charity, you may care to ask yourself the following questions:

If you are a trustee: "Would I be satisfied in committing my long-term career to working for this organisation?" or, **if you are a worker**: "If I were a trustee would I be comfortable in governing this organisation?"

There is a consensus that better governance results in better delivery of service and, therefore, improved accountability to beneficiaries, donors and other stakeholders.

Private Benefit

The point has been made earlier that charity trustees should not personally benefit from their position as a trustee. There are of course exceptions to this rule, but they are closely controlled. For example:

· If the governing document permits it, a trustee (e.g. a Chief Executive or minister, and maybe more than one) may, if it is in the best interest of the charity, be employed by the charity or remunerated for a service provided to it; see section 6.

· A professional person who is also a trustee (e.g. solicitor or accountant), may charge professional fees for specific work done at the charity's request; see also section 6.

· A charity trustee may rent a property to the charity, but the terms of the rental must be supported by professional valuation advice and agreed between the trustee and the remainder of the board.

The Charities Act 2011 underlines the fact that charities must exist for the public benefit. There have been occasions where the Charity Commission has closed down a charity and removed it from the Register on the basis that the level of public benefit (as opposed to the private benefit to the trustees and members) is insignificant. (NB: this would not apply to a small church with a small membership; provided that the church keeps its doors open to the general public.) Fundamentally, it is a question of degree and the test is "does the organisation exist primarily for the advantage of its members, or is the membership an administrative convenience or merely an effective way of delivering charitable benefits?"

The question is sometimes asked as to whether a church can legitimately provide social activities that may be enjoyed free of charge by those attending the church. For example can a church provide a harvest supper free of charge to its members or are they getting personal benefit? Given that social activities are usually a by-product of the main purpose of the church (the advancement of religion), normally such social activities are merely ancillary to the main religious activity, and provided that the private benefit is not the main purpose of the charity, it is unlikely to be a problem for the Charity Commission. However, as set out in section 3 HMRC is taking a contrary view!

Charity trustees should bear in mind that where one or more trustees are benefitting in some financial way from the charity, there arises the possibility for a conflict of interest. Where a conflict of interest exists, there is a danger that decisions may not be made on the basis of what is in the best interests of the charity, but rather what may or may not benefit one or more of the trustees. It is essential that the trustees should develop a protocol for the disclosure of potential conflicts of interest that individual trustees may have, so that the trustee affected is excluded from certain discussions and decisions. See also section 6.

The charity's board of trustees are advised to consider adopting a code of conduct which covers the trustees' behaviour and relationship towards the charity. The NCVO produce a model contract for charity trustees and all trustees should sign this and ensure that new trustees sign it as well.

In section 6 the point was made that directors and trustees owe a fiduciary duty of care and skill towards the charity, and they must also act in what they honestly believe to be the best interest of the charity. Failure to observe this fiduciary duty can result in directors/trustees incurring serious personal liability.

In the event that the director/trustee is involved in a property transaction with the charity, then special provisions apply and the charity must take legal advice at the first possible opportunity. This governs not only a transaction between a trustee and the charity but also one between a connected person and the company. See section 11.

Lack of Independence

For an organisation to be a registered charity, it must be independent (i.e. it exists to carry out its stated charitable Objects and not for the purpose of advancing any decisions, guidance or proposals for any other person or organisation). Furthermore, charity trustees must have an unfettered discretion to reach decisions that they believe (on the basis of professional advice where necessary), are exclusively in the best interests of the charity.

It follows that any attempt by an outside party to control or overly influence the decision-making process of the charity must be resisted. This principle can cause conflict in cases where the direction and policy for an individual charity may be coming from another "branch" of the organisation that is registered in the UK or overseas.

A review of the reports of the Charity Commission Inquiries shows instances where it have found evidence that a UK charity has been "controlled" by an outside organisation, notwithstanding that the outside organisation may have similar purposes or contribute financially towards the UK charity, or have been set up by a common founder.

The ways in which UK and overseas organisations may "partner" towards a common objective are set out in section 10. However, the fundamental principle is that the trustees of a UK charity must not be fettered in any way in reaching their decisions.

In cases where an outside body seeks to appoint one of more of the trustees, then that trustee must not exist to promote the interests of the body appointing them. A funding body may try to insist upon appointing a trustee in order to protect its interest and as a condition of providing the funding. If the charity agree to this, the trustee must ensure that he works with the board to make decisions in the best interest of the charity. Each charity must only act exclusively in the best interests of the charity.

Funding Failure

Given that most charities' income can be dependent upon many factors outside their control, it follows that charities will at some point or other face financial uncertainty. If a charity finds itself in financial difficulties, it is important that the trustees take prompt and careful action before the risk of insolvency and potential personal liability becomes unavoidable.

A charity can be deemed insolvent when:

· either it is unable to pay its debts as they fall due; and/or
· where the value of its assets is less than the amount of its liabilities (taking into account its possible and prospective liabilities).

In addition, directors of charitable companies are subject to the provisions of the Insolvency Acts 1986 and 2000. Those Acts do not specifically apply to unincorporated charities, but, for the purposes of this discussion, trustees of unincorporated charities should apply the same standards as if they were directors of a charitable company.

In principle, each trustee of a charity shares responsibility for a liability created on behalf of that charity, so long as the decision to incur the liability was taken at a properly convened meeting. In the normal course of events, trustees can expect to be reimbursed from the charity's assets in respect of those liabilities that have been properly incurred. In circumstances where a trustee has retired from the board, they can still expect to be indemnified from the assets of the charity, unless the liability arises from a contract of employment. (Any claim against the trustees under a contract of employment is against the trustee body at the time the claim is made and not against the trustee body that existed when the contract started).

In the event there are insufficient assets in the charity to meet the liability, then the trustees may have to meet the debts and liabilities personally.

Each year when the charity's accounts are independently examined or audited (depending on the level of income), those undertaking the examination or audit will apply a test for solvency and then state whether or not the charity has sufficient resources available to meet its immediate and short-term liabilities. If the examiner/auditor advises that the charity does not pass that simple test, then they may refuse to sign off the accounts until or unless steps are taken to address the issue. Given, however, that as accounts are usually prepared in arrears (i.e. some months after the end of the financial year), the charity may have received a large gift or received good income during the months following the end of the financial year. The auditor can insert a note to that effect (known as a "Post Balance Sheet Event") in the accounts to explain why he considers that the charity is still solvent.

The charity may hold Restricted Funds (i.e. monies given for a specific purpose) and while these will boost the cash balance, they cannot be used for general expenditure and therefore, notwithstanding their existence on the balance sheet, the charity may still be insolvent as it cannot pay its ordinary liabilities as they fall due.

Insolvency can arise over a period of time (in which case the trustees should have been alert to the tell-tale signs of falling income or rising expenditure), or it may happen suddenly where a major grant is withdrawn. The former may be preventable, the latter less so.

Ultimately, it is for the trustees constantly to monitor the overall financial performance of the charity, and to this end:

- regular financial management reports (in an understandable format) should be provided to them;
- the preparation and agreement of an annual budget and cash flow projection at the beginning of each financial year should be undertaken. This projection should be regularly monitored throughout the year in question against the actual income received;
- if the charity is too heavily dependent on one or two funding sources then urgent steps will need to be taken to create other funding streams, so that the charity is not prejudiced if one or more of the main funding sources dries up;
- any long-term contracts that the charity has should be reviewed, and if possible renegotiated, to ensure the charity can withdraw from them should the need arise. For example, if the trustees feel that the charity's financial performance is diminishing year on year they may decide that new staff are hired on annual contracts, rather than open ended ones;
- any long-term contracts that the charity is proposing to enter into (a lease on a property or long-term loan), should be undertaken only once the charity has taken independent professional advice. In the case of a charity taking up a loan, it will usually be necessary for the trustees to receive independent advice from a person suitably qualified, and the advice will address the issues of the suitability of the funding source for the charity and its likely impact on the charity's cash flow etc;
- the charity needs to make proper provision for VAT, PAYE and National Insurance. These are statutory liabilities, and if the charity fails, the trustees may be required personally to make good any shortfall. It is certainly not good practice for the charity to withhold payment of one or more of these statutory taxes in order to improve cash flow;
- the trustees should ensure that restricted funds are not spent on unrestricted matters. This can amount to a breach of trust and the trustees can be required to personally make good the shortfall;
- a prudent board of trustees would adopt a reserves policy. This involves setting aside a sum of money that would be sufficient to fund the day-to-day operations of the charity for, say, a period of three to six months. By having this buffer, it means that if sources of funding cease, the charity will still have sufficient funds to achieve an orderly wind-down of its activities.

Specific steps that the charity can take to reduce the potential for financial exposure where income is consistently short of the required level include:

· reducing the charity's expenditure to a level below the sustainable income ;
· launching an emergency appeal (donors would need to be made aware that new funds will be used to pay the charity's debts);
· attempting to renegotiate contracts and other commitments;
· transferring some of the activities of the charity to another like-minded charity;
· considering a full merger of the charity with another charity;
· raising interest-free loans from the charity's supporters;
· re-mortgaging the charity's main asset to release funds;
· seeking the Charity Commission's consent to borrow from any Permanent Endowment funds that the charity possesses;
· entering into an informal arrangement with the charity's creditors to either defer payment of a debt or reduce the size of the claim. Such an arrangement needs to be made legally binding on the creditors, and therefore professional advice needs to be obtained.

If, notwithstanding the foregoing, the trustees are faced with an insolvency situation i.e. the charity cannot pay its debts as they fall due and there is no reasonable prospect of the situation improving, then the following steps need to be taken:

· professional advice needs to be sought from the charity's accountant and from a Licenced Insolvency Practitioner. The advice received should be preserved in writing and any remedial steps strictly followed.
· the trustees should take steps to minimise the potential loss by reducing or stopping some of the charity's activities;
· the trustees may take the decision to wind up an unincorporated charity. Directors of a charitable company will need to place the company into liquidation (in conjunction with the Licensed Insolvency Practitioner).
· If the charity winds up or ceases operations, the Charity Commission must be informed so that it can remove the charity from the Register.

In the case of a charitable company, it may be possible to enter into a voluntary agreement with the company's creditors, for them to accept either a delayed or reduced payment; again, an Insolvency Practitioner or other professional needs to be involved.

By and large, the Charity Commission does not become involved in issues relating to restructuring or refinancing of charities. The Charity Commission will certainly take an interest, as the charity Regulator, in order to find out the reasons for insolvency. Where there is a suspicion of mismanagement or maladministration, it may decide to open an Inquiry. It also has the power to appoint an Interim Manager where it feels the present trustees have not acted properly or where it perceives there to be a risk to the charity's property. The Interim Manager serves in the role of a trustee for the duration of their appointment and, ultimately, this often ends in the appointment of new trustees who will take the charity forward.

In circumstances where the charity has launched a specific fundraising project, for example, to buy a new building or undertake a particular activity in furtherance of the charity's Objects, and that fundraising campaign does not raise sufficient money then the issue of what happens to the monies raised is dealt with in section 23. However, notwithstanding the failure to raise the appropriate level of funding, the charity may be contractually obliged to fulfil a contract for which it no longer has the resources. For example, it may have exchanged contracts on the lease or purchase of a property or it may have hired a venue and undertaken publicity in anticipation of a major project. The question, therefore, is how can this liability be settled? If the charity has sufficient general funds, then potentially they can be applied towards settling the liability. If the charity has insufficient funds then its options would include:

· trying to raise a short-term loan or re-mortgage an asset;
· attempting to negotiate to withdraw from the contract – even if agreed damages are paid;
· issuing an appeals letter to its major donors.

If the potential liability is out of all proportion to the charity's assets then that in turn may result in an insolvency situation. It is recommended that professional advice, together with advice from the Charity Commission, is sought.

Disallowed Expenditure

See section 3.

Tainted Charity Donations

These apply in circumstances where a donor (or someone connected to the donor) enters into an arrangement to make a donation to a charity from which the donor will obtain financial advantage.

The Tainted Charity Donation Rules do not apply to:

· a donation to a charity where no additional arrangements are being entered into;
· a donation under Gift Aid that is within the Gift Aid benefit limits;
· where the benefit of the donation has already been taken into account in the calculation of the relief due for the donation to the charity of shares or property.

The Tainted Charity Donation Rules will ensure that the usual tax reliefs are not available because the donor has entered into an arrangement with the charity to obtain a financial advantage from that charity in return for the donation.

There are three conditions that must be met before a donation to a charity can be regarded as a tainted one:

· The donation to the charity and the arrangements entered into by the donor are connected.
· The main purpose of entering into the arrangement is for the donor or someone connected to the donor to receive a financial advantage directly or indirectly from the charity.
· The donation is not made by a company that is wholly owned by the charity.

The Tainted Charity Donation Rules have largely replaced the previous Substantial Donor Rules.

HMRC

One of the main advantages of charity registration is the tax breaks that are available. Relief from income tax, corporation tax, capital gains tax and stamp duty tax are a valuable contribution to the charity's activities – to say nothing of Gift Aid. With the benefit, however, comes an obligation on the charities and that is to ensure that all of their income is expended for purposes that are exclusively charitable.

HMRCs monitor charities and their expenditure to ensure that monies are expended for purposes that are exclusively charitable. In Section 1 of this book, the thirteen main charitable purposes (Objects) are set out. Broadly, HMRC will be concerned to ensure that each item of expenditure by a charity is in furtherance of at least one of those Objects (it does not necessarily have to be the Object(s) for which the particular charity exists!).

If HMRC subsequently finds that a charity has expended its resources on items that are not exclusively charitable, then they treat such expenditure as non-charitable expenditure and can recover tax at the appropriate rate on the sum expended. They do this by way of scrutinising a charity's accounts once they are filed, and will write to the charity seeking clarification on particular items of expenditure before drawing a conclusion.

For charities that exist to advance religion, HMRC considers that such definition includes:-

- the provision of places of worship;
- raising awareness and understanding of religious beliefs and practices;
- carrying out religious devotional acts;
- carrying out missionary and outreach work.

HMRC is of the opinion that advancement of the Christian faith does not include acts that are simply in keeping with expected Christian behaviour, such as generosity of spirit.

Some of the areas that HMRC takes particular interest in include:

- **Employment** – in addition to reviewing employment records, they are particularly interested in any payments that are made to volunteers – see Section 15.
- **Expenditure** – areas such as travel expenses, loans to staff, trading for non-primary purpose, as well as welfare payments made to needy members of a Church have all attracted their attention and, in some cases, been disallowed for charitable expenditure.
- **Money sent overseas** – for a fuller treatment on this subject please see Section 21.
- **Accounting records** – missing vouchers, incomplete documentation or lack of adequate explanation have all led to items of expenditure being disallowed.
- **Entertaining** – the provision of meals, which is an integral part of a religious activity (for example, an alpha meal) would be allowable as a

charitable expense. A party for church members using the charity's funds would not.

- **Sale of merchandise** – sale of recordings of the church's service would be regarded as within the purposes of the charity. Selling merchandise such as T-shirts or baseball caps would not.

In the event that a charity's income is spent on non-charitable purposes, then the tax exemptions are removed and the charity must pay tax on an amount of income equivalent to the value of the non-charitable payments.

HMRC have also demonstrated a reluctance to grant tax relief on expenditure that is partly for charitable purposes and partly for non-charitable purposes.

Other areas of non-charitable expenditure can include:

- a loan to a third party (e.g. a member of staff);
- payment to an overseas body where the charity has not taken reasonable steps to ensure the payment will be applied for charitable purposes (see Section 21);
- trading income from non-primary purpose trading;
- payments not specifically authorised by the terms of the charity's governing document;
- payments made that are specifically prohibited by the charity's governing document.

If, as a result of a review of a charity's accounts HMRC decide to investigate further, they will instigate a compliance check. This can be done either over the telephone or in writing, and HMRC will inform the charity exactly what they are checking. During the period of a compliance check, the charity should not stop sending returns or making payments to HMRC when they are due, although they may find that HMRC suspend Gift Aid claims until the outcome of the compliance check.

If HMRC find that the compliance check has not satisfactorily answered their questions, then they could decide to open a formal inquiry. Again, they will write to the charity and state their intention to do so and set out the areas they are interested in.

At this point, it is recommended that the charity should appoint a professional advisor to liaise with HMRC, particularly as the outcome of such an inquiry could be very expensive as far as the charity is concerned.

If, as a result of the formal inquiry HMRC decide that there are items of expenditure, made by the charity for non-charitable purposes, then their powers include:

- the ability to charge a penalty of up to 100% of the sums in issue;
- a claim for back tax together with interest on that sum;
- suspension of Gift Aid;
- extrapolation – this means that if, for example, HMRC find that 5% of a charity's expenditure in the year in question was for non-charitable purposes, and then they can claim that the same percentage would apply to other years as well. Bearing in mind HMRC can go back seven years in their investigations, it means that the payment that the charity may have to make for the year in question could be multiplied by seven.

Steps that a charity could take to minimise non-charitable payments being made would include:

- enacting specific policies, binding on all members of the charity (trustees included), concerning expenditure;
- internal control systems;
- checking before making grants and to overseas bodies;
- refusal to make any payments without proper and complete vouchers/ receipts;
- undertaking a risk management analysis.

Malpractice

Whether the trustees know or suspect that the charity has been affected by malpractice (of whatever form) they should:

- meet together and agree that there is an issue to investigate;
- appoint an independent professional to investigate the matter (usually an accountant or lawyer). Such investigation to include how the situation arose and the likely impact of it on the charity;
- report the matter immediately to the Charity Commission (and forward it a copy of the investigator's findings);
- consider whether the matter should also be reported to the police or other statutory bodies e.g. HMRC;
- proceed in the light of the advice received;

- provided that the effects of the malpractice can be ring-fenced from the general activity of the charity, take any necessary steps to prevent a reoccurrence.

Failure to Comply with Legislation

This section should be read in conjunction with section 26 "Risk Management".

The trustees (whether the charity is an unincorporated charity, CIO, or a charitable company) are liable for a breach of trust that results from the breaking of the law. Simply put, a breach of trust occurs when the trustees act in a way that is not authorised by the charity's governing document or permitted by charity law. For example: engaging in unlawful activity; spending charity monies on activities that are outside of the charity's stated objective or entering into contracts and liabilities against professional advice.

It is for the Charity Commission to decide whether or not to order a charity trustee to reimburse the charity for a loss that may have arisen as a result of a breach of trust. Under the Charities Act 2011 the Charity Commission has power to relieve a trustee or auditor from liability for breach of trust, if it is satisfied that the trustee has acted honestly and reasonably and therefore ought fairly be to excused for the breach of trust. However, that relief does not apply to any personal contractual liability of a charity trustee. So, for example, if the trustee joins in a finance agreement to purchase a vehicle in the name of and for the charity, yet the governing document did not allow for such agreement to be entered into, then while the Charity Commission could excuse the trustee on the basis that he acted honestly and reasonably, he will still be personally liable as a signatory to the finance contract if the charity has insufficient funds to make the payments.

Trustees will also be personally liable for any payments that are due under legislation and for which the charity cannot pay (see above with regard to PAYE, National Insurance etc.).

Fundamentally, it can be stated that if charities do not comply with current legislation, they risk not only the sanction that non-compliance will bring but also the possibility of an injunction and claim for damages. These in turn attract the attention of the Charity Commission, which then leads to an Inquiry and the possibility of sanctions being imposed. All of which is extremely time consuming, costly and ultimately damaging to the charity, its

25

reputation and the achievement of its charitable Objects.
Remember ignorance of the law is no defence.

Governance Dispute

See section 5.

Compliance

See section 8.

SECTION 26

Risk Management

Identification and Management

Risk management has been defined as the process of measuring or assessing risk, and developing strategies to manage it.

Fundamentally, charities exist for the public benefit, and are often involved in innovative and practical activities in order to facilitate change for the better in the desired area of activity; some of these activities may be deemed "risky". In the commercial world, company and business spending is often constrained by the overriding need to make profit, whereas charities exist to spend their resources to achieve their charitable Objects.

Charities do get involved in activities that others, for whatever reason, have decided to avoid. Indeed, many of today's well-known charitable organisations who have been, and are, so effective in making change, started off with the founders taking risks in order to address the issues on which they had decided to focus.

Risk, however, is not necessarily something to be avoided (even in today's risk-adverse culture). Rather, charity trustees need to be encouraged to focus on the nature of the risk which its very mission requires it to face, if it is to be true to its charitable Objects.

While all charities face risk (albeit to varying degrees), the trustees and key workers in the charity should engage in a process of risk analysis, maybe by Spotting the risk, Assessing the risk and then Solving the risk, S.A.S.

Spot It!

The following is a list of examples of possible areas of risk that affect charities today. Each charity will need to address those that are most relevant to its own situation. The list is not exhaustive.

Financial
- A drop in income over a sustained period;
- withdrawal of funding by a major grant-maker;
- lack of return on investments;
- failure of a charitable project or a trading subsidiary;
- fraud, corruption, or money laundering;
- HMRC disallowance of expenditure;
- Gift Aid investigation.

Governance and Management
- Loss of the Chief Executive or other "key" leader or manager;
- dispute amongst board members

or other failure by the board to give clear leadership and direction;

- conflict of interest;
- Charity Commission/HMRC Inquiry;
- qualified Audit Report;
- IT systems failure;
- a claim from a third party;
- failure to adapt to the changing needs of the charity's beneficiaries;
- Health and Safety issue;
- Data Protection breach.

Staff Issues

- Key members of staff in dispute or leaving;
- employment tribunal claim brought by a staff member;
- breach of Health and Safety/Equal Opportunities/Data Protection or other legislation;
- employee/trustee theft;
- Safeguarding breach.

Miscellaneous

- Exposure to foreign currency fluctuation;
- kidnap or ransom of overseas staff worker;
- overseas government change of law or policy;
- underfunded pension commitments;
- adverse publicity.

Assess It!

Many charities undertake a SWOT analysis (strengths, weaknesses, opportunities and threats) for the charity as whole. Fundamentally, it is important to assess the magnitude of the risk in order to decide whether it can be managed, accepted or needs to be avoided.

Part of the assessment process is to decide both the severity of the potential loss and also the probability that the loss will occur. For example, if a charity was attempting to assess the implication of losing a major grant, the potential severity of the loss would be fairly easy to ascertain, but the probability of it happening may be more difficult to project. In these circumstances, the charity should make an educated guess in order to implement a risk management programme. It is important that the "guess" and the reasons that were considered in arriving at that guess, are recorded in the charity's records should they ever need to be referred to in the future.

Best practice would be for a charity board to undertake a risk management assessment, and given the diversity of most charities, this assessment is likely to result in the revealing of several areas of risk which will then need to be assessed. Once a definitive list has been produced then that will need to be prioritised, so that the charity does not spend all of its time in risk management to the detriment of its pursuit of its charitable Objects!

A sample risk management matrix is set out in Appendix 3 together with a summary work plan, enabling the level of risk to be assessed on a scale of 1 (low) to 5 (high) in both likelihood of occurrence and severity of impact. This, in turn, will enable the charity to prioritise attention to those areas that pose an unacceptable risk yet, at the same time, make provision to deal with those that are of lesser risk, albeit still important.

Solve It!

The solution to the risk, once it has been "spotted" and "assessed", can be broken down in to four main categories.

- **AVOIDING THE RISK**

  While avoidance may be the ultimate answer to all risks, it can also mean losing out on the potential gain to the charity that accepting the risk may have permitted. That said, however, there are some risks that the charity may decide are just too great for it to accept safely.

  A review of the cases where the Charity Commission has intervened in the affairs of a charity, will reveal examples of charities accepting a risk that they would have been (albeit in hindsight) better advised to avoid.

  It should be emphasised here that each charity is different (because each is made up of a unique combination of people, resources and opportunities). Therefore, the fact that one charity succeeds in a risky venture, does not necessarily mean that another charity will be similarly successful, if it replicates that charitable activity. Each charity must undertake and execute its own risk management strategy based on the particular circumstances that present themselves to it.

  There are some occasions when the charity just cannot decide whether it should proceed with a level of risk or not. Short of deciding the matter by drawing lots, this is surely a situation where independent professional advice should be taken by the trustees and that advice followed.

  An example of risk avoidance could include a charity deciding not to work in a particular country in view of the risks to its personnel or from government interference; or of a church not proceeding with the acquisition of a property, in circumstances where the church was concerned that the level of income needed to repay a large loan could be affected by a fluctuation in the church's attendance.

- **REDUCING THE RISK**

The charity may decide to accept a level of risk but put in place steps to reduce the level of risk or the likely implication of a loss. An example of this (using the above illustration), would be the church deciding to proceed with its property acquisition, having succeeded in securing a commercial tenant for part of the building, that would bring in an income for a set period to assist the church to meet its mortgage repayments.

- **RETAINING THE RISK**

This involves the charity reaching a definite conclusion that it could accept the risk concerned, having calculated that, even if the event itself took place, the organisation would be able to survive.

Using the above example of the church property project, retaining the risk would be where the church had decided that, even if its income fell during the period of the loan, then it would have the resources (or perhaps the trustees and key workers would agree to ensure it had the resources), to make the loan repayments for a certain period of time. During this period, the trustees would decide whether the loan itself could be restructured over a longer period (thereby reducing the monthly payments) or whether it would be preferable to sell the building to clear the indebtedness.

- **TRANSFERRING THE RISK**

This is where the risk itself is actually transferred to a third party. An obvious example is where the charity can take out insurance to offer a level of indemnity, in the event of the risk materialising. In today's insurance market it is possible to insure a good many risks, including kidnap and ransom, theft of the charity's assets, indemnity for trustees against a claim, and legal expenses, as well as the standard policies that cover fire and damage to properties, public liability, etc. Banks offer a facility to "hedge" likely exposure to currency fluctuations, which is an important issue for charities who move significant amounts of money overseas on a regular basis.

Once the charity has prepared a risk management matrix, this needs to be reviewed on a regular basis, at the very least annually, as some risks pass and are replaced by new ones.

Ultimately, it is considered part of the trustee board's role to ensure that an adequate risk assessment and management programme is in place. In medium to large charitable organisations, the trustees are unlikely to be involved in the day-to-day implementation of it, as this will be delegated down to senior management. In small to medium-sized charities they may well have a more "hands on" approach.

However, risk management is not something that is limited to the trustees and/or senior management. It is considered that everyone in the charity (even the volunteers), needs to be aware of these issues and to participate in the implementation of the risk management programme of the charity.

The current SORP requires the trustees of charities with a gross income of £250,000 per annum, to report on risk management in their Annual Report, which forms part of the charity's audited accounts, (trustees of smaller charities are encouraged to make a similar statement as a matter of best practice). The Charity Commission will be looking for such a report to clarify that:

· the trustees acknowledge that they are responsible for risk management;
· an overview of the risk identification process has been adopted;
· major risks that have been identified, have been assessed;
· adequate systems have been established by the charity to address those risks (avoidance/reduction/retention/transfer).

The charity's Auditors are not required to formally audit the risk management statement in the accounts, although if they become aware (from the work done during the audit), of some inconsistencies in what the trustees are saying in their Annual Report, they may need to qualify their Audit Report, if their reservations on the risk management statement cannot be resolved!

The Charity Commission provides some helpful examples of trustees' Annual Reports which are available via their website.

Other Steps in Risk Management

Other practical steps that charities can take to assist in the risk management process include:

· **A legal audit** – a review by a firm of lawyers experienced in representing charitable organisations will address areas within the charity that are not covered by the normal financial audit. Many charities have found such a legal audit of great assistance in clarifying the main areas of risk. The charity can then follow through with their own risk assessment and management. A review by an external organisation invariably reveals things that, although clear to them, have been less than obvious to those within the charity.

- **Professional advice** – independent professional advice is essential when charities are considering activities which are outside of their normal day-to-day functions. A good example that faces many charities concerns a project, perhaps, to acquire or develop a property for the charity's use. Even if the charity board has representatives of the surveying, architectural, legal or accounting professions thereon, it is considered wise for the charity to bring in independent professional advice from outside on such matters. It is not unknown for there to be instances where in the enthusiasm of the charity to acquire or develop a building for its use, decisions are made which are then substantially challenged by the independent advisors, who are subsequently retained!
- **Trustee Indemnity Insurance** – while not a "get out of jail free card", it is considered essential by many trustee boards to provide a level of indemnity for the trustees against the risk of personal liability arising from breach of trust, together with the likely legal costs that would be involved in responding to a challenge. It should be noted, however, that such insurance does not protect charity trustees from all types of personal liability.

Trustee Indemnity Insurance

Before trustee indemnity insurance can be taken out, the following needs to take place:

- The board needs to assess that there is a risk that the trustees could be held, albeit in extreme circumstances, to be personally liable and that, notwithstanding the implementation of a specific risk management programme for the charity, the risk remains.
- The governing document must not prohibit the charity from taking out and paying the premiums on trustee indemnity insurance for its trustees. The Charities Act 2011 provides the trustees with legal authority to take out Trustee Indemnity Insurance, provided that they are satisfied that it is in the best interest of the charity (not the trustees!), for it to be taken out. In other words, there must be a clear advantage to the charity. There is nothing to stop the trustees taking out the indemnity themselves, however, and splitting the costs of the premiums between them.

Trustee Indemnity Insurance will not normally cover liability in the following circumstances:

- The personal liability of trustees of unincorporated charities as a result of contracts that they have entered into on behalf of their charity.
  For example, if trustees of an unincorporated charity entered into a mortgage deed to assist in acquisition of a property for the charity, then if the charity defaulted, it is likely the trustees would still be personally liable under the personal covenant they will have made in the mortgage deed itself.
- Any redundancy payments that may be payable to employees of the charity.
- Any liabilities under a lease that the charity has (for example repair or maintenance of the building or dilapidations).
- Liability for fraud or dishonesty by employees of the charity;
- Fines or damages that the trustees have to pay.
- The costs of an unsuccessful defence to a criminal prosecution arising out of fraud, or dishonest or reckless misconduct, of a trustee.
- The charity's liability arising from conduct that the trustee knew, or should have known, was not in the interests of the charity.

Currently it is estimated that there are in excess of 600,000 charity trustees serving on the boards of approximately 165,000 charities that are registered with the UK Charity Commission. The aggregate annual income of these charities exceeds £70bn. Yet the instances whereby trustees are made personally liable are usually in single figures each year.

Mergers, Collaboration, Takeover, Conversion and Cessation of Charities

27

Charities who are seeking to increase the size and influence of their work, reduce overheads, eliminate overlap and maximise efficiency, can view a possible merger, or collaboration with another like-minded charity, as an attractive proposition; conversely, some charities are forced to consider merger/collaboration for other diverse reasons such as financial distress, loss of key people or at the insistence of a major funder.

Certainly, it is very wise for charities to consider whether they can achieve more for their beneficiaries through working closely with other charities in the same sector. This can be achieved in one of two ways:

· through a merger with another charity with similar Objects (effectively combining the assets and liabilities of two charities into one unit);
· by collaboration (where two or more charities agree to work together on a common project, yet remain as separate organisations).

Merger

A merger can be achieved by:

· two or more charities transferring their assets and liabilities to a new charity that is established by them with similar charitable Objects. Charities proposing to do this should take professional advice to ensure:
  · the respective governing documents of the charities merging actually permit the merger;
  · neither charity holds any Permanent Endowment (assets held by the charity on the basis that only the income and not the capital can be spent on the charitable Objects). However the Charities Act 2011 may offer a resolution to the issue of Permanent Endowment; see appendix 1 paragraph 19;
  · any Restricted Funds can be passed over to the new charitable body;
  · the employees of the charity are properly consulted and the requirements of employment legislation are met (see section 15);
· or one charity transferring its assets and liabilities to another and then the transferring charity closing down and being removed from the Register;
· or one charity (or its trustees) actually becoming the trustees of the other charity.

The Charity Commission's consent is not needed for a merger. However, it will become involved if one or other charity has insufficient powers to effect the proposed merger. In such cases, they can be expected to work with the charities to achieve the merger, including, for example, issuing a Scheme to amend the Objects or deal with Permanent Endowment.

The Charity Commission will become more actively involved in any reorganisation of a CIO. Two or more CIOs that wish to merge must apply to the Charity Commission for the amalgamation, and for the incorporation and registration as a charity, or for a new CIO to be their successor. Following amalgamation, each of the old CIOs must give notice of the proposed amalgamation to all those who would be affected by it and send a copy of that notice to the Charity Commission. Any persons claiming to be affected by the proposed amalgamation then have opportunity to make written representations to the Charity Commission by a specified date. The Charity Commission has the final authority in approving or refusing the application for amalgamation. If the Charity Commission grants the amalgamation then the new entity will be registered, and all the rights and liabilities of the old CIO transferred to the new one, and each of the old CIOs are then dissolved.

Special care needs to be taken by charities that have an active membership structure. The governing document may require the members' consent before a merger can be effected.

In addition to consulting professional advisers, it is strongly recommended that any charity seeking to merge with another should go through a proper due diligence exercise on that other charity, in order to understand fully the history, make-up and methods of operation of the other charity. While in the long-term a merger can possibly save money, in the short-term, time and money will need to be spent to effect an integration of management information systems, accounting systems, contracts and administration generally.

Under the Charities Act 2011 the Charity Commission is required to maintain a public Register of Mergers. Once the transfer of property involved in the merger has taken place, then notification must be given to the Charity Commission, by the charity trustees, clarifying the date the merger took place and confirmation that appropriate arrangements have been made with regard to the payment of any liabilities of the transferring charity. This is particularly important if either of the merging charities receives, or expects to receive, legacy income. By registering the merger, then future legacies and gifts can be transferred to it. It is important to take legal advice before deciding to register the merger, as gifts in some supporters' wills state that the monies must go to someone else if the original charity ceases to exist!

The Charity Commission can make a Scheme on the application the charities wishing to merge, providing for the charities to be administered as one charity. Under this method the original charities will still exist.

Unscrambling a merger will be difficult to achieve, particularly if the original charities no longer exist! Conceivably, the newly merged charity could however be divided into two or more new charities. Perhaps before entering into a merger it is wise to remember that you cannot unscramble scrambled egg!

Collaboration

A collaboration or partnership is not limited to the charitable activity itself; it may, for example, concern the combining of administration, working together on a fundraising project, sharing an asset, outsourcing specific services or a specific joint venture.

Fundamentally, in collaborative relationships, the trustees must always act in the interest of the individual charities that are collaborating, as each charity will be maintaining its independence throughout the relationship.

Whatever form the collaboration takes, the details should be properly recorded in a written document, approved by the respective boards of trustees and signed by a trustee from each charity participating. If the charity's governing document does not permit collaboration with another charitable organisation, then the Charity Commission will need to be consulted. In certain circumstances, it may be wise for a more formal legal structure, for example a charitable company, or jointly owned trading company, to be put in place to facilitate the collaboration.

On a practical level, it will be important to ensure that there is an adequate mechanism for disengaging from the relationship should it not prove to be beneficial to both charities.

Takeover

When a larger charity takes over a smaller one, diplomatically it may be called "a merger", but in reality it is a takeover!

Unlike a commercial organisation, a charity has no shareholders or owners who would benefit from any premium paid. If the acquiring charity is to pay any money at all, it is usually to enable the other charity to discharge debts and liabilities, in order that it may close with a zero balance sheet.

Professional advice needs to be taken on the terms of the proposed takeover to ensure for both the acquirer and the other charity that the transaction is in the best interests of each, and is on terms that are fair and reasonable in all the circumstances. (The comments made earlier in this section about Permanent Endowment Funds and other Restricted Funds apply equally to a takeover).

Conversion from One Charitable Entity to Another

The trustees of an unincorporated charity may decide to incorporate and become a charitable company. The process involves the preparation of a specially drafted Memorandum and Articles of Association. Standard form Articles from a company formation agent are not advised. The Objects expressed in the Articles of Association should be identical to those in the governing document of the unincorporated charity. Otherwise, not all of the assets of the unincorporated charity can be transferred over. For example, if the unincorporated charity has charitable Objects of "the advancement of religion" and the Articles of the new charitable company also include "the relief of poverty" as a charitable Object, then monies given to the unincorporated charity cannot be used for the "relief of poverty" activity.

The company is formed at Companies House and an application made for its registration with the Charity Commission. The trustees of the unincorporated charity may have authority under the governing document to pass a resolution to transfer all the assets and liabilities of the charity (subject as above), over to the new charitable company (this includes any freehold or leasehold property, staff contracts, grant contracts etc.).

Final accounts are prepared for the unincorporated charity and once they are filed with the Charity Commission, that charity is removed from the Register. An application can be made for the merger to be included in the public Register of Mergers. It is usually possible to retain the name of the old charity and register that for the new charitable company.

When a merger has been registered, gifts and legacies that have been left to the charity that has closed down can, as a result of the merger, be automatically transferred to the new charitable entity that has replaced it.

Cessation

Trustees of small unincorporated charities (where the income in the last financial year does not exceed £10,000), have power to transfer the property of that charity to one or more other charities, or to amend the charitable Objects and administrative powers of the charity. However this provision does not apply to a small charity that holds designated land (e.g. a church hall), or is a charitable company.

The trustees however can only resolve to do this, if they are satisfied that it is in the interests of furthering the purposes of the transferring charity, and that the recipient charity has charitable Objects that are substantially similar. The resolution itself needs a majority of not less than two-thirds of the transferring charity's trustees.

Once the resolution has been passed, a copy is sent to the Charity Commission, together with a statement stating the trustees' reasons for passing it. The Charity Commission may direct the charity to give public notice of the resolution. Provided the Charity Commission has no objections to the resolution, the resolution itself then takes effect 60 days following receipt of a copy by the Charity Commission.

If the charity has Permanent Endowment then the Permanent Endowment can be transferred to the recipient charity (or charities), provided the recipient charity meets certain requirements with regard to its charitable Objects.

If the small unincorporated charity (whose income in the previous year does not exceed £10,000), does not wish to pass its assets on to another charity, but finds that its existing charitable Objects are no longer attainable, then providing it meets the tests as set out above, it may resolve that the charitable trusts of the charity should be modified, by replacing one or all of the purposes of the charitable Objects of the charity with other charitable Objects specified in the resolution. The procedure for passing the resolution is the same as set out above and again a copy sent to the Charity Commission and, subject to the Charity Commission's response, it takes effect at the end of 60 days following receipt of the resolution by the Charity Commission.

The Charities Act 2011 also gives the trustees of an unincorporated charity the ability to modify any of the powers given to the trustees in the governing document, or to regulate the procedure to be followed in connection with the charity's administration. Care needs to be taken that any alterations do not affect any clauses of the governing document which are expressed to be unalterable without the consent of the Charity Commission, (for example, altering its Objects or its dissolution clause).

The Charity Commission publishes information dealing with the cessation of small charities and their removal from the Register.

Closing a Charity

Charities close for a variety of reasons. Any charity wishing to do so first needs to dispose of its remaining funds, either by spending them in furtherance of the Objects (if that is possible), or transferring them to another charity with the same Objects. The charity will need to clear all its debts and liabilities beforehand and then can close in one of the following ways:

- **UNINCORPORATED CHARITY**
  The governing document should be checked to ensure the trustees have power to wind up the charity.

· If it is a membership charity then it will be necessary to call a members' meeting to get authority to close the charity down.
· If the charity has an income of less than £5,000,000 in the previous year and/or assets under £100,000,000, then it can use the charity Commission's online charity closure procedure.
· If the governing document does not give power for the trustees to close it down, Charity Commission consent may need to be obtained.
· If the charity has Permanent Endowment then that too will need to be spent or transferred before the charity is closed.

There is a legal requirement on trustees to tell the Charity Commission if a charity ceases to exist. It will then remove it from the Register of Charities.

- **CHARITABLE COMPANY**
  Once the charitable company has spent all its assets on its Objects, the Charity Commission can be informed via the online closure process. Remember that the company will need to be removed from Companies House Register as well.

- **CIO**
  The CIO and its members will need to make a dissolution resolution and once this is passed the trustees then make a declaration confirming that all debts and liabilities have been settled and confirming how any assets have been dealt with on dissolution. A copy of the resolution is then given to every member, employee, and trustee of the CIO and an application made to the Charity Commission, who will then publish a notice on the Register stating that there is an application to close the CIO. Subject to any representations it may receive, the CIO will be removed from the Register three months later

and will then automatically cease to exist.

Irrespective of the method used to close down the charity the trustees must arrange for its accounting books and records to be kept for at least three years after they were made (in case of a charitable company or CIO), and at least six years after they were made, for unincorporated charities. However bear in mind that HMRC can go back seven years in their enquiry into an organisation.

SECTION 28

Miscellaneous

Charity Commission Schemes

On occasions, a charity may need to consider making changes to its governing document. Such changes may be to the charitable purposes (Objects) or to the administrative provisions given to the trustees to carry out those Objects (Powers).

An alteration to the charity's Objects will require the consent of the Charity Commission. The Commission has the power to change Objects by making a Scheme.

The charity's Powers can usually be altered by the trustees themselves, using provisions that are given to them by the governing document. If the trustees do not have the necessary provisions in the governing document, then the Charity Commission can make a Scheme, thereby empowering the trustees to amend the administrative provisions, or indeed to confer additional Powers that are not currently available in the governing document.

It is helpful to look at this in more detail.

Essentially a Scheme is a legal document made by the Charity Commission where it is satisfied that there is good reason for it to change the charitable Objects of the organisation, appoint new trustees or authorise trustees to carry out particular actions. Examples of when a Scheme will be appropriate include:

· where the original Objects of the charity can no longer be carried out in a way laid down in the governing document, for example when a group of people who were originally to benefit from the charity no longer exist;
· where the Objects have been fulfilled or are no longer attainable;
· where pursuing the Objects will not utilise all the charity's income or property;
· where the Objects use outdated definitions of either location or classes of people who will benefit;
· where the Objects are no longer a useful way of using the funds or property;
· where two or more charities with similar Objects wish to merge but lack the legal power to do so.

The Charities Act 2011 permits a more liberal approach to be taken when a charity applies to the Charity Commission for guidance in how such monies can be used. The Charity Commission will take into account current social and economic circumstances and also the spirit in which the original gift was made. This can include authorising the charity to pass monies on to another charity, with a duty imposed on the trustees of the recipient charity to ensure that the gift is applied as closely as possible to the original purposes for which the monies were raised.

In instances where the Charity Commission is requested to agree new Objects, it will apply the legal doctrine of "cy-prés" (close to), by taking account of the underlying intention of the existing Object and of current social and economic circumstances. For example, if a charity's Object is to provide a chapel in a small village, which subsequently closes because the demographics have reduced the number of people who would use it, the application of the cy-prés doctrine would allow the building to be sold and the proceeds used to purchase a chapel in another town, where there is a need for such provision.

Excepted and Exempt Charities

An **Excepted** charity is a charity with income of under £100,000 per year that belongs to a specified group and does not have to register with the Charity Commission or submit annual returns but is otherwise regulated by the Charity Commission. Examples of excepted charities include churches and chapels belonging to some Christian denominations, as well as Scout and Guide groups.

The Charities Act 2011 now requires some of these charities to register with the Charity Commission, providing that their income is in excess of £100,000 per year. Excepted charities with an income of under £100,000 will continue to come under the Charity Commission's jurisdiction, which means for example, that their trustees have the same responsibilities as trustees of registered charities.

Exempt charities include organisations which previously had not been required to register with the Charity Commission, because they were overseen by other public bodies, for example Academy Trusts, universities, further educational corporations and some national museums. The Charities Act 2011 now requires that these charities be regulated by a "Principal Regulator" to ensure their compliance with charity law. They are exempt from registration by the Charity Commission, so long as they are regulated by another Principal Regulator. If they are not, then they are no longer exempt and must register with the Charity Commission.

Unregistered Charities

The Charities Act 2011 defines a "charity" as an institution that is established for charitable purposes only and is subject to the control of the High Court in the exercise of its jurisdiction. The Act goes on to say that every charity must be registered with the Charity Commission unless:

· it continues to be an exempt charity;
· it continues to be an excepted charity, by the specific order of the Charity Commission, and whose gross income does not exceed £100,000 per year;
· it is a not excepted yet its gross income does not exceed £5,000 per year

Where a charity is required to be registered, it is the duty of the charity trustees (i.e. those that have the conduct and management of the charity), to apply for that registration to be made.

Some very small churches have registered their buildings under the Places of Worship Act 1855, and such registration has been accepted by HMRC as being sufficient to allow the church to administer a Gift Aid scheme.

SECTION 29

Evaluating Effectiveness

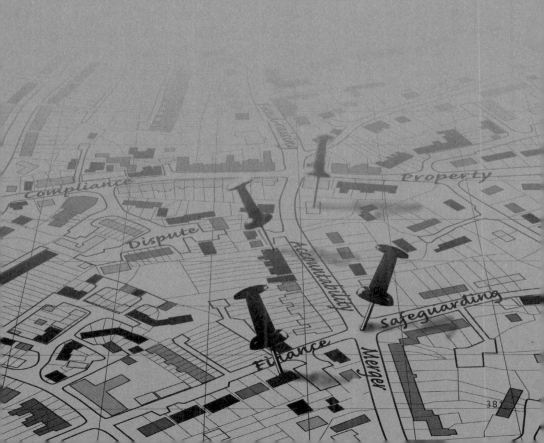

Many charities consider that their most pressing task is to raise enough money to enable the charity to function from year to year. However, in recent years the Charity Commission, perhaps picking up on public sentiment, is encouraging charities, and their trustees, to take time to measure how effective the charity is against its stated charitable purposes. The accountability that charities have to their donors, potential partners and ultimately beneficiaries requires that the charity's effectiveness is both measured and monitored on an ongoing basis.

The trustees of a charity should regularly review the charity's effectiveness against its stated Objects, consider the challenges the charity is facing, review whether the charity's structure is effective and consider carefully any changes that may be necessary.

In a changing and uncertain economic climate, no charity is immune to financial problems, and sadly the best efforts of trustees and staff may not be sufficient to overcome very serious problems that may result in the charity having to close.

Even if the charity seems to be functioning well, the trustees should never become complacent and should constantly review its Risk Management policy in the light of prevailing circumstances. See section 26.

The Trustees Annual Report, contained in the annual accounts, is an excellent forum for charity trustees to demonstrate the measured effectiveness of the charity's work in the particular year that the accounts cover.

Steps to Evaluate the Effectiveness of a Charity

Notwithstanding the fact that each charity is unique in terms of size, make-up and activity, it should be possible to adopt the following checklist of questions to help evaluate the effectiveness of most charities:

- Are the stated Objects, activities and values of the charity clearly set out and understood by its trustees, workers, volunteers and beneficiaries?
  - Does the charity regularly review the governing document, policies and plans to ensure they are up to date and developing in line with both the charity's work and the changing times?
  - How does the charity define "success" against the stated Objects, activities and values?

- How truthfully does the charity communicate its success to its donors and beneficiaries?

- Is the charity compliant with the legal and accounting regulations that affect it?
  - When did the charity last submit its inner workings to outside legal and accounting input (a legal audit or financial appraisal)?
  - Does the charity understand and observe all regulations that affect the arena of its activity, and the way in which it operates?
  - Does the charity strive to apply "best practice" to its operations and output?
  - How does the charity respond to complaints or negative experiences, e.g. employment claims by departing staff or adverse postings on social media/internet?
  - Does the charity have adequate safeguards in place to prevent fraud?

29

- How effective is the governance and management of the charity when benchmarked against other comparable charities?
  - Does the board have the right mix of skills, experience and knowledge for the charity?
  - Does the charity provide ongoing training and evaluation for trustees and staff?
  - Do the trustees work together harmoniously and effectively and solely for the charity, without conflict of interest?
  - Are the staff and volunteers valued, empowered and held accountable?
  - Is the Chief Executive/minister understood, supported, valued and accountable?
  - Are the managers empowered and guided to work effectively and within correct boundaries?
  - Does the charity have appropriate and robust systems in place to control risks, assets, expenditure and other liability?
  - Does the charity practice effective communication with those who have an interest in the charity, including staff and volunteers?
  - Does the charity's trustee board need to monitor the charity's affairs more closely, for example, by meeting more frequently?
  - Are difficult or unpopular decisions (if needed) taken appropriately and without procrastination?

- How accountable is the charity to donors, beneficiaries and the authorities?
  - Is information disclosed on a "need to know" basis or is the charity open and transparent?
  - Does the charity provide a forum to enable its beneficiaries and members to influence and vote for change?
  - Are the accounts and annual returns accurate, clear, full and filed on time?
  - Does the charity open up its programmes to allow review by outside professionals or donors?
  - Do the staff and volunteers have input to this evaluation on the charity's effectiveness?
  - Is the charity making the best use of its staff and volunteers?

- How effective is the charitable activity (programmes, services, products etc.) in achieving the Charitable Objects?
  - How effective in terms of financial cost?
  - How effective in terms of resources (people and/or assets applied)?
  - Could more be achieved or could the activity be more effective if the charity worked together with other like-minded charities?
  - What performance indicators are built into the programmes and activities? Who developed the performance indicators? Are they realistic?

- Is the charity reactive or proactive?
  - How does it respond to change that is imposed on it, for example by legislation or financial constraints?
  - Does the charity accurately foresee change in the needs of its beneficiaries and therefore voluntarily respond by adapting to meet those changes?
  - Are the plans and policies regularly reviewed in order to adapt them to meet changes?
  - Does the charity interact with other charitable bodies and learn from or work with them, where there is significant advantage in so doing?
  - Does the charity keep up to date and make good use of technology?
  - Is there any benefit to be gained by collaborating with another charity in some areas of the charity's activities?

The Charity Commission has developed a "best practice" leading to their endorsement of a charity's quality standards in areas such as accountability, governance, structures, conflicts of interest, policies and their ability to manage their staff and volunteers. It is called the Charity Commission's Quality Standards Endorsement Programme. Primarily, this is to encourage umbrella bodies to develop a set of quality standards to which the members of the umbrella body commit. Once the Charity Commission agrees that the quality systems meet its bench mark for comprehensive, robust and objective assessments, which encourage compliance and accountability, then the Charity Commission will endorse those standards and expect the umbrella body and its members to keep to them rigidly. There are reputational and other tangible benefits to be gained from such an endorsement.

29

Appendices

APPENDIX 1

What to Do When ...

1. The charity needs to appoint a new trustee

When a suitable candidate has been found it is wise to take up at least two character references on the potential new trustee. The charity should also take steps to ensure that the proposed trustee is not disqualified from acting in that capacity (see Section 6)

A Disclosure and Barring Service (DBS) check must be undertaken. See section 8.

The charity should ensure the proposed trustee fully understands the charity's objects and the responsibilities that they are taking on.

Specific requirements:

- Check the governing document to see who can appoint a new trustee (if no one exists with the right to appoint a new trustee, then an application may need to be made to the Charity Commission).
- A formal Deed of Appointment is recommended for an unincorporated charity, particularly if the charity owns property.
- The Charity Commission should be notified.
- Consider whether any freehold or leasehold property belonging to the charity is held in names which include the outgoing trustee and which should be transferred into the name of the new trustee.
- Ensure that the appointment is recorded in the charity's minute book.
- The bank mandate may need to be changed.

If it is a charitable company then notice of the appointment needs to be filed at Companies House (Company Form AP01.)

2. A trustee retires, resigns or dies

Written notice should be given by the trustee leaving, and that notice should be recorded in the charity's minute book. It is also necessary to notify the Charity Commission.

A formal Deed of Retirement is suggested as being appropriate, for an unincorporated charity. If the trustee is one of those named on the title of the charity's freehold property, then the Deed of Retirement or a transfer document will need to be registered at the Land Registry to remove that trustee's name. Legal help will need to be sought if the trustee is a named party to the charity's lease or a party to the charity's mortgage deed, as it may be more difficult to extricate the leaving trustee from such an arrangement. If the trustee was a party to the charity's bank account then the mandate will need to be changed.

In the case of a charitable company, notice of the retirement or resignation will need to be filed at Companies House (Company Form TM01). There is no special form for a trustee retiring from a CIO.

The charity must consider whether or not the retirement or resignation will reduce the number of trustees to below the minimum number as stated in the charity's governing document. If it does, then immediate steps need to be taken to appoint a replacement trustee to ensure that the charity can continue to function. (See section 6.)

If a trustee dies then it is important for the charity to obtain a copy of the death certificate which can be used to remove the trustee's name from the any legal documents. Notification of the death should also be given to the Charity Commission and , if applicable, Companies House.

3. The identity of the trustees is not clear

Enquiries can be made of the lawyers and accountants for the charity to see whether they have any records that may assist. In addition the Charity Commission may be able to access details from their archives. If the charity has held land, then the title deeds to that land may disclose the last known active trustees.

The Charity Commission has the ability to determine who are the members of a charity, but such a determination is not fully binding unless it is endorsed by the High Court. In other words the trustees so nominated by the Charity Commission, can be challenged and any actions and decisions they have taken can be unravelled, unless their appointment has been ratified by the High Court.

4. The charity trustees desire to remove a trustee from the board

The governing document of the charity may well specify the procedure to be followed if the majority of trustees wish to remove a trustee from the board.

Fundamentally, there needs to be good reason for this.

In the case of a charitable company the majority board members have a right under the Companies Act to remove a director, irrespective of what else may be written in the Articles. However removing that person as a director may not remove them as a trustee in such circumstances.

The Trustees Act 1925 may allow the majority trustees to remove a trustee even if the governing document itself does not give them that power. Professional advice should be sought if the governing document is unclear as to the ability of the majority trustees to remove a trustee.

If the charity has a voting membership then the members may be entitled to vote for the removal of a trustee.

5. Trustee numbers fall below the minimum permitted

The governing document of the charity will specify the minimum number of trustees necessary to form a quorum. Failure to maintain that number means that the charity cannot operate lawfully. The practical application of failure is that decisions made by the board (save perhaps for the decision to appoint an additional trustee

A1

or director) are invalid. The Charity Commission has the power to co-opt additional trustees to make the charity board quorate if the existing trustees are unable or unwilling to do so.

6. There is non-attendance or non-involvement by a trustee

Charity trustees have a duty of care to use reasonable care and skill to ensure that the charity is well run and efficient, and to consider taking external professional advice on matters where there may be a material risk to the charity.

Given the above and the general level of responsibility on charity trustees, it is considered that trustees who are habitually absent from board meetings (say missing three or more consecutive meetings without good reason), are seriously abdicating their responsibilities and should be asked to leave the board (or be removed if they do not agree), for their good as well as the good of the charity.

Trustees who, while they may attend board meetings, fail to "engage" or identify positively with the charity's work, may also be a negative influence on the board. It is advised that steps be taken to identify the reason for the board member's non-involvement. For example, some trustees serve out of a sense of duty, or perhaps have been seconded to the board in an ex officio capacity?

One way in which boards can ensure that each member is engaged and fully focused on the interest of the charity, is for the chairman to conduct board appraisals with individual members of the board on an annual basis. Such appraisals can either be based on an informal discussion, or formalised, perhaps by using a pre-agreed questionnaire. The board chairman also needs to be evaluated, and this is perhaps best done by two other senior members of the board, using the same approach as that for the general board members.

A board member who was formally engaged and enthusiastic and who becomes withdrawn, (perhaps through a negative experience with the charity), will need sensitive handling, particularly as any sense of injustice may quickly spread to other members of the board and senior staff. See also section 6.

7. One trustee cannot agree with a majority decision of the board

Trustee boards take decisions acting collectively and as a team. The decisions do not need to be unanimous as a majority decision is sufficient (unless the charity's governing document says otherwise).

If one or more of the trustees cannot agree with a majority decision on an issue, and the issue is a significant one, the dissenting trustee(s) will need to consider:

- whether the decision in question is of such fundamental importance to the charity or the trustee that their

continued involvement on the board has been undermined;

- if the decision involves the expenditure of a large sum of money or the entering into of a major contract, whether the dissenting trustee is prepared to shoulder ultimate responsibility with the rest of the board if the decision goes wrong. If they are not so prepared then they may need to resign immediately;

- that the minutes of the board meeting clearly record their dissenting opinion and vote on the issue in question.

It is suggested that a wise and skilful board chairman would, in the instance of a major decision, come alongside the dissenting trustee(s) to ensure that any reaction does not undermine the decision itself or the ongoing work and the reputation of the charity. See also section 6.

8. There is a dispute between board members

While board members should strive for "unity in diversity", this is not always achievable and there are, therefore, occasions when a conflict can negatively affect the function of the board and compromise the ability of the charity to achieve its stated Objects.

Steps that might prevent disputes escalating include:

- ensuring that each member of the board clearly understands his or her role and area of responsibility; and obligation to act in the best interests of the charity;
- periodic reminders from the chairman of trustees that the board acts jointly and a trustee does not have power individually, unless it has been specifically delegated by the board;
- focusing the board on serving the charity and achieving its charitable Objects;
- reminding any defaulting members of their agreed responsibility under a trustee code of conduct (see section 6).

Notwithstanding the above, if a dispute escalates to the stage where it threatens the unity of the board and is potentially undermining the charity itself, then additional steps may include:

- bringing in an outside independent mediator;
- considering the removal of the trustees in dispute from the board. (Check the governing document to ensure the correct procedure is followed.)

The Charity Commission does have limited powers to intervene but it will only do so in cases where:

- the way in which the charity is being run is putting significant assets of the charity at risk;
- the charity's income is not being used for its charitable purposes;
- the trustees are not acting in accordance with the charity's governing document or charity law.

The Charity Commission will not get involved in doctrinal disputes, employment matters or disputes between the charity and other people who have entered into contracts with it. See also section 3.

A1

9. Trustees claim they are not consulted

Trustees who validly make this claim are in a very serious and vulnerable position! Given that trustees are ultimately responsible for what happens in a charity, the board is negligent if it allows a situation to arise whereby a Chief Executive, minister or a senior management team are making all the decisions without the knowledge or involvement of the trustees.

Clearly, trustees in this position have a simple choice; either they can resign en mass (with the attendant turmoil that it will cause in the charity until the new board is appointed), or they can address the issue involved and ensure that the correct method of governance and accountability is thereafter implemented.

A governance audit may be helpful in

order to understand fully who is exercising power within the organisation. Ultimately, it is a question of how seriously the charity trustees are prepared to take their responsibilities. See also section 6.

10. There is a conflict between the "spiritual" and the "legal"

The Charity Commission will not get involved ... or arbitrate over interpretation of doctrine or spiritual responsibility in the life of a charity. Fundamentally, the trustees are responsible in law for controlling the management and administration of the charity. In the event of a conflict between the "spiritual" and the "legal", then unless the issues can be resolved by competent mediation, ultimately the trustees are responsible for the charity. If the trustees are distinct from the persons responsible for the "spiritual", there is always the possibility that the beneficiaries may side with "spiritual" leaders, leaving the trustees to administer an "empty" charity! See section 20.

11. Payment is to be made to a trustee

The general principle is that a trustee must not benefit in any way from their connection with the charity. There is an exception to this principle where the governing document specifically allows a payment to a trustee or allows them to do business with the charity. Full details are set out in section 6.

A trustee in breach of this principle can be made liable to repay to the charity any salary or benefits they have received. This applies even if the trustee has resigned as a trustee before, or at the time, they took up the employment, unless the charity can clearly show that the trustee has not obtained the employment by reason of their being a trustee and that there will be no ongoing conflict of interest.

If the governing document does not allow a payment to be made, yet the charity wishes to make such a payment, then the Charity Commission in certain circumstances has the power to authorise an alteration to the governing document, providing that the charity's trustee can demonstrate that there is a clear advantage to the charity in the payment being made to the trustee.

The Charities Act allows payment for goods or services that a trustee provides to a charity over and above the trustees normal duties. (See section 6.)

12. The trustees wish to delegate their responsibilities?

Subject to the provisions of the charity's governing document trustees usually have the power to delegate certain responsibilities to a committee or to individuals. Responsibilities that can be delegated include:

- the implementing of a decision that has been made by the board;
- the investment of assets;
- raising funds for the charity.

Notwithstanding any power to delegate that is contained in the governing document, the trustees have final responsibility for everything that is done in the charity, including things done by those to whom a responsibility has been delegated.

The person or group to whom a responsibility has been delegated should always make the fact of that delegation known to any third parties whom they deal with, thereby reducing the risk of their being held responsible by the third party. See also section 6.

13. It is difficult to recruit new trustees

Charities that are finding it difficult to recruit new trustees may consider:

- advertising the opportunity together with brief details of the role, in general and denominational publications;
- approaching specific people in either the geographical area or the particular sector that the charity is involved in and asking them either to make the need known or suggest potential candidates;
- the possible appointment of a custodian trustee for the charity's building;
- a merger with another like-minded charity.

14. The trustees wish to make an *ex gratia* payment

Fundamentally, a charity's funds can only be spent in accordance with the governing document and in order to further the stated charitable Objects.

An *ex gratia* payment (Latin - out of Kindness) is one where the trustees, although not having a legal obligation, nevertheless feel there is a moral obligation on them to make a payment to a party, yet there exists no power under the governing document for the payment to be made, nor can the trustees justify it as being exclusively in the interests of the charity.

Charity trustees wishing to make an ex gratia payment must first seek the consent of the Charity Commission. In addition, the Charity Commission has the power to authorise a payment which the trustees have no legal obligation or power to make, but believe that such payment will result in benefit to the charity.

Trustees who take the Charity Commission's advice on such matters, and proceed in accordance with that advice, are generally protected from any personal liability for breach of trust (provided they have not misstated the facts or withheld material information from the Charity Commission before the advice is given).

An example of an *ex gratia* payment that may need to be paid would be where a charity received a gift in a will that, because of a legal technicality or an oversight on the testator's part, resulted in a larger gift than the testator really intended and, as a result some other person will be deprived of money or property which the testator intended them to receive.

The charity may be legally entitled to keep the whole of the gift and the trustees may conclude that they have a moral obligation to make a payment out of the monies they have received, to ensure that the testator's original intentions were complied with. In these circumstances the trustees will need to get the prior written consent of the Charity Commission before the *ex gratia* payment can be made.

An example of a possible *ex gratia* payment that may not need to be made is where the charity wishes to pay a sum in excess of £1,000 to a retiring founder trustee in recognition of all that they have done in setting up the charity. Again Charity Commission approval would need to be applied for, although in those circumstances it is unlikely to be given.

A1

15. The charity wishes to purchase a leaving present for a retiring trustee

It is permitted to purchase "a modest token of appreciation" to a retiring trustee using the charity's funds. Provided that the expenditure is not excessive, it is likely to generate goodwill with the retiring trustee and everyone to whom they show the present!

16. The charity wishes to spend money to do something that is outside its "Objects"

Consider whether:

- a payment would qualify as an ex gratia payment – see Appendix 1 paragraph 14;
- it is applicable to apply for a Charity Commission Scheme – see section 28;
- a Cy-prés Scheme is relevant – see section 28;
- an application to the Charity Commission for specific advice is needed;
- the governing document permits the charity to make a gift of monies to another charity, which is itself empowered to apply it for the charitable Object that is not authorised by the donor charity's governing document.

17. The Objects for which the charity has been set up are no longer possible

If the charity's Objects are no longer achievable, they can be changed, and where charities do not have the power themselves to make that change, the Charity Commission can assist.

In some cases a charity may need to change its Objects completely and in other cases it may be sufficient for the charity to change the way that it works. See Section 28 as to how these amendments can be made.

As an alternative to the above, the trustees may consider that there are other like-minded charities who are still working effectively in achieving the same charitable Objects. The trustees may wish to consider amalgamating the charity with other such charitable organisations, rather than changing the charitable Object completely just for the sake of perpetuating the original charity. Sometimes it is not the Objects themselves that are unobtainable but rather the existence of some other limiting factor in the particular charity, which is preventing that Object from being achieved (see Section 27).

18. The charity can no longer spend "Restricted Funds"

Restricted Funds are funds held by the charity that are subject to specific restrictions that may have been imposed by the donor, or by the terms upon which those funds were raised, for example a church that raises funds specifically for a new roof would hold those funds as "Restricted Funds".

Options for the charity, if they can no longer spend Restricted Funds, include returning the money to the donors (if they can be ascertained) or applying to the Charity Commission for a Scheme authorising the money to be spent on a wider charitable Object within the charity.

As mentioned in section 23, it is a wise move at the start of any fundraising campaign for a specific purpose, to agree in writing with the donors that any surplus funds left after the project has been completed, can be applied to the general purposes of the charity.

19. The charity has Permanent Endowment

These are restricted funds given to a charity where the donor has imposed a condition that they must be held permanently as part of the capital of the charity. The income from the capital is useable in accordance with the donor's instructions. Permanent Endowment can be cash, shares, land or buildings. Unincorporated charities may be permitted to spend all or part of the Permanent Endowment as income for the Objects of the charity as set out in the governing document. However Charity Commission consent may be required.

Larger unincorporated charities are also given power to spend capital that had been given for a particular purpose, provided that the value of the capital exceeds £10,000 and the charity has an annual gross income in the last financial year of at least £1,000. The Charity Commission needs to consent to this. However, If the Permanent Endowment was not given to the charity (i.e. the charity itself created it) then Charity Commission consent is not necessary.

Charitable companies cannot hold Permanent Endowment.

20. The Governing Document of the charity needs amending

In the case of a charitable company, any alteration to the Articles of Association that (1) changes the Objects clause, or (2) states what is to happen to the assets of the charitable company upon its dissolution, is ineffective, unless the Charity Commission has given their prior written consent.

If the Charity Commission consents to the alteration, then the charitable company will need to pass the appropriate resolution and file a copy of that resolution together with the revised Articles of Association with both Companies House and the Charity Commission.

In the case of an unincorporated charity, the governing document is likely to contain provisions concerning any intended alteration of it. The trustees should seek the Charity Commission's consent before altering the governing document in any of the two areas listed above.

The trustees of unincorporated charities and the directors of charitable companies can pass resolutions to alter the administrative parts of their governing document, for example, to vary the number of trustees needed to form a quorum at meetings.

21. The "Leader" will not be accountable

For the reasons set out in section 5 this is not a situation that the charity's trustees can allow to continue for long. Not only does the leader need to agree to be accountable (in word and deed), but the trustees need to be holding that person accountable.

A review of the reports of the Charity Commission Inquiries shows the danger of having a senior person (whether or not that person is also a trustee), acting in an independent way to the exclusion of the charity's trustees. Practical steps to address such a situation could include:

- Attempting to agree areas of responsibility and cooperation between the board and the leader.
- The possibility of involving a third party to help bring alignment.

A1

If the above steps fail to resolve the situation, then the trustees may need to consider either the future of the leader or ultimately their own position.

22. There is a vote of no confidence in the "Leader"

Charities should be careful before electing to go down the route of dispensing with the services of the leader. With appropriate support and/or mediation, the trustees should actively consider the possibility of allowing the leader to continue. It is only in the most serious of cases (where there is either gross misconduct or the continuance of the leader in their role is incompatible with the culture and harmony of the charity), that the parties should go their separate ways.

If the board or the members of the charity (if the charity is regulated by members), have lost confidence in the leader then the following options are available:

- If the person is an employee who does not have written particulars of employment then the charity will be in some difficulty, given that they are required as employer to provide a statement of the terms of employment. It is likely that, if the decision to terminate the employment were challenged, then an employment tribunal would impose a liability on the trustees for their failure under employment law.
- If the person is hired by the charity under a contract of employment then, depending on the terms of the contract, and after taking appropriate legal advice, the board as employer can consider terminating the contract.
- If the person is not employed (and therefore does not have a contract) then, depending on the governing document, it may be possible to pass a resolution agreeing to dispense with that person's services.
- If the person is also a trustee, then depending upon the governing document, a board resolution to remove that person from trusteeship may be possible.

In cases of gross misconduct (financial, Safeguarding, criminal), then the trustees are empowered to take immediate steps to terminate the employment in order to protect the assets, reputation and ongoing work of the charity. If the misconduct is of a moral nature, then advice will need to be taken as to whether the issue is one entitling the trustees to terminate the employment. See section 15.

23. There is a claim against the charity

Claims against the charity can come from various sources:

- A claim about the services that the charity provides (quality).
- A claim from an employee (discrimination).
- A claim concerning the charity's work with vulnerable persons (Safeguarding).
- A claim concerning the charity's administration/finances (malpractice).
- A claim about the way the charity is carrying on its work (negligence).
- A claim that the charity is in breach of the law (non-compliance).
- A claim concerning the charity's behaviour (nuisance).

Claims concerning the charity's services and their inner workings need to be taken seriously and responded to. Many charities now have a claims policy and procedure that is implemented when a complaint is received.

If the claim concerns an employment issue or one made on behalf of a vulnerable person, then the charity must engage outside professional assistance at the earliest possible opportunity, in order to respond correctly to the claim.

If the claim alleges that the charity is in breach of the law then professional help will need to be sought. Charities rely heavily upon their reputation and registration as a charity implies a degree of trustworthiness and integrity. If a charity is in breach of those standards, then very often the whole charitable sector can suffer if the complaint is not handled correctly. As a result, a section of the public may end up with a less than positive impression of the way in which charities are administered.

Churches who occupy buildings in breach of the established planning use for that building, or who fail to insulate the property properly to prevent sound becoming a nuisance to adjoining owners, damage the reputation of like-minded charities in the eyes of the planning authorities who have to enforce Planning Acts. In addition, it is a poor reflection of the standards and principles that those churches claim to embrace.

If the charity needs either to commence court proceedings, or to defend them, it is good practice to notify the Charity Commission beforehand and obtain prior authorisation to use charity funds to meet the costs of legal action. Failure to do so may risk the trustees being made liable for these costs. If court proceedings escalate and a considerable amount of the charity's monies are expended on them, then the trustees risk the Charity Commission's questioning as to whether such expenditure was a good use of the charity's funds. If the Commission is notified at the outset, then any issues are raised by them at an early stage in the proceedings.

A1

24. There is a compliance failure

Accounts/annual return/AGM

Charities with total income or total expenses in excess of £25,000 are required to prepare an Annual Return and Accounts and file them with the Charity Commission within 10 months of the end of the charity's financial year. The Statement of Recommend Practice (SORP) outlines the methods and disclosures that are required and both the Annual Return and the Accounts need to comply with these specific requirements. (See section 22)

The Charity Commission actively encourages charities to submit their Accounts and Annual Return on time and to that end they:

- enter the dates that the Accounts and Annual Returns are filed on the charity's entry on the Register (remember that the Register is a public document),

and can be viewed "on line");

- identify those charities that are persistently in default of submitting the Accounts and Annual Returns on time;
- consider taking regulatory action if the charity persistently fails to submit its Accounts on time.

Once the accounts are filed, they cannot be retrieved and replaced and therefore it is essential to ensure that they are approved by the entire board and are correct.

Charities should ensure that their accounts are prepared well before the ten-month deadline following the end of the financial year. To this end the charity can assist by ensuring that all accounting records are in order, bank statements and certificates of closing balances (at the end of the financial year), are to hand and that all the books are delivered to the Auditor within a few weeks of the end of the financial year. If the Auditors are warned that the books are coming they can programme the Audit into their work schedule and avoid a last minute rush to deliver the signed accounts before the end of the ten-month period.

While audited accounts are a historical record, they are likely to be of more benefit to the charity in a management function if they can be produced within a month or so of the end of the financial year. Many charities use the audited accounts as a fundraising tool (particularly to support major grant requests), and therefore their timely production can only assist.

Depending on the governing document and/or the nature of the charitable organisation, it may not need to hold an Annual General Meeting. The Companies Act 2006 removed the requirement for private companies to hold an AGM.

However, directors of charitable companies need to balance that possible relaxation with their obligation for open and transparent governance. In the circumstances, it may be considered preferable to hold a specific meeting to give the charity's members the opportunity to participate.

Unincorporated charities may be required by the provisions of the governing document to hold an AGM. Charities that have an active membership (be they an unincorporated charity or a charitable company), will be keen to hold one as that is an important method of accountability and communication to its stakeholders and beneficiaries. See section 9.

25. The charity wants to undertake a "mega" project

Decisions concerning projects which are of a size that is out of all proportion to the normal capacity of the charity or to those projects which the charity has undertaken to date should be approached in the following way:

- A check should be first made to ensure that the project is consistent with the charity's Objects and therefore permitted by the governing document.
- An evaluation should be undertaken by or on behalf of the charity's board focussing on the timescale, cost, (financial and staffing) and the ultimate benefit of the project to the charity. This would also include financial projections and the availability of funding.
- Outside specialist advice should be obtained on both the financial implications and the viability of the project itself. If the project is in a sphere of activity that is not usually undertaken by the charity, then specialist professional consultancy should be taken up.

- A risk assessment should be undertaken and its conclusions built into the project.
- When all the information is to hand the board should make their independent decision as to whether the charity should undertake the project. Proper records of all discussions and reports should be kept.
- The charity should decide internally as to who will "manage" the project (it is suggested that a minister is not the appropriate person to "manage" a church redevelopment project), and set up an adequate reporting and accountability structure while the project is being undertaken.
- Consideration as to whether the project could be undertaken in stages may be relevant, in order to minimise risk.
  See section 11.

26. An urgent response is needed from the Charity Commission

There are occasions when a charity needs an instant response from the Charity Commission, particularly on issues relating to possible fraud or money laundering.

The Charity Commission has realised that previous turnaround times were not adequate and it established "First Contact". This has been set up as a central point of contact for all requests for services from the Charity Commission. In addition, it provides general advice and guidance from an advisor.

27. The charity is facing an unusual/new challenge

Given that charities operate in a continually changing environment, it is likely that they may from time to time face unusual and new challenges. The critical issue is how the charity will respond to these. The following issues may be relevant:

- Does the charity's governing document allow the charity to undertake the new challenge being offered?
- Will the new challenge provide public benefit?
- If it takes up the new challenge, will that adversely affect the present charitable Objects?
- Does the charity have the expertise among its existing trustees and/or staff to cope with the new challenge?
- If the charity's donors have given monies for the present charitable activity, how will they react if a new challenge is adopted?
- Does the charity need to bring in outside professional support, perhaps on a consultancy basis, to enable it to have the necessary expertise to respond to the new challenge.

A1

28. The risks to the charity are too big

If, following a risk assessment, the charity concludes that the risks facing it on a day-to-day basis are too large to be safely accommodated by the charity, then the options include:

- discontinuing the activity or the particular project that presents an unreasonable risk;
- (if it is a specific project) joining with another charity(s) in order to reduce the overall exposure;
- the purchase of suitable insurance;
- ring-fencing the risk by using a specially formed company to undertake the project and thereby reduce the overall risk for the charity.

The greatest risk to the charity may be from "within" rather than "without". If the charity lacks strategy, adequate governance, management or experience, then steps will need to be taken to mitigate the risk from those "internal" issues whereupon the previously perceived risks from "without" may seem to be manageable after all. See section 26.

29. The charity runs out of money

As we have seen in section 25 a charity can be unable to pay its bills as they fall due even though it is holding substantial monies (for example if those monies are held on a special trust and cannot be applied to the general day-to-day expenditure).

Charities who have taken the steps outlined in section 25, yet nevertheless find they have reached a stage whereby there is no reasonable prospect of sufficient income being generated, should in the short-term, to enable the debts to be discharged as they fall due, consider the following:

- Immediately take accounting and legal advice.
- Consult with a Licenced Insolvency Practitioner.
- Consider whether or not the charity should approach other charities with a view to being taken over.
- Investigate whether or not the charity has any other assets that can be realised to provide temporary respite while a more permanent solution is explored.

The Charity Commission will appoint an Interim Manager only as part of a formal Inquiry into a charity and where it feels it is necessary to protect the assets of the charity, or to resolve a badly administered charity. The Charity Commission will not appoint an Interim Manager just because the charity is running out of money. Indeed it applies a "proportionality" test before such an appointment, to ensure that the charity has the necessary funds to pay for an Interim Manager, and that any negative results from the appointment do not outweigh the anticipated gain.

Prudent trustees should ensure that they have taken appropriate steps long before the charity actually runs out of money. Indeed, failure to do so may call into question their conduct (be they trustees or directors), which could in turn result in personal liability attaching to them.

30. VAT is an issue

Registered charities in the UK are not automatically exempt from paying VAT.

Charities may, however, be able to obtain VAT relief when purchasing certain goods and services, even if the charity is not registered for VAT. Examples (but not an exhaustive list) include:

- aids for the disabled;
- buildings and construction;
- equipment for producing talking books and newspapers;
- medical and scientific equipment;
- advertising and goods connected with the collecting of donations for the charity.

To claim this VAT relief, the charity needs to complete a special declaration and an eligibility certificate is then given to the supplier, who will not charge VAT on the purchase, so long as all the conditions relating to the relief have been met.

If the charity has a turnover from business supplies that is above the current VAT registration threshold, then the charity is required to register for VAT as if it were a normal trading business. Once registered, the appropriate VAT treatment will need to be given to income received and supplies made.

Charities can take advantage of the online inquiry form (CHYchaEnq) to seek guidance from HMRC on matters relating to VAT.

HMRC has detailed information about all VAT and other tax issues relating to charities.

31. There is a "problem"

Depending on the nature of the "problem", trustees should consider whether it is an issue that just affects the internal workings of the charity, or one that affects the charity's beneficiaries or the public at large.

If it is internal, (e.g. a personality issue)

the trustees should endeavour to resolve the issue using their personal skills and experience and ensure that the charity is well run and efficient.

If the problem is one that affects the potential beneficiaries or the public at large (e.g. fraud, Safeguarding or mismanagement) then the trustees will need to consider:

- involving outside professional input (lawyers, accountants, Safeguarding specialists);
- whether the matter should be reported to the statutory authorities (Companies House, HMRC, Social Services, Police etc);
- asking the Charity Commission to assist the trustees in investigating the issues and working with them to put things right.

Failure by the trustees to respond properly to a problem situation could result in the trustees being made personally liable for any debts or losses that the charity incurrs.

Charity trustees may wish to consider establishing a "whistle-blowing" procedure for staff and volunteers. The charity itself would benefit from having a process whereby allegations of fraud, abuse, health and safety breaches, poor employment practice and malpractice in general, are notified before the charity suffers real harm. A written policy statement from the trustees making it clear that reports of malpractice are acceptable, and will be taken seriously and handled discreetly, is an important and necessary component in a successfully run charity, particularly where staff and volunteers work among vulnerable people or in difficult and challenging circumstances.

When a problem is discovered, the facts and circumstances surrounding the issue and the trustees' proposals for resolving them, need to be properly recorded in the charity's minute book. If the charity then takes outside professional advice, copies of such advice should be included with the minutes, so that a paper trail is in place should the trustees' actions be subsequently questioned.

A1

32. There is a "suspicion" of someone or something

If the charity becomes suspicious of a donor's intention it should:

- Report the suspicions to the Charity Commission and/or the police.
- Ensure that none of the charity's assets, premises, staff or volunteers could be used for activities that either may, or may appear to, support or condone any illegal activity.
- Beware lest it commits an office under S19 of the Terrorism Act 2000. If trustees receive information that leads them to believe that a person may be involved in an activity (for example raising money or using property), for the purpose of

terrorism, such suspicion or knowledge must be disclosed to the police immediately.

- Formally seek the Charity Commission's advice. The person who makes a written application to the Charity Commission for an opinion and who receives that opinion and acts on it, is regarded as having acted prudently, i.e. the trustee is unlikely to fact subsequent criticism;
- report to the police and the Charity Commission any fraudulent solicitations received via letter or email (often from overseas).

33. The charity has a problem with a key staff member

Carefully review the contract of employment for the staff member concerned.

In conjunction with that contract, consider the appropriate response from the charity to the problem that has arisen.

If the charity's disciplinary procedure is to be invoked, then the staff member needs to be given the opportunity to be accompanied by a "friend" to any consultative meeting.

It is important to ascertain the root cause of the problem. It may, for example, result from the omission by the charity to provide a safe and stable working environment or to properly support the staff member, particularly overseas. Consider the impact to the overall work of the charity caused by a disaffected or marginalised key staff member.

Given the nature of the charitable activity, it is likely that many of the charity staff identify very strongly with the Objects of the charity. This, in turn, leads to a sense of ownership in the charity, which may be reflected in the fact that the staff member has made a personal sacrifice in order to be involved with it. If there is a breakdown in the relationship between the charity and an employee, it is likely that the sense of betrayal and hurt felt by the staff member will run deep. Charities need to respond very delicately in the whole area of employer/employee relationship. Statistically charities that adopt a more consultative and participatory approach to human resource issues are less likely to have significant problems with key staff members. See section 15.

34. There is a "request" for compliance from an overseas government

Charities working overseas from time to time find themselves facing demands from a national government, which may be directed at one particular charity, all charities working in that country, or perhaps those that come from a specific country or who are undertaking a specific kind of work. This can result from insensitive behaviour by the charity; or the government deciding that it does not want details of the social needs of its citizens reported by charities in the West; or outright jealousy that the charity can secure grants from international governments, or build and equip schools and hospitals to a better standard that can be done locally. (I have seen first-hand examples of all of these, and others, in acting for charities working in various parts of the world).

When facing a "request" for compliance from an overseas government that the charity deems unreasonable, the following steps are open to it:

- The board of the charity in the UK need to be made fully aware of the issue, in order to determine whether or not the charity can and should comply.
- The trustees should take legal advice.
- An application should be made to the Charity Commission for advice and guidance.
- The charity may be advised to discuss the issue with the British Embassy in that particular country, as their commercial section may have local wisdom and advice.
- Discussions may be conducted with the appropriate government department in the country in question.
- It may be helpful to open discussions with other like-minded charities and NGOs in the country to see whether they are similarly affected. If they are, then there may be opportunities to combine forces in a united presentation

to the government on behalf of all the charities/NGOs.

If the above fails to resolve the issue in a satisfactory way, and the trustees (acting on the advice they have received), decide that they cannot comply with the request from the overseas government, then they may opt to adjust their operation accordingly in order to keep on the right side of the law.

Remember the government in a particular country may not share the charity's sense of importance of the specific work being undertaken in that country. It has been found to be unwise to threaten the government with the withdrawal of the organisation from the country, as that may have been the game plan for that government all along!

35. The word "Limited" is unnecessary in the charity's title

A charitable company can be exempt from using "limited" in its name where:

- all profits and income are to be spent in promoting the charity;
- no dividend is paid to its members;
- if the company is wound up, all assets are transferred to a similar organisation.

Usually this exemption is claimed at the time the company is formed at Companies House, although it is possible to pass a special resolution to effect this change after the company has been formed.

Many faith-based charitable companies have found it helpful to their charitable Objects to have excluded "Limited" from their name, as the word limited tends to have commercial implications.

36. The charity works with vulnerable beneficiaries

Charities that are either working with children and/or concerned with the care of vulnerable adults, in circumstances where the trustees have access to such children and/or vulnerable adults in carrying out their normal duties, need to pay special attention to the requirements for Disclosure and Barring Service (DBS) check on the trustees, to ensure that a trustee is not disqualified from working with children and/or vulnerable adults.

Fundamentally each charity and its trustees must decide whether they are legally allowed to carry out DBS checks, The burden is on the charity and its trustees to ensure compliance. It is an offence to offer a regulated position (e.g. the position of trustee of a children's charity), to an individual who is disqualified from working with children, even if the person offering the position did not know that the candidate was disqualified.

It is not possible for most charities to undertake these checks themselves and therefore "umbrella bodies" that are directly authorised by the DBS to carry out these checks are used. Groups such as CCPAS have a wide experience of undertaking this work for churches and Christian organisations, as well as a thorough understanding of all the issues relating to Safeguarding.

37. The media asks for an interview or quote

In this media-driven age, many charities look to maximise their exposure in the media by way of promoting their work and soliciting funds. Issues relating to the use of social media are dealt with in section 15.

On occasions the media may contact a charity to:

- seek a quote/opinion on a matter that is topical at the time;
- seek a response from a charity that may be working in a particular country or situation where a disaster or other event has taken place;
- provide some film footage showing the charity at work.

In such circumstances, charities need to be aware that what the charity thinks it is saying to the media, may not appear in the printed or broadcast version in the same format! Ultimately the media use information gleaned to support the particular story or slant that they are keen to communicate. Many charities have been "used" and have been hurt or suffered reputational damage as a result of responding to what they considered was an innocent request from the media.

Charities are advised to seek the input from someone sympathetic to the charity who is also experienced in the media, before responding to a request for an interview or a "comment". Alternatively, a charity can agree a "media statement" that sets out the charity's position, which is then given to the media outlet without any further comment. If a copy of that statement is posted on the charity's website, then its supporters can compare what the charity said with what the media ultimately reported and draw their own conclusions!

38. The charity features negatively in the media

Despite the charity's best intentions, policies and plans, sometimes a negative story about the charity, one of its staff or its work generally, appears in the media. As a result, the charity is faced with damage limitation. Possible steps would include:

- Preparing a full and accurate statement setting out the charity's position on what has been reported; sending this to the charity's major donors and supporters and any grant funders and maybe the Charity Commission (if the media has made a serious allegation).
- Posting a copy on the charity's website and having it available for distribution to other media outlets that may approach the charity for a response.
- Writing to the media outlet which had reported the story and challenging their version of events, if they are inaccurate.
- Refraining from a temptation to consider suing the media outlet in defamation: they will have deeper pockets to pay lawyers than will the charity!

Provided the charity's donors and supporters are not adversely swayed and pursuing its Objects has not been affected, then the old maxim that "there is no such thing as bad publicity" might just apply?

39. You don't know what to do!

Have you ever looked at a letter or a computer screen or listened to a person and thought, "I am not sure what to do in this situation"? Don't worry, you are in good company!

It might be a Safeguarding issue, a letter from the charity's bank, a potential claim against the charity or a notification from HMRC or the Charity Commission, ignoring the matter (however tempting) will not make the issue go away.

As a lawyer, I probably earn more from charities that have ignored issues than I would had they come to me straight away, so why am I saying this? Simply that a quick call to the right person for advice can often lift the burden and bring clarity and direction. It can prevent a bad situation getting a lot worse.

There are probably three phone numbers that those running a charity should have on speed dial: the accountant, the lawyer and CCPAS (for Safeguarding issues). If none of those three can solve the issue, they will be able to direct you to those who can.

40. It all gets too much!

Despite the noblest aims and ideals of the charity, the commitment and enthusiasm of its key workers and volunteers and the personal affinity that the trustees may share with its charitable Objects, there are occasions during the trustee's period of service when the weight of responsibility, expectation and demand becomes too great.

This can be the result of:

- unreasonable demands that the charity is putting upon the trustee;
- the difficulties that the charity may be going through;
- chronic lack of cash that is preventing the charity from functioning properly;
- personality issues within the board or between the board and key staff;
- ill health;
- the pressures of the trustee's other activities.

Whatever the issue, the reason behind it needs to be identified and addressed for the sake of both the trustee and the charity. If a satisfactory resolution cannot be found, it is probably in everyone's best interest for the trustee to consider resigning (or withdrawing from trusteeship for a period).

Solomon (one of the wisest men who ever lived), stated that "there is a time for everything". There may come a time when a particular trustee needs to step down from responsibility because it has all got too much. There may be a time when all the trustees may decide that the charity has run its course; that it would be in the best interests of everyone (including the charity's beneficiaries), if the charity ceased and its assets were passed over to a like-minded charity. Perhaps faith-based charities are more inclined to "stick it out" in the hope that things may change. However, it may be clear to all onlookers that the charity is just perpetuating its existence, living off past glories and really does not have a bright future ahead of it.

A1

APPENDIX 2

Sample
Forms of Non-Conformist Church Government

Explanatory Notes

I have set out in the following chart six examples of church structures from the perspective of someone who has been involved with many churches experiencing problems and have set out my comments in view of the damage caused when leadership/churches fail. I accept that some of this may be controversial and that I may have missed some of the nuances/details of some churches whose characteristics I have summarised.

Ultimately no system of church government is perfect as it largely depends upon those who administer it. However, some structures are clearer and more accountable than others, mainly because they separate the responsibilities in a way that is clear to all, building in appropriate accountability.

In any structure people need to know to whom they should go and what will be done. By dividing the "legal" from the "spiritual", (trustees and leadership) it enables that to be done.

There are examples of very well run, successful churches that use each of the models I have listed in the chart. However, any successful versions of numbers one and six are probably more down to the quality and *bona fides* of the persons in charge than the strength of the structure itself.

Each of the six scenarios set out are largely dependent on the availability of capable leaders who can give time to the role. If the church has the correct governance structure with clearly defined roles and is efficiently set up, then the time requirements for any role should not be onerous for any leader.

Churches who purposely invest time and resources in developing leaders (perhaps from an early age) are likely to find less difficulty in recruiting suitable candidates for the leadership roles. How many trustee boards deliberately include some members under 30 years of age?

Today any church structure has to face two fundamental challenges:

- How will it deal with its duty of compliance and separate the "legal" from the "spiritual"?
- What happens if there is failure in the leadership?

I have seen in particular that version 5 in the chart has stood up well in a crisis, both because of the close accountability of those involved and also the ability that it gives to limit the fallout from failure and to take decisive action.

Church structures

Church Structures 1	Advantages	Disadvantages
• Pastor/Minister, Elders and/or Deacons, • Membership meets once a year but has no real influence as Elders/Deacons appoint themselves. • Voting is on practical matters e.g. budget and decoration. • Deacons and Elders have no set period of service. They are often also the trustees of the charity.	• Simple structure works providing the leaders are good. • Decisions made quickly.	• No/little accountability. • No ability for members to "influence" leadership. Too much authority vested in the minister. • Membership can get restless/frustrated and then leave, especially if the church grows and new people have no say in development. • If leadership "fails" then church likely to split or close because membership leave. • Elders/deacons can get weary of the ministry and see no way out. • No separation of trustees (governance) from spiritual leadership (management).
2		
• As above but membership meet often though have no real "vote". Decisions made on consensus and presented by leadership for the church to "agree". • In some cases the church may relate to a "regional minister" who can influence how this church should function. • No separation of trustees from spiritual leadership.	• As above. It works if leaders are good and church continues to grow. • Attractive to "members" who do not want to get involved in the practical details of church. • If leadership fails the fall out can be ameliorated by the influence of the regional minister.	• Members have no real influence in decisions and can feel they are financing the leaders' dreams. • If members unhappy then they leave – easily. • Comments above as per separation of governance from spiritual leadership. • Elders/deacons can get weary of the ministry and see no way out.

A2

Church Structures 3	Advantages	Disadvantages
• Membership fully participates in the church. • Each member can influence via their vote and participate in making almost every decision. • A small amount of delegated authority given to the leaders. • Trustees might be separate from spiritual leadership or trusteeship of property held by outside trust corporation.	• Democratic – everyone has the capacity to be heard and to vote. • Decisions not made by leadership on their own. • Sense of participation and family.	• The need to call regular meetings to endorse/ make decisions. • Difficulty in securing a quorum for a meeting. Possibility of partisan voting. • Difficulty of large meeting in making decisions, especially "big" decisions. • Need to update full membership list annually with Companies House. • Problem of absent trust company who holds title to the property. • Senior leader can feel lonely, even vulnerable (as can't be certain things will work out as desired).

4		
• Minister and other leadership voted on by the membership. • Members get to vote on all major decisions (congregational government). • Limited authority given to minister and leadership team to make decisions. • Elders/Deacons serve for limited terms and can be removed by membership. • Trustees usually drawn from the same group of spiritual leaders.	• Democratic. • Leadership can be challenged by members. • If leadership fails, membership usually stays in place because they have influence. • There is a measure of holding leaders to account.	• Partisan voting by membership can replace leaders. • Decision-making can be drawn out plus difficulties of quorum/ percentage votes for major decisions. • Members often asked to make decisions that effectively rubber stamp what leaders have done. • Question as to whether membership are fully engaged and take ownership of the decisions they are asked to endorse, e.g. the budget. • Possibly no separation of governance from management. • If problems arise, the damage may be irreversible before a meeting can be called to agree a way forward. • Leadership can feel thwarted by some members perpetually opposing motions. • Factions can more easily form.

Church Structures	Advantages	Disadvantages
5		
• Membership appoints trustees to deal with compliance and Elders/Leadership team to lead the spiritual. • Trustees appoint the minister who is accountable to them for his job description. • Minister builds leadership team and together they lead the spiritual, leaving trustees to deal with legal compliance. • Trustees are accountable to church membership as are the spiritual leaders; membership ultimately holds the power of influence. • Separation of trustees from spiritual leadership is clear and defined.	• Separation of legal and spiritual. • Minister works alongside his team yet is accountable to trustees. • All leadership/trustees accountable in small accountability structure. • Membership have influence and feel valued. • If leadership fails, then trustees are separate enough to be able to contain damage.	• Partisan voting and difficulties with quorum for church meetings for major decisions.
6		
• Minister controls everything – appoints Elders/Deacons but he is "the Minister" especially if present for 10 or 15 years. • Membership has little or no influence and is expected to follow minister's leadership unquestioningly in everything. • Trustees and other key team leaders likely to be Minister's family/friends and/or the Elders/Deacons.	• Minister free to work out his or her passion/vision without hindrance.	• Possibility of spiritual and physical abuse. • No accountability. • "Members" come and go and breed a "we come to church to get, not give" attitude. • If leadership fails there is no plan B to rescue the situation. • Compliance is down to the minister and if he does not do it, it does not get done. • Easy for minister to become proud - "my church" especially if church grows to say more than 150. • Likely to be succession problems when minister leaves or retires.

A2

APPENDIX 3

Sample
Risk Management Matrix
Schedule of Potential Risk Areas

Potential Risk	Potential Impact	Mitigation
A. Governance and Management		
1. Company lacks direction, strategy or forward planning.	Issues are addressed piecemeal with no strategic reference. Financial management difficulties.	Creation of a strategic plan setting out key aims, objectives and policies. Creation of financial plans and budgets. Funding plan. Managing of financial and operational performance. Feedback from funders. Time out for creative thinking.
2. Board of Directors lacks necessary skills.	Company is too reliant on a few people. Decisions are made bypassing the Board. Company fails to grow and its impact is restricted.	Skills review. Competence framework and job descriptions. Trustee training. Recruitment process.
3. Conflicts of interest.	Decisions may not be based on relevant considerations. Compliance failure.	Understanding of the law. Protocol for disclosing potential conflicts of interest.
4. Loss of key staff.	Experience and skills lost. Operational impact on key projects. Loss of contact base and corporate knowledge.	Succession planning. Documentation of systems, plans and projects. Training programmes. Recruitment processes.

Potential Risk	Potential Impact	Mitigation
5. Reporting to the Board (accuracy, timeliness and relevance).	Inadequate information results in poor quality decision-making. Failure of the Board to fulfil its control function. Board becomes remote and ill-informed.	Agreed reporting format. Timely and accurate project reporting. Timely and accurate financial reporting. Proper project assessment and authorisation procedures. Regular contact between Board and managers. Accountability of senior staff.

B. Operational Risks

Potential Risk	Potential Impact	Mitigation
1. Contractual risk.	Onerous terms and conditions. Liabilities for non-performance. Non-compliance with Company's obligations. Loss of reputation. Financial implications.	Cost/project appraisal procedures. Authorisation procedures. Professional advice on terms and conditions. Performance monitoring arrangements. Insurable risks cover.
2. Complaints from a Donor.	Loss of income. Reputational risks.	Quality control procedures. Complaints procedures. Benchmarking of service.
3. Funding.	Cancellation or curtailment of programmes.	Review of adequacy of financial returns achieved (benchmarking). Development of appropriate fundraising plan. Buy-in from Board and senior managers.
4. Employment issues.	Employment disputes. Health and Safety claims. Equal opportunity issues. Low morale.	Recruitment processes. Adequate staff training and development. Health and Safety training and monitoring. Staff appraisals and exit interviews.
5. Volunteers.	Need for supervision and training. Vetting and reference procedure. Indirect cost to charity.	Assessment of role and competences. Vetting procedures. Training and supervision procedures. Development and motivation.
6. Health, Safety and Environment.	Staff injury. Product or service liability. Inability to operate.	Knowledge of law and regulation. Compliance officer and training. Monitoring and reporting.

A3

Potential Risk	Potential Impact	Mitigation
7. Disaster recovery and planning.	Destruction of property, equipment, records through fire, flood, etc.	Insurance. Disaster recovery plan for alternative accommodation.
10. Procedural and systems documentation.	Lack of awareness of procedures, policies and obligations. Actions taken without proper authority.	Proper documentation of policies and procedures. Audit and review of systems. Adequate staff training and accountability.
11. Information Technology.	Systems fail to meet operational needs. Failure to innovate or update systems. Loss/corruption of data. Lack of technical support. Breach of confidentiality.	Appraisal of system's needs and options. Security and authorisation procedures. IT recovery plan. Data back-up procedures and precautions. Use of service and support contracts. Outsourcing. Insurance. Authorisation procedure.

C. Financial Risks

1. Budgetary control and finance reporting.	Budget does not match key objectives and priorities. Decisions made on inaccurate financial projections or reporting. Decisions made on unreliable financial data. Inability to meet commitments or key objectives.	Budget linked to business planning and objectives. Timing and accurate monitor reporting. Proper costing procedures. Adequate skills base to produce and interpret key budgetary and financial reporting.
2. Reserves policies.	Lack of liquidity to respond to new needs or opportunities. Inability to meet commitments or plan objectives. Reputational risk.	Reserves policy linked to business plans, activities and identified financial and operating risk. Regular review of policy. Establishment of reserves fund.
3. Cash flow sensitivity.	Inability to meet commitments. Lack of liquidity to cover variance. Impact on operational activities.	Adequate cash flow projections. Identification of major sensitivities. Adequate information flow from operational managers. Monitoring arrangements and reporting. Availability of reserves.
4. Dependency on income sources.	Cash flow and budget impact of loss of income source.	Identification of major dependencies. Adequate reserves policy. Diversification plans.

Potential Risk	Potential Impact	Mitigation
5. Fraud or error.	Financial loss. Reputational risk. Regulatory action. Impact on funding. Loss of staff.	Financial control procedures. Authorisation limits. Security. Insurance. Accountability.

D. Environmental/External Factors

1. Public perception.	Impact on advertising income. Ability to access funding.	Communications with supporters and beneficiaries. Quality financial and factual reports. PR training/procedures.
2. Adverse publicity.	Loss of donor confidence or funding. Loss of influence. Impact on morale of staff. Loss of viewers/advertisers.	Complaints procedure (internal and external). Proper review procedures for complaints. Crisis management strategy. Nominated spokesperson and message.
3. Relationship with Members.	Distance in relationship may impact on funding and support available, as well as reputation.	Regular contact and briefings to major funder. Project reporting. Show "added value."
4. Compliance Risk. Data Protection Act. Child Protection. Employment law. Health and Safety.	Fines, penalties. Loss of opportunity to undertake activity. Action for negligence. Reputational risk.	Identification of key legal and regulatory requirements. Allocation of responsibility for key compliance. Monitoring and reporting. Accountability.
6. The Tyranny of the Urgent.	Burn-out. Loss of morale. Failure to achieve charity's potential. Poor service delivery.	Allocation of time for blue-sky thinking. Accountability. Adequate reserves and personnel to enable thinking time. Improvement of management and reporting structure. Ability to learn.

A3

Sample
Risk Management Work Plan

Risk Area	Likelihood of Occurrence	Severity of Impact	Overall Risk	Control Procedures	Retained Risk	Monitoring Process	Responsibility	Further Action Inform	Date of Review
Reduction of Income	5 (High)	5 (High)	25	Early warning meeting	High	Regular contact with Board Members	CEO	Inform Board	
Fraud	2 (Low)	5 (High)	10	Insurance	Policy excess	Review Insurance	COO	Review date	
Conflict of Interest	1 (Low)	2 Low	2	Board policy	Low	Board Minutes	All	Disclose in Accounts	

APPENDIX 4

Annual Governance Health Check

Five Essential Questions to Ask

1
Are the charitable Objects being carried out for the public benefit?
· Is the main thing the main thing?
· Can we show public benefit?

2
Are the accounts and Annual Return(s) being filed on time?
· When are the filing dates?
· Who will do the filing and ensure it is on time?

3
Policies/Safeguarding
· What policies do we need/have ?
· Are they up to date?

4
Trustee **meetings**
· Are they regular?
· Are they properly run?
· Are they accurately minuted?

5
Finance – Income and Expenditure
· Is there a budget?
· Is income monitored?
· Is expenditure for charitable purposes only?

A4

APPENDIX 5

Definitions

"AGM" · The Annual General Meeting of the charity, open to all members.

"Alternate Director" · A person appointed by a Director to act on their behalf in their absence. Only possible if the Articles of Association of the company permit this.

"Annual Report" · The report made by the trustees and forming a part of the annual accounts of the charity explaining how the charity has carried out its Objects for the public benefit during the year in question.

"Annual Return – charitable company" · A document filed annually with Companies House on the anniversary of the Date of Incorporation. Filed online. Failure to do so results in a fine.

"Annual Return – charity" · Filed with the Charity Commission, but only if the charity's income is in excess of £10,000 a year. Due within ten months from the end of each financial year. No financial penalty for lateness but the Charity Commission may remove the charity after six months.

"Articles of Association" · A document set out in the format required by the Companies Act and which forms the governing document of a charitable company.

"Audit" · An official examination and verification of financial accounts and records of a charity. Charities with income under £1 million per annum can opt for an independent examination instead of an audit.

"Beneficiary" · A legal term referring to a person who is eligible to benefit from a charity's work. Usually the beneficiaries of a charity will be defined in the governing document.

"Board" · Collective term that describes the duly appointed directors or trustees of a charity.

"Breach of Trust" · Means a breach of any duty imposed on a trustee. For charity trustees, these duties may be imposed by the provisions of the charity's governing document, laws and regulations, or Orders of the Court or the Charity Commission. A duty is something which trustees have to do. It is distinguished from a power which trustees may or may not choose to use.

"Capital" · Resources belonging to the charity which the trustees are legally required to invest or retain and use for the purposes of the charity. It may also include Permanent Endowment.

"Chair" · The trustee or director who is appointed to lead the charity's meetings.

He/she may have a casting vote in the event of an equality of votes.

"Charity" · An organisation which is established for charitable purposes only and is subject to the control of the High Court. It can be an unincorporated organisation, a charitable company, or charitable incorporated organisation, amongst others.

"Charitable Company" · A company registered under the Companies Act which is established exclusively for charitable purposes and which prevents the distribution of its assets amongst its members. A charitable company has no shareholders and is a separate legal entity from its members and directors.

"Charitable Incorporated Organisation" (CIO) · A corporate body permitted by the Charities Act which combines the benefits of being a separate legal entity from its trustees with the administrative simplicity of being regulated by one body – the Charity Commission.

"Charitable Purposes" · See "Objects"

"Charity Commission" · Corporate body set up by the Charities Act 2006, it functions on behalf of the Crown and is not subject to the direction or control of any minister of the Crown or other Government department.

"Charity Trustees" · The people having general control and management of the administration of a charity (regardless of what they are called). They may also be known as "the Executive", "the Board" or "Management Committee". In the case of a charitable company the trustees are known as Directors.

"Chief Executive" · Usually refers to the most senior member of staff within the charity. May also be known as Chief Executive Officer, Director, or General Director.

"Community Interest Company" (CIC) · A special type of company for those wishing to establish businesses that trade with a social purpose. CICs are not charities and are outside of the control of the Charity Commission.

"Company Secretary" · An officer of a charitable company responsible to ensure compliance with the duties imposed by Company Law and for the secretarial duties set out in the charity's governing document.

"Compliance" · Either the state of being in accordance with established laws and guidelines for the charitable sector or the process of becoming so.

"Conflict of Interest" · Any situation in which a trustee's personal interests/loyalties could prevent them from making a decision only in the best interests of the charity.

"Connected Person" · A trustee, the donor of any land to the charity, a child/parent/grandchild/grandparent/brother or sister of any trustee or donor, an officer or employee of the charity or any spouse or civil partner of any of the above, or a person carrying on business with any of the above people.

"Constitution" · The written document which establishes the purpose for which an organisation is set up and the principles and rules by which it will be governed. This can be contained in a Conveyance, Trust Deed, Will, Articles of Association or other written document.

A5

"Corporate Members" • Include companies, local authorities and other public bodies or organisations for which a nominated representative holds a right to vote at the charity's annual general meeting on behalf of the organisation they represent.

"Corporate Trustee" • A company or corporation that is appointed a trustee of a charity e.g. an NHS Trust which acts as a trustee of an NHS charity.

"Custodian Trustee" • A company appointed to have the custody (but not the management) of trust property. A Custodian Trustee is not a charity trustee and has no say in the administration of the charity.

"Cy-prés" • A legal doctrine under which the trusts of a charity may be formally modified to allow them to be used for a purpose that is as near as possible to the provisions of the original trust.

"Designated Funds" • Funds of the charity that the trustees have "designated" for a particular project or use without restricting those funds legally, e.g. monies set aside by the board to renew the charity's IT system.

"Directors" • Those who hold office of a charitable company whose office is controlled under the Companies Acts. Also known as trustees, and subject to the provisions of the Charities Acts.

"Disclosure & Barring Service" (DBS) • The organisation that provides a disclosure service concerning information held by the police together with information held under the Protection of Children Act, Protection of Vulnerable Adults Act and lists maintained by the Department for Education and Skills.

"EGM" • Extraordinary General Meeting (sometimes also called Special General Meeting) and relates to any general meeting of the members of the charity that is not an AGM.

"Endowment Funds" • Funds which the charity's trustees are required to invest and use for the charity's Objects. They may be "expendable" (i.e. useable in their entirety) or "permanent".

"Excepted Charities" • A charity that is excepted from the need to register with the Charity Commission but is to all intent and purposes subject to their jurisdiction e.g. Scout and Guide Associations.

"Exempt charities" • Charities which are not supervised or monitored by the Charity Commission and are accountable to some other statutory body e.g. registered friendly societies are accountable to the Financial Conduct Authority.

"*Ex officio* Trustee" • Means trustee by virtue of their office. Normally this relates to positions such as the vicar of a parish, the mayor of a town, etc. *Ex officio* trustees have the same responsibilities as other charity trustees.

"Fiduciary Duty" • Obligations imposed to promote loyalty or faithfulness. For example, a trustee's duty not to put himself in a position of potential conflict of interest with the charity.

"General Meeting" • A general meeting of the members of the company. Also known as the Annual General Meeting

"Gift Aid" • A gift to a charity by a UK tax payer under this scheme enables the charity to claim the repayment of basic rate Income Tax. If the tax payer pays higher-rate tax then they will get the additional tax relief. A gift made to charity by a company under this scheme enables the company to get the tax relief.

"Governing Document" · Any document that sets out the charity's Objects and details of how the charity is to be administered. Sometimes known as a "Trust Deed", "Constitution", "Articles of Association", "Rules", "Conveyance", "Will", "Royal Charter", "Scheme".

"HMRC" · Her Majesty's Revenue and Customs

"Incorporated Association" · See Incorporated Charity.

"Incorporated Charity" · A charity that is established as a corporate body. This includes a charitable company, a body incorporated by an Act of Parliament or bodies incorporated by Royal Charter.

"Information Commissioner" · The independent authority set up to promote access to official information and to protect personal information.

"Interim Manager" · Appointed by the Charity Commission during a formal Inquiry usually after discovery of misconduct or maladministration in the charity. They manage the charity to the exclusion of the trustees until such time as responsibility can be passed back to a board of trustees (usually a new board) to take the charity forward.

"Malpractice" · This could be where a person who is under a duty to act in a specific manner fails to follow the generally accepted professional standards, and as a result, loss or damage is caused to the charity itself.

"Members" · An individual, corporate body or other charity who has agreed to belong to the charity. The members'

rights and responsibilities will usually be set out in the governing document.

"Mission" or **"Mission Statement"** · A statement designed by a charity to explain why it exists and/or what it intends to do.

"Non-charitable expenditure" · Expenditure not incurred exclusively for charitable purposes, any payment to an overseas body where the charity has not taken appropriate steps to ensure it will be for charitable purposes, an investment or loan by the charity which is not a qualifying one, or a transaction with a substantial donor.

"Non-Governmental Organisation" (NGO) · An organisation established for benevolent or philanthropic purposes for the benefit of the public, independent of central or local government control and which does not belong to those who run it or are employed by it.

"Non-primary purpose trading" · Trading which is carried on with the main aim of raising funds for a charity.

"Objects" · The legal purpose(s) for which a charity exists as stated in its governing document. The Objects direct how the charity's assets must be used. For example "The Advancement of Religion".

"Official Custodian for Charities" · The holder of this office is appointed by the Charity Commission to hold land or assets, as a custodian trustee, for charities in respect of any land or assets which are vested in the official Custodian by means of a Charity Commission Scheme or Order.

"Order" · A legal document made by the Charity Commission which can

A5

confer new powers on a trustee body or appoint or remove trustees.

"Permanent Endowment" • The property of a charity which must be held permanently, sometimes to be used for furthering the charity's Objects, (e.g. a building) sometimes to produce income for the charity.

"Powers" • A charity's powers are the authority that the charity has to enable it to carry out its Objects. Powers are not charitable in themselves and are usually set out in the charity's governing document in a clause immediately following the Objects.

"**Primary Purpose Trading**" • Trading carried out by a charity in the course of fulfilling the primary purpose of the charity e.g. goods produced by the beneficiaries of a disability charity.

"Quorum" • The minimum number of people entitled to attend and vote that must be present at a meeting in order that valid decisions can be made. The number of people required for a quorum is usually set out in the governing document.

"Register of Charities" • The Register maintained by the Charity Commission containing the names of every registered charity and such other information as the Charity Commission thinks fit (this is also known as "The Register"). This other information will include a working name, the Objects of the charity, financial year-end and the name and address of the correspondent for the charity. In practice the register will also include more general information about the charity.

"Reserves" • Income of the charity which is not yet spent, committed or designated. It does include Permanent Endowment, Restricted Funds and Designated Funds.

"Reserves Policy" • A policy developed by the trustees and contained within the charity's Annual Accounts, explaining why the charity is holding a particular amount of reserves, usually equating to between three and six months operating costs, or whatever figure the trustees believe would enable an orderly wind-down of the charity, in the event that funding ceased.

"Restricted Funds" • Funds or property held and administered as a separate trust by or on behalf of a charity e.g. monies raised by or given to a charity on condition they are used only for a particular purpose e.g. to purchase a specific building.

"Safeguarding" • Protecting people's health, wellbeing and human rights and enabling them to live free from harm, abuse and neglect.

"Scheme" • A legal document granted by the Charity Commission giving approval to change any aspect of a charity's Objects or administrative provisions.

"Secretary" • The person appointed to be the secretary of the charity. If no such person exists then the person who calls the meetings and/or takes the minutes at the meetings.

"Social Enterprise" • A type of non-profit business that employees people and earns income to help address perceived social or environmental issues.

"SOFA" • Statement of Financial Activities. A charity's SOFA shows all the incoming resources becoming available during the year and all its expenditure for the year, and reconciles all the changes in its funds. The SOFA should account for all the funds of the charity and should be presented in columns representing the different types of funds.

"SORP" · Statement Of Recommended Practice for Accounting and Reporting by charities.

"Special Trust" · Funds or property held and administered on its own separate trust by or on behalf of a main charity for any special purposes of that charity. It follows that the Objects of a special trust must be narrower than those of the main charity.

"Spiritual Abuse" · The control of one individual by another in a spiritual context.

"Structure Document" · See Governing Document.

"Trading Subsidiary" · A non-charitable trading company, limited by shares, owned by the charity, in order to carry out a trade with a view to generating funds for the charity.

"Trust Deed" · The document setting out the charity's Objects and describing how it will be administered. This can be a Constitution, Conveyance, Will, Royal Charter, Statement of Rules, Scheme of the Charity Commission, Articles of Association or other formal document.

"Trustees" · See Charity Trustees

"Trustees' Annual Report" · See Annual Report

"Trustee Board" · The charity's governing body which may also be called the Board of Directors, Executive Committee or Committee.

"Unincorporated Charity" · A charitable trust or a charitable unincorporated association. Its main characteristic is that the charity is not a separate legal entity from its trustees (see Charitable Company).

"Unrestricted Funds" · Monies which are expendable in furtherance of the charity's Objects (also known as General Funds).

"Vision" · The goals, aims or Objects towards which the charity is working.

"Vulnerable Persons" · Children or vulnerable adults (person suffering from a substantial learning or physical disability/a physical or mental illness including addiction to alcohol or drugs/a significant reduction in mental capacity).

"Working Name" · The name or an acronym under which the charity is more commonly known. This name may be completely different from the official name entered on the Register of Charities.

A5

421

APPENDIX 6

Useful Addresses

Centre for Effective Dispute Resolution (CEDR)
International Dispute Resolution Centre
70 Fleet Street
London EC4Y 1EU
Tel: 020 7536 6000
www.cedr.com

The Charity Bank Limited
Fosse House
182 High Street
Tonbridge
Kent TN9 1BE
Tel: 01732 774040
www.charitybank.org

Charity Commission
P O BOX 211
Bootle
Liverpool L20 7YX
Tel: 0300 066 9197
www.gov.uk/government/organisations/
charity-commission

The Charity Commission for Northern Ireland
257 Lough Road
Lurgan
Craigavon BT66 6NQ
Northern Ireland

Christian Copyright Licensing International
Chantry House
22 Upperton Road
Eastbourne
East Sussex BN21 1BF
Tel: 01323 436100
www.ccli.com

Churches' Child Protection Advisory Service
Child and adult protection, support, training and policy/practice issues including work with sexual offenders.
Tel: 0845 120 4550 or 01322 517817
Email: info@ccpas.co.uk
Web: www.ccpas.co.uk

Circles of Support and Accountability
A community support system for sex offenders. Circles UK is the national body supporting the development, quality, coordination and effectiveness of Local Circles.
Tel: 0118 950 0068
Web: www.circles-uk.org.uk

Companies House
Crown Way
Cardiff CF14 3UZ
Tel: 0303 1234 500
www.gov.uk/government/organisations/
companies-house

Directory of Social Change
352 Holloway Road
London N7 6PA
Tel: 0845 077 7707
www.dsc.org.uk

Disclosure and Barring Service
DBS Customer Services
PO Box 3961
Royal Wootton Bassett SN4 4HF
Tel 03000 200 190
www.gov.uk/government/organisations/
disclosure-and-barring-service

Fundraising Standards Board
London Fruit Exchange
Brushfield Street
London E1 6EP
Tel: 0845 402 5442
www.frsb.org.uk

HMRC Charities
St Johns House
Merton Road
Bootle
Merseyside L69 9BB
Tel: 0300 123 1073
www.gov.uk/government/organisations/
hm-revenue-customs

Information Commissioners Office
Wycliffe House
Water Lane
Wilmslow
Cheshire SK9 5AF
Tel: 0303 123 1113
www.ico.org.uk

Institute of Fundraising
Charter House
13-15 Carteret Street
Westminster
London SW1H 9DJ
Tel 020 7840 1000

Intellectual Property Office
Concept House
Cardiff Road
Newport
South Wales NP10 8QQ
Tel: 0300 300 2000
www.gov.uk/government/organisations/
intellectual-property-office

Lucy Faithfull Foundation
A national child protection agency working with adult male and female perpetrators of child sexual abuse. Lucy Faithfull Foundation runs Circles of Support (see also in this listing). Also runs Stop it Now! – a national campaign that aims to prevent child abuse by encouraging offenders to seek help.
Tel: 0808 1000 900
Email: help@stopitnow.org.uk
Web: www.stopitnow.org.uk

The National Council for Voluntary Organisations (NCVO)
Society Building
8 All Saints Street
London N1 9RL
Tel: 020 7713 6161
www.ncvo.org.uk

NSPCC
A national child protection charity.
Helpline: 0808 800 5000
Email: help@nspcc.org.uk
Web: www.nspcc.org.uk

Office for Civil Society
(formerly Office of the Third Sector)
1 Horse Guards Road
London SW1A 2HQ
www.civilsociety.co.uk

A6

Office of the Scottish Charity Regulator (OSCR)
2nd Floor
Quadrant House
9 Riverside Drive
Dundee DD1 4NY
Tel: 01382 220446
www.oscr.org.uk

Performing Rights Society
Causeway House
Bocking End
Braintree
Essex CM7 9HB
Tel: 01376 552525
www.braintree.gov.uk

Phonographic Performance Limited
1 Upper James Street
London W1F 9DE
Tel: 020 7534 1000
www.ppluk.com

Regulator of Community Interest Companies
CIC Regulator
Room 3.68
Companies House
Crown Way
Cardiff CF14 3UZ
Tel: 029 20346228
www.gov.uk/government/organisations/
office-of-the-regulator-of-community-
interest-companies

Contributors to this book

Beavis Morgan
Chartered Accountants
82 St John's Street
London EC1M 4JN
Tel: 0207 417 0417
www.beavismorgan.com

Churches Child Protection Advisory Service (CCPAS)
PO box 133
Swanley
Kent BR8 7UQ
Tel: 0845 120 4550
www.ccpas.co.uk

EQ Investors
Centennium House
100 Lower Thames Street
London E3R 6DL
Tel: 020 7488 7110
www.eqinvestors.co.uk

Wellers Law Group LLP

65 Leadenhall Street
London EC3A 2AD
0207 481 6381
www.wellerslawgroup.com

and at

Tenison House
Tweedy Road
Bromley
BR1 3NF
Tel: 020 8464 4242

Second Floor
50-52 London Road
Blighs Meadow
Sevenoaks
Kent TN13 1AS
01732 457575

Butler House
Guildford Road
Great Brookham
Surrey KT23 4HB
01483 284567

Index

I